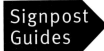

Signpost
Guides

WASHINGTON DC

AND VIRGINIA, MARYLAND AND DELAWARE

The best of Washington, DC, and Virginia, Maryland and Delaware, from the Appalachian Mountains to the sandy beaches of the Atlantic, including early colonial towns and battlefield sites, with suggested driving tours

Tom Bross, Patricia Harris, David Lyon, Timothy Nollen, Barbara Radcliffe Rogers and Stillman D Rogers

The Globe Pequot Press

Thomas Cook Publishing

Published by Thomas Cook Publishing
A division of Thomas Cook Holdings Ltd
PO Box 227
Thorpe Wood
Peterborough PE3 6PU
United Kingdom

Telephone: +44 (0)1733 503571
Fax: +44 (0)1733 503596
E-mail: books@thomascook.com

For further information about
Thomas Cook Publishing, visit our website:
www.thomascook.com

Published in the USA by
The Globe Pequot Press
PO Box 480
Guilford, Connecticut USA
06437

ISBN 0 7627 0695 3

ISBN 1 841570 32 X

Text: © 2000 Thomas Cook Publishing
City maps: © 2000 Thomas Cook Publishing
Road maps supplied by Lovell Johns Ltd, OX8 8LH
Road map data © 2000 MapQuest.com Inc., Mountville, PA 17554
City maps prepared by Polly Senior Cartography

Publisher: Donald Greig
Commissioning Editor: Deborah Parker
Map Editor: Bernard Horton
Series Editor: Christopher Catling
Copy Editor: Matthew Brown
Proof-reader: Hugh Davis
Written and researched by: Tom Bross, Patricia Harris, David Lyon,
Timothy Nollen, Barbara Radcliffe Rogers and Stillman D Rogers

Managing Director: Kevin Fitzgerald

About the authors and acknowledgements

Tim Nollen, who contributed the chapters on Washington and on northern and western Virginia to this book is a Washingtonian by upbringing, with a long-time affinity for the hills of old Virginia. He lived in Prague for several years in the 1990s, where he wrote three guidebooks to the vibrant towns and peoples of the Czech Republic. This work expanded into full-time guidebook and newspaper writing on European destinations from Spain to Lithuania. Now home again in DC, he writes on a part-time basis, contributing primarily to guides on East Coast destinations. In a perfect world, he'd be listening to bluegrass music in front of a campfire. Tim would like to thank the many tourist offices in Virginia for their wealth of information, as well as Josh and Katie Nickerson and Aja Mala.

Barbara Radcliffe Rogers and **Stillman D Rogers** are the authors of more than a dozen books about places from New England to South Africa. Among their recent volumes are *The Adventure Guide to Maryland and the Chesapeake Bay* and the forthcoming *Baltimore Alive*. For this book, they contributed the Maryland chapters. They wish to express their thanks to Lee Ann Chearney, Anne Mannix, Connie Yingling and Charles and Shirley Radcliffe, Marylanders all.

Tom Bross contributed Canadian and New England chapters to previous Thomas Cook guidebooks. For this Signpost volume, he covered central and eastern Virginia, plus North Carolina's Outer Banks. He'd like to thank Julia Scott (Virginia Tourism Corp), Doretha Vaughan (Metro Richmond CVB), Patricia MacDonald (Williamsburg Area CVB), Debby Padgett (Jamestown-Yorktown Foundation), Susan Tipton (Northern Neck Tourism Council), Karen Hedelt (Fredericton Office of Economic Development and Tourism), Kelly Larkin (Norfolk CVB), Hester Waterfield (Virginia Beach Dept of Convention and Visitor Development), Rebecca Cutchins (Portsmouth CVB), Sam Martinette (Hampton CVB), Suzanne Pearson (Newport News Tourism Development Office) and Carolyn McCormick (Dare County, NC, Tourist Bureau) for their help.

Patricia Harris and **David Lyon** are authors and contributors to several Thomas Cook guides on Canada, New England and Spain and write extensively on art, food and travel for a range of print and online media. For this volume, Pat and David contributed the introductory chapters as well as chapters on Pennsylvania and Delaware. They would like to thank Ellen Kornfield of the Philadelphia Convention and Visitors Bureau for her sage advice.

Contents

About Signpost Guides

Thomas Cook's Signpost Guides are designed to provide you with a comprehensive but flexible reference source to guide you as you tour a country or region by car. This guide divides Washington, DC, Virginia, Maryland and Delaware into touring areas – one per chapter. Major cultural centres or cities form chapters in their own right. Each chapter contains enough attractions to provide at least a day's worth of activities – often more.

Star ratings

To make it easier for you to plan your time and decide what to see, every sight and attraction is given a star rating. A three-star rating indicates a major attraction, worth at least half a day of your time. A two-star attraction is worth an hour or so of your time, and a one-star attraction indicates a site that is worth visiting, but often of specialist interest. To help you further, individual attractions within towns or theme parks are also graded, so that travellers with limited time can quickly find the most rewarding sights.

Chapter contents

Every chapter has an introduction summing up the main attractions of the area or town, and a ratings box, which will highlight its appeal – some places may be more attractive to families travelling with children, others to wine-lovers visiting vineyards, and others to people interested in finding castles, churches, nature reserves, or good beaches.

Each chapter is then divided into an alphabetical gazetteer, and a suggested tour or walk. You can select whether you just want to visit a particular sight or attraction, choosing from those described in the gazetteer, or whether you want to tour the area comprehensively. If the latter, you can construct your own itinerary, or follow the author's suggested tour, which comes at the end of every area chapter.

The gazetteer

The gazetteer section describes all the major attractions in the area – the villages, towns, historic sites, nature reserves, parks or museums that you are most likely to want to see. Maps of the area highlight all the places mentioned in the text. Using this comprehensive overview of the area, you may choose just to visit one or two sights.

One way to use the guide is simply to find individual sights that interest you, using the index, overview map or star ratings, and read what our authors have to say about them. This will help you decide whether to visit the sight. If you do, you will find plenty of practical

Symbol key

- ℹ Tourist Information Centre
- Advice on arriving or departing
- P Parking locations
- Advice on getting around
- Directions
- Sights and attractions
- Eating
- Accommodation
- Shopping
- Sport
- Entertainment

Practical information

The practical information in the page margins, or sidebar, will help you locate the services you need as an independent traveller – including the tourist information centre, car parks and public transport facilities. You will also find the opening times of sights, museums, churches and other attractions, as well as useful tips on shopping, market days, cultural events, entertainment, festivals and sports facilities.

information, such as the street address, the telephone number for enquiries and opening times.

Alternatively, you can choose a hotel, with the help of the accommodation recommendations contained in this guide. You can then turn to the overall map on pages 10–11 to help you work out which chapters in the book describe the cities and regions closest to your touring base.

Driving tours

The suggested tour is just that – a suggestion, with plenty of optional detours and one or two ideas for making your own discoveries, under the heading *Also worth exploring*. The routes are designed to link the attractions described in the gazetteer section, and to cover outstandingly scenic coastal, mountain and rural landscapes. The total distance is given for each tour, and the time it will take you to drive the complete route, but bear in mind that this indication is just for driving time: you will need to add on extra time for visiting attractions along the way.

Many of the routes are circular, so that you can join them at any point. Where the nature of the terrain dictates that the route has to be linear, the route can either be followed out and back, or you can use it as a link route, to get from one area in the book to another.

As you follow the route descriptions, you will find names picked out in bold capital letters – this means that the place is described fully in the gazetteer. Other names picked out in bold indicate additional villages or attractions worth a brief stop along the route.

Accommodation and food

In every chapter you will find lodging and eating recommendations for individual towns, or for the area as a whole. These are designed to cover a range of price brackets and concentrate on more characterful small or individualistic hotels and restaurants. In addition, you will find information in the *Travel Facts* chapter on chain hotels, with an address to which you can write for a guide, map or directory.

The price indications used in the guide have the following meanings:

$ budget level
$$ typical/average prices
$$$ de luxe

PENNSYLVANIA

Page 200

Page 192

Hagerstown

MARYLA

Fred

Page 78

Page 70

WEST VIRGINIA

Winchester

Strasburg

WASHINGTON, DC

P

Arlington

Warrenton

Pag

Harrisonburg

Culpeper

VIRGINIA

Page 122

Staunton

Frederic

Page 90

Charlottesville

Page 21

Page 114

Lynchburg

Page 102

Richmond

Roanoke

Appomattox

Willia

Petersburg

Danville

Fra

NORTH CAROLINA

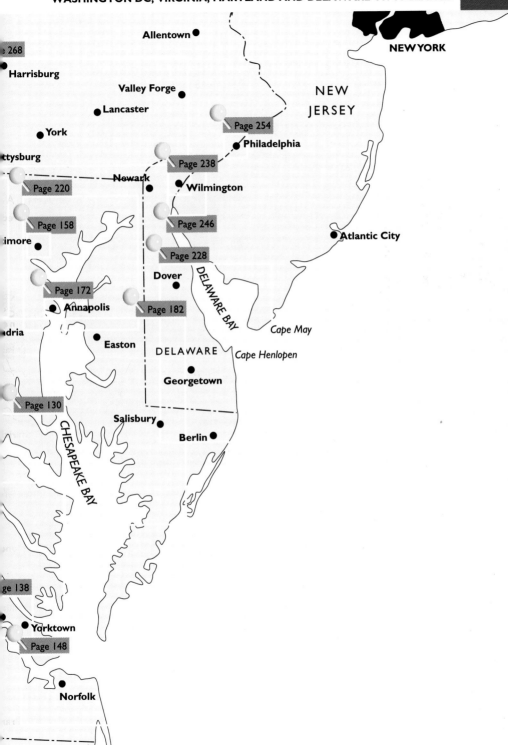

Allentown

NEW YORK

e 268

Harrisburg

NEW

JERSEY

Valley Forge

Lancaster

York

Page 254

tysburg

Philadelphia

Page 238

Newark

Page 220

Wilmington

Page 158

Page 246

imore

Atlantic City

Page 228

Dover

Page 172

DELAWARE BAY

Annapolis

Page 182

Cape May

dria

Easton

DELAWARE   Cape Henlopen

Georgetown

Page 130

Salisbury

CHESAPEAKE BAY

Berlin

ge 138

CHESAPEAKE BAY

Yorktown

Page 148

Norfolk

Above
Washington's Capitol

Introduction

Washington, DC, is a rarity in the world: a planned, intentional, dedicated capital. Philadelphia (and, briefly, other places) served as the seat of government in the formative years of the Republic when Washington was little more than muddy farmland on the banks of the Potomac River. The creation of a splendid marble city full of grandeur and pomp was an act of political will – and some would say that wilful politics has been its lot ever since.

As proud as we Americans are of our representative democracy, we make a national sport of deriding officials elected from other districts or representing the 'other' party. In this context, the word 'Washington' is a pejorative. Yet roughly 20 million people come from around the world to Washington, DC, each year, not so much to see the US government at work, but to marvel at the power and the glory of official Washington.

For all our protests to the contrary, we Americans *do* love our national capital. Ask us about the Smithsonian Institution, and we will beam and tell you that it is the nation's attic, full of some of our people's finest memories. Mention the White House or the US Capitol, and we will speak with awe – not necessarily of the officials who live or work there, but of the symbolic majesty of the structures themselves. Ask about 'the Wall', as we persist in calling the Vietnam Veterans' Memorial, and we grow inarticulate with choked-back tears over one of the most powerful pieces of abstract sculpture ever set on public soil. Washington is much, much more than the seat of American government; it is a city full of touchstones of American life.

Yet Washington is only a place to begin, especially for the fly-drive traveller, whose best plan of attack is to see Washington first or last, to be shed of the responsibility and inconvenience of an automobile in the city. The term used in this book, 'Capital Region', traditionally refers to Washington, DC, and the contiguous areas of Maryland and Virginia, but the scope of this book is broader, embracing all of Maryland, most of eastern Virginia, the tiny state of Delaware and a crescent of southeastern Pennsylvania. With so many rich destinations so close, it seems a shame to restrict oneself to official Washington and its satellite communities within the Beltway. The marble monuments and processional boulevards of the American capital are wonderfully augmented by the country roads, tidewater villages, rolling farmlands and craggy mountains of the broader region. City and countryside alike are part of the experience. The Capital Region found in this volume is richly diverse in topography, culture, activities and attractions – a little like the United States itself.

Washingtonians like to pretend that their city is neither Northern nor Southern, invoking diplomatic neutrality. They are being disingenuous. The entire Capital Region is stamped with some of the South's finest hallmarks. Washington is a Southern city, and its ways were set in the era before air conditioning made the South fully habitable in the summer and capable of year-round industriousness. In those days a certain manner evolved: the famous Southern hospitality, the languid Southern approach to time and even the drawn-out enunciation of the Southern accent.

Like much of the wider USA, the Capital Region has a sometimes troubled, always colourful past. The inhabitants of Williamsburg, Virginia, play their 18th-century roles to perfection in a community where time has been truly stopped. At the same time, the 21st-century folk of Annapolis, Maryland, and New Castle, Delaware, see nothing anachronistic about walking down their cobbled streets past Georgian houses. The past has a way of rebounding in Virginia's Tidewater, where grand old plantations bear mute testament to a feudal agriculture based on slave labour. Old ways of life drift into view in tiny villages along Maryland's Eastern Shore, where fishermen harvest oysters from sailing boats using long hand tongs. It is a case of picturesque traditions persisting in the name of scientific conservation and sound resource management. On the Amish farms of southeastern Pennsylvania, field hands still walk behind horse- or ox-drawn ploughs and ride into town on horse-drawn buggies with large reflective safety triangles mounted on the back. Perhaps no segment of the past so occupies the Capital Region as the Civil War. The horrors of those four difficult years between 1861 and 1865 resound down the generations, and the war's battlefields and cemeteries still mark the face of the region as indelibly as a tattoo.

Below
Elfreth's Alley, Philadelphia

Be careful, traveller, not to become lost in the Capital Region's past and overlook the timeless beauty of the countryside, from the gentle peaks of the Blue Ridge Mountains to the coves and inlets of the Eastern Shore. Long rolling plains of rich farmland seem to embody the American promise of the New World, while the Atlantic beaches of Maryland and Virginia suggest another kind of Promised Land, where frolic is never done. Follow the narrow paths into Delaware's marshes at dawn to see thousands of waterfowl gathered in a feathery peaceable kingdom. Take the ferry out to see the wild ponies of Assateague Island galloping down the beach. Pull off the Skyline Drive to sit with binoculars and watch a bald eagle, America's national bird, ride the thermal lifts from the sunny side of the hills.

Travel facts

Accommodation

Tourist offices can provide information about lodgings in every style and price, but cannot usually make bookings.

Most major chain hotels can be found in urban centres, along with more distinctive historic properties. At chain hotels and motels of every price, expect a clean, comfortable, relatively spacious room with one or two double- or queen-sized beds and a private bathroom. Some independent hotels and motels provide a lower standard, but many are well maintained, and have more character. Motels often line major auto routes and display 'vacancy' signs if rooms are available. Most chains have freephone reservation telephone numbers.

Bed and breakfasts can be more personal than hotels and offer an opportunity to meet other travellers. Enquire whether bath facilities are shared or private and whether a 'full' or 'continental' breakfast is served.

Country inns bridge the gap between hotels and bed and breakfasts – more charm and personal attention than a hotel; more services and amenities than a bed and breakfast.

Camping facilities for tents and recreational vehicles (RVs) are plentiful. Those in state or national parks and forests are the quietest and most primitive – facilities may be limited to pit toilets and cold showers. Private sites usually offer more amenities, but may be crowded with RVs.

Airports

Four major airports serve the Capital Region: Washington/Dulles International Airport; Ronald Reagan Washington National Airport; Baltimore/Washington International Airport; and Philadelphia International Airport. All have foreign exchange and banking services, car-hire facilities and public transport to the nearest city. Information booths help travellers with transport, lodging or touring, but cannot make bookings and usually have limited hours.

Children

The Capital Region's beaches and natural areas and some museums will appeal to children. For museums and transport, check for children's rates, often segmented by age, eg, under 3 free, 6–12 years $3, 12–18 years $4. Some attractions offer family rates.

Except for some luxury inns, most lodgings welcome children and

Room bookings

It is most difficult to find a room in tourist destinations from Memorial Day (end of May) to Labor Day (early Sept) or during special events. September and October are becoming increasingly popular with travellers. Thomas Cook or any good travel agent can handle room bookings, air tickets and local transportation. Advance bookings require a voucher or credit card number. Ask for discounts if you are a senior citizen, belong to a motoring club or are travelling off-season.

Local or state taxes on accommodation range from 1 to 13 per cent.

Above
Washington National Airport

Thomas Cook Foreign Exchange Bureaux

Thomas Cook Travellers Cheques free you from the hazards of carrying large amounts of cash. Thomas Cook Foreign Exchange bureaux are listed below. They all provide full foreign exchange facilities and will change currency and travellers' cheques (free of commission in the case of Thomas Cook Travellers Cheques).

Washington, DC Thomas Cook branches:

50 Massachusetts Avenue
Airport
Washington
2002
Tel: (202) 371-9219
Fax: (202) 789-5399

1800K St North West
Washington
20006
Tel: (202) 872-1428
Fax: (202) 789-5399

Ronald Reagan
International
PIA Services/TCCSI
Room 276 Main
Washington
Tel: (703) 417-3200

Washington/Dulles
International Airport
Main Terminal-Upper
Level, East End
Washington
20041
Tel: (703) 572-2963
Fax: (703) 572-2964

are equipped to meet needs such as nappies, rollaway beds, cribs, video games and in some places (expensive) baby-sitters. Most chains allow children under 12, 14 and sometimes 18, to stay free in their parents' rooms.

Climate

The region's mountains are rather cooler and drier than the coast. Spring arrives in March with profuse fruit tree blossom and remains balmy into May when summer arrives. July and August temperatures frequently reach the mid-90s°F (32°–35°C). The hurricane and tropical storm season in September can mean the evacuation of low-lying coastal areas, but fall weather is pleasant between storms, with colourful foliage, especially in the mountains. In December, most of the region endures brief periods of sub-freezing temperatures and occasional snowfalls, heavier in the colder mountains and southeastern Pennsylvania.

Right
Hotel Roanoke, Roanoke

Electricity

The USA uses 110v 60hz current. Two- or three-pin electrical plugs are standard. Electrical appliances from outside North America require plug and power converters, best purchased at home. Beware of buying electrical appliances in the USA since most cannot run on 220v 50hz power. Exceptions are battery-operated or dual-voltage equipment.

Entry formalities

Citizens of Australia, New Zealand, Ireland and the UK (as well as citizens of most western European countries and Japan) need only a valid passport to enter the USA if their stay is less than 90 days, they have a return ticket and have arrived on an airline participating in the visa-waiver programme (most major carriers). Canadian citizens need only identification and proof of residence. Citizens of South Africa and most other countries must present a passport and tourist visa, obtained from a US consulate or embassy in their home countries.

Currency

US dollars are the only currency, available as notes (bills) – $1, $2, $5, $10, $20, $50, $100 – and coins – the 1-cent penny, 5-cent nickel, 10-cent dime, 25-cent quarter and, more rarely, 50-cent and dollar pieces.

Dollar travellers' cheques from well-known issuers such as Thomas Cook can be used like cash or changed easily almost everywhere. Major banks will usually exchange foreign currency. Rates of exchange and commission charges are often less favourable in hotel receptions.

Cash withdrawals and advances can be made with debit and credit cards from the ubiquitous cash machines (ATMs or MACs – Money Access Centers), but check terms and availability with the card issuer before leaving home.

Credit cards are necessary to secure car-hire and most lodging reservations, and sometimes as security for incidental lodging expenses.

Customs regulations

Personal duty-free allowances for visitors entering the USA are 1 litre of spirits or wine; 200 cigarettes or 100 (non-Cuban) cigars or 2kg of smoking tobacco or any proportionate combination of tobacco products; gifts valued up to $100 total. On your return home you will be allowed to take:

- **Australia:** AU$400 in goods (AU$200 under age 18). Travellers over 18: 1125 ml of alcoholic liquor; 250 cigarettes or 250 grams of tobacco products.
- **Canada:** C$750 in goods (provided you have been away a week or more) per year; 50 cigars plus 200 cigarettes and 1 kg of tobacco (if over 16); 1.5 litres of wine.
- **Ireland:** Goods purchased outside the EU and/or in EU duty-free shops by travellers 17 and older: 800 cigarettes, 400 cigarillos, 200 cigars, 1kg tobacco, 10 litres distilled spirits, 20 litres of fortified wines, 90 litres of wine (of which only 60 litres may be sparkling), 110 litres of beer.
- **New Zealand:** NZ$700 in goods. Travellers over 17 are allowed 200 cigarettes or 250 grams of tobacco or 50 cigars; one bottle of up to 1125 ml of spirits, liqueur or other spirituous beverages; 4.5 litres of beer or 4.5 litres of wine.
- **South Africa:** Gifts valued up to R1250 per traveller (20 per cent duty on gifts valued R1251–10,000). Travellers over 18 can take in 400 cigarettes, 50 cigars, 250g tobacco; 1 litre of spirits; 2 litres of wine; 50ml of perfume; 250ml of toilet water.
- **UK:** Goods purchased outside the EU and/or in EU duty-free shops are subject to the following restrictions: £145 goods; 200 cigarettes or 50 cigars or 100 cigarillos or 250g tobacco; 2 litres of wine; 1 litre of spirits; 50ml of perfume; 250ml of toilet water.

Information Address
requests for information
well in advance.

**Delaware Tourism
Office** 99 Kings Hwy,
Dover, DE 19901; tel:
(800) 441-8846, or
(302) 739-4271;
www.state.de.us/tourism.

**Maryland Office of
Tourism** 9th floor, 217 E
Redwood St, Baltimore, MD
21202; tel: (800) 543-1036.

**Pennsylvania Center
for Travel, Tourism
and Film** Room 404,
Forum Building, Harrisburg,
PA 17120; tel: (800) VISIT-
PA, TDD, or (800) 210-
8351, or (717) 787-5453;
www.state.pa.us/visit. Call
(800) 237-4363 to request
an edited version of the
guide in tape format.

**Virginia Division of
Tourism** 901 E Byrd St,
Richmond, VA 23219; tel:
(800) VISIT-VA, or (804)
786-2051; www.virginia.org.

**Washington, DC
Convention and
Visitors Association**
Suite 600, 1212 New York
Ave. NW, Washington, DC
20005; tel: (202) 789-7000;
www.washington.org.

Drinking

Tap water is safe, and fruit juices, carbonated and spring water and soft drinks are readily available. People drink far more (weak) coffee than tea, which is usually imbibed cold and sweetened with meals. Pennsylvania, Maryland and Virginia have a few small wineries, but their products are not broadly distributed. Microbreweries and brewpubs are found throughout the region.

The drinking age for all alcoholic beverages is 21. Pennsylvania permits beer and wine sales in retail stores but limits spirits to state-controlled Wine and Spirits Shoppes. Delaware and Maryland's Montgomery County (adjacent to DC) exercise similar control. Elsewhere in the Capital Region, alcoholic beverages are sold in wine shops, package stores and retail liquor stores. Prices are often as good or better than those in duty-free stores, especially on American products such as Bourbon whiskey.

Eating out

Breakfasts tend to be hearty, lunches casual and light and dinners large. 'Southern home cooking' means hefty portions of meat, large helpings of potato or rice and vegetables cooked very soft with salt and butter or bacon fat.

Delightful exceptions are found in the cities and in coastal regions, where fresh fish and shellfish are plentiful and delicious and the variety of ethnic cuisines can boggle even a seasoned world traveller.

Fast-food dining offers convenience and relative thrift. McDonald's, Burger King, Wendy's, KFC and Popeye's Chicken are ubiquitous. One rung higher in price and variety are chain restaurants such as Applebee's.

Above
Michie Tavern, Charlottesville

Insurance

Experienced travellers carry insurance that covers their belongings, holiday investment (including provision for cancelled or delayed flights and weather problems) and health (including evacuation home in a medical emergency). Many hospitals refuse treatment without proof of insurance. Thomas Cook and other travel agencies offer comprehensive policies. Medical coverage should be high – at least $1 million.

National Park Service
National Capital Region, 1100 Ohio Dr. SW, Washington, DC 20242; tel: (202) 619-7000; www.nps.gov.

National holidays

1 Jan New Year's Day
Third Mon in Jan Martin Luther King Jr Day
Third Mon in Feb Presidents' Day
Last Mon in May Memorial Day
4 Jul Independence Day
First Mon in Sept Labor Day
Second Mon in Oct Columbus Day
11 Nov Veterans' Day
Fourth Thu in Nov Thanksgiving
25 Dec Christmas

Expect to pay $4–$10 for breakfast (more at hotels), $6–$15 for lunch and $15 and up per person for dinner before tax or tip.

Festivals

Washington DC's Cherry Blossom Festival begins in late March. Washington, DC, and Philadelphia stage extensive Independence Day (Fourth of July) festivities, while even small towns celebrate with parades and fireworks.

Re-enactments and commemorative events occur throughout the year at historic sites and battlefields. In rural areas, agricultural fairs take place from late August into October.

See route chapters for local festivals.

Food

The 'Pennsylvania Dutch' cuisine of southeastern Pennsylvania features meals suitable for hard-working farmhands. Among the specialities are relishes, fruit pies and a sugar pie called 'shoo-fly pie'. The Philadelphia cheese steak is a sandwich of thinly sliced beef, grilled onions and melted cheese on long Italian rolls.

Both sides of the Chesapeake Bay claim the best oysters and crabs, while Tidewater Virginia mussels are noted for their sweetness. Crab cakes and fried oysters are found throughout the region, and fried soft-shell crabs are a favoured local delicacy.

Health

Hospital emergency rooms handle life-threatening medical problems. Treatment will be swift and top-notch, with payment problems sorted out later. For mundane problems, doctors' offices or health clinics can provide care.

Non-USA national health plans are not accepted by USA medical providers, so some form of health insurance coverage is mandatory – at least $1 million of coverage is essential.

Bring enough prescription medicine for the trip and carry a copy of all prescriptions. No inoculations are required, and the Capital Region is basically a healthy place to visit. When visiting state and national parks or other natural areas, check for posted warnings about rabies, Lyme disease or other local health risks.

Maps

State, regional and city maps are produced by the American Automobile Association, known as AAA ('Triple A'), and distributed free to members at AAA offices. Most automobile clubs world-wide have reciprocal agreements with AAA to provide maps and other

member services. Be prepared to show a membership card. State tourism offices also provide excellent touring maps.

Museums

Many major museums open seven days a week all year. Others close Mondays, and all close New Year's Day, Christmas and Thanksgiving. Hours are generally 0900 or 1000 to 1700 or 1800. Some museums have longer summer hours and stay open one evening. Some offer reduced or free admission on one day. Smaller museums, particularly outside tourist areas, may be open limited days or hours and may close in winter.

National parks

National parks abound in the Capital Region, apart from Delaware – see the individual chapters.

Opening times

Office hours are generally Monday to Friday 0900 to 1700. Some tourist offices also open on Saturday morning all year and on weekends in summer. Many banks open from 0900 or 1000 to 1500 or 1600; some may open one evening and on Saturday morning. Petrol stations open from early till late; some open 24 hours on major routes. Large stores and shopping centres open at 0900 or 1000 Monday to Saturday and usually close between 1900 and 2100, with shorter hours on Sunday.

Packing

Everything you could ever need is available, so don't pack too much. In fact, USA prices on many goods may seem low. Do pack all medicines, glasses and contraceptives and keep duplicate prescriptions to verify your need for medication.

You can buy whatever you forget, but useful items include mini-binoculars, a magnifying flashlight for reading maps and examining marks on antiques, and a Swiss Army knife.

Postal services

Post offices are open Mon–Fri morning and afternoon, although hours may vary. Major USA Postal Service branches are open Sat and a few on Sun. Stamps may be purchased from machines in some pharmacies

Spectator sports

Washington, DC:

The MCI Center: the Wizards (basketball), Mystics (women's basketball) and Capitals (hockey);

Jack Kent Cooke Stadium, Raljon, Maryland: the Redskins (American football);

RFK Stadium: United (soccer).

Baltimore:

Oriole Park at Camden Yards; the Baltimore Orioles (baseball);

PSINet Stadium: the Baltimore Ravens (American football).

Philadelphia:

Veterans Sport Stadium: the Philadelphia Phillies (baseball); the Eagles (American football);

First Union Complex: the Flyers (hockey), the 76ers (basketball), the Kicks (soccer).

Useful telephone codes

911 – emergency calls to fire, police or ambulance;

0 – operator;

411 – information: charged;

011 – international dialling: followed by the country code (omitting the first zero if there is one) then the local number;

800/877/888 – freephone codes;

900 – information or other services, often premium-rate.

Country codes

Australia – 61
New Zealand – 64
Republic of Ireland – 353
South Africa – 27
United Kingdom – 44

and convenience stores and from some ATMs. Letters and cards with correct postage may be dropped in blue boxes outside postal branches or on street corners; parcels over 1lb must be handled by a postal clerk. All USA mail must include the 5-digit zip, and the 4-digit suffix speeds delivery. Mail everything going overseas as air mail (surface mail takes weeks).

Public holidays

On national holidays, post offices and government offices close, as do many businesses and shops. Large department stores usually stay open and often have sales. Convenience stores, supermarkets, liquor stores and petrol stations generally remain open (sometimes with curtailed hours). Workers often take short holidays, so tourist destinations can be crowded.

Nearly everything closes at New Year, Thanksgiving and Christmas.

Public transport

Amtrak (*tel: (800) 872-7245 or (202) 906–4971*) provides passenger rail services linking New York to Washington via Philadelphia and Baltimore, with some trains continuing south through Richmond. **Greyhound Bus Lines** (*tel: (800) 231-2222 or (202) 289-5160*) and **Peter Pan/Trailways** (*tel: (800) 343-9999 or (202) 371-2111*) provide long-distance, and in some cases, local bus services to major cities and smaller towns. Ask your travel agent to enquire about discount passes for non-US residents.

The bi-monthly *Thomas Cook Overseas Timetable* contains timetables for trains and buses, plus some ferry services, and much additional travel information.

Reading

Most museums and National Park visitor centres have substantial book selections in their stores. Useful outdoors guides include the appropriate Appalachian Mountain Club trail guides for Virginia and Maryland. A broad variety of materials can be found at **Borders Books and Music** *1801 K St NW, Washington, DC; tel: (202) 466-4999.*

Shopping

Clothing can be a bargain, particularly at discount stores or factory outlets, and photo equipment is generally less expensive in the USA than in Europe. Prices on alcohol, tobacco and perfume are often lower in retail stores than in duty-free shops. Do your homework on prices before you go, and shop around.

Capital Region souvenirs include folk art and crafts (particularly

Opposite
Rossetti's *La Bella Mano* in the Delaware Art Museum

Tipping

Most people performing services expect a tip. As a general guide:

restaurant bills – 15–20 per cent;
airport and hotel porters – $1 per bag;
valet parking attendants – $2;
bartenders – 50 cents to $1 per drink;
hairdressers/taxi drivers – 10 per cent;
restroom attendants – 25–50 cents.

Toilets

The most common terms are 'restroom' or 'bathroom', though 'toilet' or 'washroom' are also used. Few people recognise 'WC'.

Most businesses, including bars and restaurants, reserve restrooms for clients. Petrol stations provide keys to customers to access restrooms. Public toilets are not common along city streets. The larger tourist information centres and roadside rest stops often have them. Hotels, museums and other tourist attractions are the most dependable.

quilts) from the Pennsylvania Dutch region, antiques and small collectibles (notably 20th-century American pottery), and reproductions of objects in the collections of Colonial Williamsburg, Winterthur and similar domestic life museums.

The USA has no VAT. Each state (except Delaware) imposes its own tax on sales of products and meals, ranging up to 7 per cent. In some jurisdictions, groceries are exempt from sales tax but ready-to-eat foods are not. Pennsylvania exempts clothing.

Stores

Woodward & Lothrop and Hecht Co. are the major department stores in Washington, DC. All cities in the region have numerous shopping malls, often in restored historic buildings. Most have food courts for inexpensive dining.

Outlet malls are common in the Capital Region. Individual stores are owned by the manufacturer and offer discounts of 20–70 per cent off retail prices for clothing (including Calvin Klein, Donna Karan, Tommy Hilfiger, J. Crew) and housewares (Lenox, Dansk, Waterford/Wedgwood). Most merchandise is first quality although often last season's stock, a discontinued line or a line made for outlet sale. Examine irregular merchandise carefully.

Telephones

Dialling instructions are in the white pages telephone directory. Phone numbers are seven digits, preceded by a three-digit area code when calling outside the local area. (The area code must always be dialled in Maryland.) For long-distance calls in the USA and Canada, dial 1, then the area code, followed by the local number.

Above
Apples, honey and cider at a roadside stall

Information for travellers with a disability

SATH (Society for the Advancement of Travel for the Handicapped) *347 Fifth Ave., Suite 610, New York, NY 10016; tel: (212) 447-7284; www.sath.org.*

RADAR *12 City Forum, 250 City Rd, London EC1V 8AF; tel: 020 7250 3222.*

Safety and security

Violent crime throughout the Capital Region is on the decline. Safety is a matter of exercising common sense. Never publicly discuss travel plans or money or valuables you are carrying; keep to well-lit and well-travelled areas; do not wear expensive jewellery or carry expensive cameras or large sums of cash; do not make cash withdrawals from ATMs in deserted areas. Use a hidden money-belt for valuables and travel documents. In the unlikely event you are 'mugged', do not resist.

If you encounter trouble, dial 911 on any telephone for police, fire and medical assistance.

Above
Society Hill bookshop, Philadelphia

Pay phones are located at petrol stations, on street corners or inside restaurants, hotels and public buildings. Local calls usually cost 35 cents; a computer voice will announce when additional coins are needed. Prepaid phone cards are available at pharmacies, news stands, convenience stores and post offices. Lodgings often surcharge the cost of calls from rooms.

Time

Capital Region clocks are set to GMT minus 5 hours, called Eastern Standard Time (EST). From the first Sunday in April until the last Sunday in October, clocks go forward 1 hour to Eastern Daylight Time (EDT).

Travellers with disabilities

State and federal laws require that all public businesses, buildings and services be accessible by handicapped persons, ie, the buildings must have access ramps and toilets designed for wheelchair users. Most cities and towns have ramps built into street crossings, and most city buses have provisions for wheelchair users. Outside Washington, DC, many older facilities and historic sites don't yet comply with the standards.

Some theatres offer assisted listening devices and some attractions provide large print information materials.

Special controls for drivers with disabilities are seldom an option on hired vehicles.

The booklet 'Washington Welcomes Disabled Travelers', is available from the Washington, DC Convention and Visitors Association.

Driver's Guide

Breakdowns

Should a breakdown occur, pull to the side of the road where you will be visible but out of the way of traffic. Switch on hazard lights and, if it is safe to do so, raise the bonnet and trunk lids. Change a tyre only if you're out of the flow of traffic.

Dial 911 from any telephone to summon emergency medical or police assistance. Report your telephone number, problem, location and any need for medical assistance. Emergency phone boxes are usually placed at frequent intervals along interstate highways. If one is not visible, stay with the vehicle and wait for a patrol car to stop to render assistance.

Accidents

In the event of a collision, always stop. (Penalties for failing to stop can include imprisonment.) If either vehicle is damaged or any person injured, immediately report the accident to state police if it occurred on a state or interstate road, or to local police. Everyone involved should exchange the numbers of drivers' licences, car registration, insurance coverage information and address and telephone number for further contact. The police will also require this information. Collisions with property or personal damage must also be reported to your car-hire company.

Automobile clubs

Many non-North American auto clubs have reciprocal privileges with the AAA, including touring books, road maps, discounts at hotels and motels and some roadside assistance. Emergency towing is not always included. For information on services, ask your own club or request *Office to Serve You Abroad, American Automobile Association, 1000 AAA Drive, Heathrow, FL 32756-5063; tel: (407) 444-7700.*

Caravans and camper vans

Convenient as it may be to drive around in one's lodging, caravans and camper vans also pose some difficulties. Most communities require that they be parked in a proper campground before using them as a place to sleep, and some communities prohibit roadside parking, especially after dark. Some urban car parks lack the overhead clearance to accommodate caravans. Very large caravans must follow posted road regulations for trucks, which generally ban them from high-speed or passing lanes.

Car hire

Hiring a vehicle provides you with freedom to travel as you please with a vehicle you can leave behind when you depart. Whether booking a fly-drive package or making independent arrangements, plan well in advance to ensure getting the type and size of vehicle you desire. Unlimited mileage is standard on most auto-rental contracts, but not on RVs.

Subcompact cars are rarely available and make poor long-distance touring vehicles under USA driving conditions. Compact or economy

cars are usually the least expensive, with small price increases for intermediate cars. Full-size and luxury vehicles are more expensive to hire and operate. Most USA rental cars come with either two or four doors, an automatic transmission and air conditioning. Intermediate and larger vehicles are often equipped with cruise control, allowing constant-speed long distance travel. Some vehicles may be equipped with four-wheel-drive (4WD), a necessity for traversing some unpaved roads in the mountains or along seashores where permitted.

Most rental companies require that the driver be at least 21 years of age (some specify 25), hold a valid driver's licence and use a credit card to secure the value of the vehicle. Before leaving the hire agency, be certain that you have the car registration and all rental documentation. Also be sure you know how to operate the vehicle (there's nothing more maddening than running low on petrol and being unable to find the fuel tank lid). If possible, ask for a vehicle without obvious rental company identifiers, as thieves often target such cars.

Driving conditions

The worst driving conditions in the region involve winter snow, or heavy rain and high winds during the fall storm season. Drive with low-beam headlights at all times as a safety precaution. Avoid using main beam in snow, rain or fog as it can blind other drivers (or yourself with reflected glare). If visibility is poor, pull over and wait for the storm to pass. The danger of hydroplaning arises during sudden heavy rain, particularly at speeds above 35 mph.

Driving on snow takes skill, and if you are unfamiliar with stopping, turning and negotiating skids on snow, practise in a vacant car park before venturing out on the road. Apply brakes lightly but repeatedly to stop on snow. Hired cars are generally equipped with all-season tyres, which do not grip well in more than 1 inch of snow. During winter, keep the petrol tank topped up in case you become stuck. If you are stranded, stay in the vehicle, place a red flag on the antenna or door handle, try to keep warm with blankets, and do not run the engine any more than necessary. Make sure the exhaust pipe is not clogged with snow. Useful winter driving gear includes a blanket, a windscreen ice scraper, a small shovel and a bucket or bag of sand. Serious snowstorms are infrequent in the region; as a result, municipalities are often poorly equipped to clear the roads.

Documents

A valid driver's licence from your home country should be on your person at all times. Vehicle registration and, where applicable, a valid car-hire contract must be in the vehicle when it is underway. Proof of liability insurance must also be supplied in the event of an accident.

Information

In addition to automobile clubs, drivers will find the roadside tourist centres of each state useful sources of maps and road condition updates.

Drinking and driving laws

Driving under the influence of alcohol or other drugs is illegal throughout the USA. Intoxication is defined as 0.08 per cent blood alcohol in most states. If a police officer stops you and suspects you may be impaired, you may be asked to take an instant 'breathalyser' test. You are permitted to refuse the test, but doing so means automatic suspension of your driver's licence.

Fuel

Petrol ('gas' or 'gasoline') is sold by the gallon (3.82 litres) at prices posted in cents and tenths of a cent – usually ranging from 119.9 cents to 185.9 cents, with a great deal of volatility based on season, location and Middle Eastern politics. All gasoline sold in the Capital Region is unleaded and most also contains various additives to decrease emissions of sulphur and nitrogen oxides. Diesel fuel is sold at separate pumps. Most fuel pumps are self-service, and many accept credit and bank cards for payment. 'Full-service' pumps sometimes charge as much as 20 cents more per gallon.

Below
Motorcyle policeman

Insurance

Third-party liability insurance is required throughout the region. In practice, coverage far in excess of the minimum is desirable. Visitors from outside the USA are wise to take out top-up liability coverage – check with your travel agent or hire car agent – which covers liability up to $1 million. Car hire agencies also ask drivers to take out collision damage waiver (CDW) or loss damage waiver (LDW). Declining makes the driver personally responsible for damage to the vehicle. CDW is often included as part of a fly-drive package. USA and Canadian drivers may be covered by their own insurance. Some premium credit cards also provide CDW as a free benefit when using the card for car hire.

Parking

Public car parks are generally indicated with a blue sign carrying the letter 'P' and a directional arrow. Rates are posted at the entrance. Urban garages are often expensive but may give discounts to shoppers or theatre-goers who have their timecards stamped with a validation sticker. Coin-operated parking meters are in effect in most areas, with rates ranging from $1 per hour in urban areas to as little as 25 cents per hour in small towns. Parking is forbidden near a fire hydrant, a red or yellow kerb or in front of a wheelchair access ramp. In urban areas, kerbside parking may be banned during morning and evening commuting hours. If you violate parking regulations or let a meter expire, expect to be issued a citation. If you do not pay it, the car hire company may charge the fine to your credit card along with a substantial penalty.

Police

Police cars signal drivers with flashing blue or blue-and-red lights and sometimes with a siren. While most police vehicles are marked, some highways are patrolled by unmarked cars. When signalled, pull over to the side and have your driver's licence and vehicle registration ready for inspection. Roll down the window but do not leave the vehicle unless requested. You have the right to ask an officer for identification.

Road signs

International symbols are used for many road signs but sometimes differ from European symbols. All language signs are in English. Signs may be white, yellow, green, brown or blue. Stop, Yield, Do Not Enter and Wrong Way signs are usually *red and white*. Warning or direction indicators are generally *yellow*. Roadwork and temporary detour signs

are generally *reflective orange*. Green indicates highway directions, blue denotes non-driving information (parking, informational radio frequencies). Brown signs are usually reserved to indicate parks, campsites and outdoor activities.

Traffic lights are red (stop), green (go) and yellow (caution). Simultaneous red and yellow lights indicate a pedestrian crossing. Unless otherwise posted, it is legal to make a right-hand turn at a red light if there is no traffic and no pedestrian-crossing light is lit. Motorists are expected to yield the right of way to pedestrians at all zebra lanes or 'crosswalks', although the law is more observed in the breach than the practice.

Seat belts

All jurisdictions in the Capital Region require drivers and passengers to use seat belts whenever a vehicle is in motion.

Security

Lock your car. Lock it when you are inside and when you leave it. Do not leave maps, guidebooks and other tourist paraphernalia in clear view. Try always to park in well-lit areas.

Above
Historic gas station

Opposite
South St, Philadelphia

Speed limits

Official highway speed limits are 65 mph in rural areas, 55 mph in urban areas. Many Capital Region drivers take these as suggestions rather than law. You are safest when moving with the flow of traffic, neither faster nor significantly slower. Note that most interstate highways also have *minimum* speed limits. Expect to be overtaken and passed on both sides if you are moving slower than the rest of traffic. This can be disconcerting but is perfectly legal in most states. On secondary roads, speed limits are much lower. When not posted, assume the limit is 30 mph in residential areas, 20 mph near schools and hospitals.

Tolls

Toll roads, bridges and tunnels are a fact of life throughout the Capital Region. On short toll roads, bridges and tunnels, drivers are expected to pay cash at the toll booths. (A good supply of quarters, also useful for parking meters, comes in handy.) On longer toll roads, drivers pick up a toll card when entering the highway and pay a variable rate based on mileage when exiting.

Getting to Washington DC, Virginia, Maryland and Delaware

Using your car

Consider going without a car during your stay in downtown Washington, as public transit is a reasonably priced and efficient way to see the major sights and parking in DC can be very difficult and expensive. Driving is even worse than parking, often confusing even the residents. If you must pick up your car at the airport, arrange parking in advance with your Washington hotel. However, if you choose to stay outside Washington in the suburbs, a car is an absolute necessity.

Reservations

It is always a good idea to book your first night's room in advance, especially from Apr through Nov in Washington and anywhere in the region during July and Aug. If you are arriving on a weekend and plan to stay outside of Washington, be sure to reserve your room in advance, as weekend getaway accommodation often fills up.

By air

International travellers to the Capital Region generally arrive at Washington's Dulles Airport (IAD), about 26 miles west of Washington in Virginia; Baltimore-Washington Airport (BWI), about 25 miles north of Washington in Maryland, or sometimes Philadelphia International Airport (PHL) in Pennsylvania. After clearing Customs and Immigration and rechecking baggage, passengers transfer for flights into Richmond or Newport News (both in Virginia) or smaller cities. If a particularly good fare is available, it is also feasible to enter the USA through New York's John F Kennedy Airport (JFK) or Newark (New Jersey) Airport (NWK), then transfer to a connecting flight.

It is also possible to travel by train from JFK or Newark airports by transferring to Amtrak's terminal at Grand Central Station in Manhattan. (Newark is closer to Manhattan and the transfer takes less time.)

Travellers from other parts of North America might also arrive at the older and smaller Ronald Reagan National Airport (NAT), 4 miles from Washington, where transfer downtown is easy on the metro.

Most international carriers service either Dulles or Baltimore-Washington international airports, with frequent daily service to the UK offered by British Air, Virgin Atlantic, United, Continental and American. Philadelphia also has direct UK flights through US Airways, often priced slightly lower than the Washington service. Many UK and European charter flights to the Capital Region use Baltimore-Washington International.

Domestic USA air service is extensive and cheaper than within Europe. There are shuttle flights into Washington hourly from Boston and every half hour from New York. Virtually every major airport in North America offers regular Washington flights, often several per day.

Car-hire facilities are found at every airport (be sure to reserve in advance) and public transport (train, bus, limousine and, at National Airport only, metro) is available into the nearest city. Travellers hiring a car will do well to look for an off-airport agency, as the airport tax on car hire can hike rates as much as 20 per cent. Agencies generally provide shuttle bus services to and from the airport.

By train or bus

Amtrak, the USA passenger rail system, offers frequent services to Washington, with more than 50 trains arriving per day at the historic and beautifully refurbished Union Station. Washington is the southern terminus of Amtrak's Northeast Corridor Metroliner service (between Boston and Washington via New York, Philadelphia and Baltimore). A premium-priced high speed service was inaugurated between New York and Washington in late 1999. Washington also serves as the eastern terminus of several east–west train lines and the northern hub of trains from Florida and Georgia. Amtrak is also a viable way to reach downtown Washington from Baltimore-Washington Airport by picking up the connector shuttle bus at the arrivals area.

Bus service to Washington is usually through Greyhound Bus Lines or Peter Pan, with connections to all major cities and many small towns. It is usually the least expensive way to reach Washington and is comparable in time to the train. Although coach services have been upgraded in recent years, bus travel remains the least comfortable and most confining.

Interstate highways

Interstate highways are always the fastest way to drive anywhere within the Capital Region but are usually the least scenic. They are convenient for travellers, as services (fuel, restaurants and motels) are found clustered at many exits. Away from the major cities, rest stops between exits offer picnic spots and some also have toilet facilities. Rest stops on toll roads generally offer food and fuel as well.

By car

The USA East Coast is virtually paved with the multi-lane roadways known as the USA Interstate Highway System. Many of these highways converge on Washington, as the seat of government. DC is surrounded by the Capital Beltway, formed by interstates I-95 and I-495. I-95 joins the circle from the south from Richmond and leaves it heading north to Baltimore, Wilmington, Philadelphia and New York. Other major interstate spurs converging on Washington are I-270, which heads south from Frederick, Maryland, to join the Beltway's northwest corner, and I-66, which comes in from the west. Major state highways connecting to the Beltway include Rte 50 from Annapolis.

Just to confuse matters, the western half of the Beltway is signposted both I-495 and I-95 ('400' series highways are circumferential connectors in the Interstate system). To get into Washington from the south, drive I-95 to I-395 and cross the 14th St Bridge into DC. From the north, stay on I-95 south to Rte 50, also called the John Hanson Hwy, which becomes New York Ave. in DC.

Above
Railroad train in Roanoke Transport Museum

Setting the scene

Land and water

The Capital Region begins in the west with the ancient rounded hills of the Appalachian Mountains. The landscape then sweeps down across rolling plains and farmland to the tidal edges of great rivers and commodious bays. It finally concludes on the eastern periphery with hundreds of miles of sandy barrier beaches facing the Atlantic Ocean.

Yet the Capital Region is also highly compact by North American standards. A determined driver can traverse it north to south or east to west in less than a full day, although no one except a fugitive would do so. Because it includes three of the major Eastern Seaboard cities – Philadelphia, Baltimore and Washington – the region is well served by major highways. Yet even the rural districts of the Capital Region support excellent road systems, making the area a prime region for fly-drive touring.

Above
Swallow Falls, near Deep Creek in Western Maryland

The most populous areas of the Capital Region lie on the water, and the rivers and bays have dictated much of the region's destiny. The great inland sea of the Chesapeake Bay is the central defining feature of the coasts of Maryland and Virginia. It divides Maryland between the heavily populated western side and the almost mythical water-world of the Eastern Shore, an area seemingly removed both in geography and chronology from the bustle of Baltimore, Annapolis and Washington. Virginia's portion of the Chesapeake, often called the Tidewater, is no less magical in its vast marshy tracks and swampy rivers that drain the interior highlands. Even the northern reaches of the Chesapeake, where the broad and deep Susquehanna River flows down through the black soil of eastern Pennsylvania's fertile farmland to empty into salt water, have an undeniable scenic appeal.

The Chesapeake was America's first great inland waterway. This bay of sandy shores and shoals quickly proved one of the New World's finest shellfish fisheries, and its protected waters encouraged a steady flow of local trade by sail. An abundance of safe harbours virtually guaranteed the emergence of great shipbuilding centres, some of which, such as Norfolk–Newport News, persist to this day.

The Chesapeake also proved essential to the opening of the continental United States because the only practical road to the interior of the continent began at Baltimore and followed the Susquehanna upriver, connecting across western Pennsylvania to the mighty Ohio Valley. When transportation technology matured, Baltimore became the eastern railhead to the west, linked by water to Philadelphia through a canal that connected the Delaware and Chesapeake bays.

The significance of the Chesapeake in the fledgling economy of the United States helped determine the siting of the District of Columbia as the new national capital. Safely sheltered from enemy warships on the Potomac River (or so the founding fathers thought), the District stood halfway down the coast of the new country, poised between the industrial and mechanical North and the agricultural South.

Overland travel by motorcar has changed all the circumstances that led to the initial heavy settlement of the western banks of the Chesapeake, for journeys to the interior that once took weeks by horse or mule now take only hours by automobile.

The Piedmont Plateau rises from the 'fall line' of the rivers flowing into the Chesapeake Bay (the point where waterfalls and rapids make them no longer navigable, even in small boats). Hardly as flat as the term 'plateau' implies, the Piedmont is a shelf of metamorphic rock that ranges from 400 to 1 200 ft above sea level. The rolling country is broken by sharp ridges and deep hollows and punctuated with loaf-shaped hills. The Piedmont extends all the way from Virginia's southern border through Maryland, into southeastern Pennsylvania at Gettysburg and around to northern Delaware. It encompasses some of the Capital Region's richest farmland, from the tobacco country of Virginia to the truck farms of Maryland to the hard-working farms of the Pennsylvania Dutch country.

The Appalachian Mountain chain rises west of the Piedmont, walling off the Atlantic coast from the continental interior. The Capital Region's portion of this long mountain system, which extends from Georgia north into Maine, includes the Blue Ridge and Allegheny mountains, with the fertile valleys of Shenandoah (Virginia) and Cumberland (Maryland) between them. The South Mountains, which encircle Gettysburg in Pennsylvania, are a northerly extension of the Blue Ridge chain. Some of the most scenic motorways in eastern North America, including Virginia's Skyline Drive, cross the sparsely populated mountain country of the Capital Region.

Below
Living history in Jamestown

Native Americans

Virtually the entire Capital Region was extensively inhabited by Native Americans when European settlers first arrived. Archaeologists group the diverse Native American peoples of the region as 'Eastern Woodlands tribes' because they shared a common cultural pattern, but they belonged to several distinct linguistic groups. The Chesapeake Bay was inhabited by about 10,000 Algonquian-speaking Chesapeakes under the general leadership of Chief Powhatan. To the north, the Lenni Lenape (called 'Delawares' by the English) and the Susquehannocks were also Algonquian peoples. The people of the Piedmont were Sioux of the Monacan and Monahoac tribes. Iroquois-speaking Nottoways inhabited southeastern coastal Virginia, while the

Cherokee occupied the highlands in the southwestern sector of the Capital Region. The recreated Powhatan Village at Jamestown, Virginia, represents in broad strokes the semi-nomadic lifestyle of these hunter-gatherer-farmers at the time of European contact.

Disease and conflict with the colonists drastically reduced the number of Native Americans in the Capital Region, and the remaining groups were further decimated during the American Revolution, having allied themselves with the British. Only the Cherokee survived as a cohesive tribe at the end of the Revolution. Although the tribe was officially removed by force from the eastern states in the 19th century, many Cherokees remained behind and were assimilated into the general population.

While there is some evidence that early colonists in Virginia adopted crops and fishing techniques from the local tribes, the principal legacy of the first inhabitants of the Capital Region has been the semi-legendary figure of Pocahontas. She was the daughter of the powerful Chief Powhatan, and her affinity for the English helped the Jamestown colonists establish a toehold in the New World. According to adventurer-explorer John Smith's sometimes exaggerated accounts of his year and a half in Virginia, Pocahontas interceded with her father to save Smith's life when he was taken prisoner by a Powhatan hunting party. She visited the English settlers often and married John Rolfe, the man who introduced the mild West Indies tobacco to Virginia that would become the state's economic mainstay. Christened Lady Rebecca, Pocahontas visited the English court with her husband, where, by all accounts, she was captivating. Only 21 years old, she died at the outset of her return trip to Virginia. Some years later her son Thomas returned to Virginia and prospered as a planter. Her story, augmented in successive retellings, remains a touchstone in American cultural myth.

Below
St John's Church, Richmond

Exploration and settlement

One of the first European captains to explore the coast of the Capital Region was the Dutchman Henry Hudson, but the first detailed maps, particularly of the Chesapeake Bay, were drawn by John Smith to promote further settlement.

Unlike New England and Florida, the Capital Region was initially colonised by many nations. The first permanent English settlement in the

Above
Historic quilt, Art Museum of
Western Virginia, Roanoke

New World was planted at Jamestown, Virginia, in 1607. Soon thereafter, Sweden and the Netherlands vied for hegemony in Delaware, with Wilmington becoming the Swedish town and New Castle the Dutch. When the Dutch got the upper hand, they let the Swedish settlers stay, and when the English gained control of the entire seaboard by 1664, they permitted both groups to remain. The community that would become Philadelphia saw the same succession, concluding with the grant to Quaker William Penn from the English king in 1681. Pennsylvania (literally 'Penn's Woods') was a great experiment in religious tolerance, and soon attracted many pacifist Mennonites of primarily German descent who later spread into other parts of the Capital Region.

Religious refugees formed a large portion of the early settlers. English Roman Catholics took refuge in Maryland beginning in 1634. Annapolis was settled in 1649 by Puritans fleeing intolerance in Virginia. The last frontiers of the region were settled in the early 18th century, when Scots-Irish immigrants flowed into the mountains of Appalachia. Even before the great waves of immigration that remade the USA in the mid-19th century, the Capital Region was already a diverse cultural stew.

Making a nation

By the time of the American Revolution, Penn's 'City of Brotherly Love', founded on the twin virtues of industriousness and tolerance, had grown into the largest, richest and most powerful city in the American colonies. It's not surprising that history tapped Philadelphia as the political as well as the economic capital of the evolving United States of America during the last quarter of the 18th century.

In 1774, representatives of the American colonies convened in Philadelphia as the First Continental Congress to air their grievances against the British Crown. When those grievances were rebuffed, the city became the first capital of a new nation in revolt. Fervour for independence ran high and fighting at last broke out in April 1775 in Massachusetts.

As relations between the colonies and the Crown deteriorated, Congress authorised a committee to draft a Declaration of Independence. Virginian Thomas Jefferson took the lead, transforming Enlightenment philosophy into a document of political action. Making some changes, Congress adopted the statement on 4 July 1776, commemorated ever since as Independence Day. (Philadelphia, predictably, pulls out all the stops to celebrate.) Soon thereafter, the representatives reconstituted themselves as the Second Continental Congress, which remained in Philadelphia (with brief refuges in York, Pennsylvania, and Annapolis, Maryland) as the national government until the Revolution was concluded with the Treaty of Paris in 1783. In 1787 delegates to the Continental Congress drafted the Constitution of the United States which was ratified first by Delaware and ultimately by all 13 states by 1789. Philadelphia's Independence National Historical Park is a compact area in the heart of the old city, dense with some of the country's most important touchstones of the Revolution, including Independence Hall, where both the Declaration of Independence and the Constitution were signed.

Below
Roanoke's History Museum

As the politics and ideology of the new nation were being forged in Philadelphia, war raged throughout the Capital Region. Many battle sites recall those difficult years with commemorative parks, but two that hold prominent places in USA history are Valley Forge, Pennsylvania, where the Continental Army endured desperate hardship over the winter of 1777–8 and emerged strengthened with resolve, and Yorktown, Virginia, where the largest of the British armies, under the command of Lieutenant General Charles, Earl of Cornwallis, surrendered to Washington's American forces, spelling the end of the war.

THEY (WHO) SEEK TO ESTABLISH
SYSTEMS OF GOVERNMENT BASED ON
THE REGIMENTATION OF ALL HUMAN
BEINGS BY A HANDFUL OF INDIVIDUAL
RULERS...CALL THIS A NEW ORDER.
IT IS NOT NEW AND IT IS NOT ORDER.

Above
Franklin D Roosevelt
Memorial, Washington, DC

Creating the capital

With the advent of peace, the US Congress set out to build a new capital worthy of a new nation. As a political compromise over payment of war debts, the district was to be situated in the South and Congress left it to President George Washington to select the spot. Washington settled on a diamond-shaped parcel near the mouth of the Potomac River close to his home, Mount Vernon, in Virginia. In 1791, Virginia and Maryland ceded land to create the District of Columbia, which Congress named in honour of Christopher Columbus. The capital city of Washington was named after the president. The initial grand plans drawn by Pierre Charles L'Enfant were slow in being realised. Congress moved into the half-finished Capitol and President John Adams into the President's House (as the White House was then called) in 1800.

Thomas Jefferson was the first president to be inaugurated in the new capital. Washington remained a muddy miasmal district in its early years, and in 1814 British forces burned both the Capitol and the White House during what Americans call the War of 1812. During that same war, a poetic-minded young man named Francis Scott Key observed the night-time bombardment of Fort McHenry in Baltimore. Seeing the American flag intact when the smoke cleared, he penned 'The Star-Spangled Banner', which became the national anthem. Washington was rebuilt from the ravages of the War of 1812, but did not take on the grandeur its original architects had envisioned until six decades later. Monuments and memorials, including those to the casualties of 20th-century wars, continue to be added even today.

Above
Charlottesville

A house divided

The great watershed in the history and the psyche of the Capital Region was not the creation of Washington, but rather the Civil War, as it was called by the victorious Union, or the War Between the States, as it was known in the vanquished Confederacy. Political rationales for the Civil War differ. In no small part, it was fought over the abolition of slavery, although equal rights unabridged by race did not became the law of the land until 98 years after the Confederacy's defeat. Other historians cast the war as the struggle for economic hegemony between the agricultural South and the industrial North. And a generation of Southern political leaders, some still in office, insist it was fought over the rights of individual states to govern themselves without interference by the federal government. At any rate, the Civil War remains a sensitive subject throughout the region, subject to much melodrama and mythology. In parts of Virginia, in particular, 'the war' still refers to the Civil War.

The conflagration of 1861–5 literally pitted brother against brother in the bloodiest war the world had seen to that point. No other part of the country was so rent as the Capital Region where Virginia, with some reluctance, joined the Confederacy and the other states, often by the slimmest of political margins, remained with the Union. Washington, capital of the Union, and Richmond, Virginia, capital of the Confederacy, stood just 106 miles apart, virtually guaranteeing that the lands between and around them would be laid waste by four years of unrelenting warfare.

Virginia, it can be argued, suffered the most. In fact, the first battle of the Civil War took place on 21 July 1861 in Manassas, Virginia, near the creek called Bull Run, and the war came to an effective close in Virginia when Confederate General Robert E Lee surrendered, on 9 April 1865, at Appomattox Court House. During the course of the conflict, more Americans died than in both World Wars combined. At Antietam near Sharpsburg, Maryland, 23,000 men were killed or wounded in a single day in 1862 in the first attempt of the Confederacy to invade the North. At Gettysburg, Pennsylvania, nearly 53,000 were killed, wounded or captured in three grim days of battle in July 1863. National, state and local parks commemorate a trauma that refuses to fade from memory. Many artefacts remain and interpretation of battle strategy and the human toll is often excellent, particularly at the larger sites. The ferocity of the fighting is still hard to grasp, but travellers may get a sense of the scope of the battles at the re-enactments staged by costumed history buffs.

A collage of cultures and styles

Although travellers often encounter a distinctly Southern flavour in the pace, food, customs and spoken accent of the Capital Region, the area has a startling diversity. At the heart, of course, is official Washington of the power brokers, where the movie-set landscape of the Washington Mall, Pennsylvania Avenue and Capitol Hill provides the backdrop for the daily interactions of some of the most influential people in the world. But Washington is more than elected officials. It was the US's first city with a majority African-American population, and issues of racial justice are always on the front burner. At the same time, the cosmopolitan clique of foreign embassy personnel guarantees an exotic tinge to Washington life, while an entire subculture of career government employees (many living in the city part-time, far from their families) ensures an active nightlife.

Baltimore and Philadelphia are vibrant metropolitan centres where extensive African-American and Italian-American populations influence the culinary and cultural traditions of city life. While nearby Wilmington, Delaware, has a similar ethnic composition, it is also strongly influenced by the glass-towered business district. Half the Fortune 500 companies (and one-third of those listed on the New York Stock Exchange) maintain their corporate headquarters in the small state. That industrial and financial power finds a genteel expression in the adjacent suburbs of northern Delaware and southeastern Pennsylvania, where some of the US's finest mansion gardens are open to the public.

The money is older along Virginia's Tidewater, where literally hundreds of plantations and grand country homes line the coastal plain from the mouth of the James River north to Richmond. Yet between the big houses of the Tidewater gentry are small villages and towns tied intimately to the ebb and flow of life along the edge of the Chesapeake. Maryland's Eastern Shore, on the far side of the Chesapeake Bay, offers a glimpse into a nearly vanished way of life, where time is measured in the shift of tides and a resident's worth is measured in his or her skill with a boat. Half fishing villages, half yacht harbours, the Eastern Shore is the Capital Region's most enduring water-world.

The title of pleasure-boat capital of the region, however, goes to Annapolis, where the traditions and contradictions of the Capital Region converge. From its 18th-century city centre, Annapolis spills down into one of the Chesapeake's busiest harbours, full of swift little day-sailors, private schooners and the no-nonsense military vessels of the US Naval Academy. In Annapolis, ancient skills of hauling canvas in the wind are augmented by the latest in satellite navigation.

No such technology is used by the region's most unusual cultural survival, the Amish and Old Order Mennonites, in the Pennsylvania Dutch Country west of Philadelphia. Less than two hours' drive from the hurly-burly of Washington, these devout farmers work their land without the aid of electricity or the internal combustion engine, a horse-and-buggy world just at the fringe of perhaps the world's most modern capital.

Highlights and touring itineraries

Spend at least four days, preferably a full week, in Washington, but don't stop there. Get out to the countryside and the other cities of the region to enjoy some of the greatest scenic and cultural variety available anywhere in the USA. These suggested routes are starting points for explorations that can last from one to three weeks each.

Above
Crownsville's Renaissance Faire

The northern history route

This route encompasses some of the major battlefields of the Civil War, several sites associated with the American Revolution and some of the prettiest farmland and gardens of the region. Drive northwest from Washington on I-270 to Frederick, Maryland, veering westward to visit the sombre Civil War battlefields of Antietam and Sharpsburg and the flashpoint of North–South hostilities, Harper's Ferry, just inside West Virginia (*pages 192–209*). Return through Frederick to drive north on Rte 15 to Gettysburg, Pennsylvania, to Gettysburg National Military Park for more Civil War history (*pages 268–81*). Continue on Rte 15 to Lancaster and tour the unusually anachronistic farming region known as Pennsylvania Dutch Country, ending at the Revolutionary War site of Valley Forge and the outlet shopping of King-of-Prussia. I-76 leads south a mere 12 miles to the US's first capital, Philadelphia (*pages 254–67*). Follow Rte 1 south from Philadelphia through small towns filled with gardens and mansions in the Brandywine Valley (*pages 246–53*), pausing to tour Wilmington, Delaware (*pages 238–45*). Follow Rte 40 south along the western shore of the Chesapeake Bay (*pages 220–7*), stopping to savour the coastal attractions. Continue south to the bustling city of Baltimore (*pages 158–71*). I-95 is the best return route to Washington.

High country

The mountains and broad valleys of the southwestern segment of the Capital Region have a wild and stunning beauty especially accentuated by colourful fall foliage. The entire route follows the mountainous backbone of Virginia. Follow I-66 west from Washington to exit 57 (Rte 50) through picturesque horse farm country to Winchester for a taste of Civil War history and country music. Follow Rte 11 south to Strasburg (*pages 70–7*), one of the region's antiquing capitals. Drive east on Rte 55 to Front Royal and follow Rte 340 south to the magnificent geological wonder of Luray Caverns. Rte 211 east connects to the Skyline Drive (*pages 78–89*). Drive south through

Shenandoah National Park to Waynesboro, detouring east to visit the university city of Charlottesville and Appomattox, where the largest Confederate Army surrendered to the largest Union force (*pages 90–101*). Double back and continue south on the Blue Ridge Parkway, an extension of the Skyline Drive to Roanoke. From Roanoke return north along Rte 11 through the Shenandoah Valley, stopping for such scenic marvels as Natural Bridge. At Staunton, consider the detour west along the designated 'scenic byways' to George Washington National Forest (*pages 78–89*). At Strasburg, return to Washington via I-66 with a stop at the Manassas National Battlefield Park, site of two critical Civil War battles.

By the water

The Chesapeake Bay and the Atlantic Ocean have stamped portions of the Capital Region with a distinctly nautical lifestyle. This route traverses both the modern resort playgrounds and the venerable waterside settlements of Maryland and Virginia, crossing Chesapeake Bay through the twin engineering feats of a long bridge and even longer bridge-tunnel. Drive east from Washington on Rte 50 to the postcard-perfect city of Annapolis (*pages 172–81*), wandering its Georgian streets and touring the US Naval Academy. Continue east across the Chesapeake Bay Bridge to Maryland's fabled Eastern Shore (*pages 182–91*), where you should eat your fill of oysters and crabs. Explore the small villages of the region, eventually returning to Rte 50 through Cambridge and Salisbury and finally to the brazen seaside resort town of Ocean City on the Atlantic. Trace the Atlantic shore southward along Chincoteague Bay and follow Rte 13 south all the way to the Chesapeake Bay Bridge-Tunnel to cross into the Hampton Roads, Virginia, area (*pages 148–57*). Consider the long detour to North Carolina's Outer Banks if you are transfixed by sea island life or enamoured of bird-watching.

Otherwise, follow Rte 17 north to Yorktown, the beginning of the end of the American Revolution, and pick up the Colonial Parkway to Williamsburg (*pages 138–47*), the most extensive restoration of colonial-era life in the USA. Drive Rte 5 north along the James River (*pages 130–7*) through plantation country to Richmond (*pages 102–13*), capital of the Confederacy. Rte 1 north leads through Fredericksburg and its historic Civil War battlefields (*pages 122–9*) back to Washington.

Washington DC

Ratings

Museums	●●●●●
Children	●●●●
Gastronomy	●●●●
History	●●●●
Shopping	●●●●
Entertainment	●●●
Nature and wildlife	●●●
Beaches	●

Visitors to Washington, DC, are often surprised both by its approachability and by its wealth of cultural attractions. Power is, of course, Washington's defining feature, and the city's architecture, characterised by stern monuments of dazzling white Greek- and Roman-inspired columns, is a statement of its eminence. Politics aside, Washington is host to a mind-boggling collection of museums and art galleries, many operated by the Smithsonian Institution, one of the finest museum complexes in the world. What's more, nearly all are free. Founded in 1791, Washington, DC – or just DC to its residents (the DC stands for 'District of Columbia', referring to Christopher Columbus) – was constructed specifically as the nation's seat of government. Its highbrow status does lend the city a certain stuffiness, but with a decidedly international population, some lively neighbourhoods and good concert life, Washington cannot fail to impress for days on end.

Getting there and getting around

ⓘ Washington, DC Convention and Visitors Association *1212 New York Ave. NW; tel: (202) 789-7000; www.washington.org.*

White House Visitor Center *1450 Pennsylvania Ave. NW; tel: (202) 456-7041; open summer daily 0700–1900, otherwise 0800–1700. Handy for general information.*

By air
Washington, DC, is served by three airports. **Dulles Airport** is the largest, and Washington Flyer buses run every half an hour to several downtown locations. The newly renamed **Ronald Reagan National Airport** is practically in the centre of town, and handles shorter domestic routes; the easiest way into town is on the Metrorail subway system. **Baltimore/Washington International Airport**, on the southern fringes of Baltimore, is served by regional rail and Amtrak (catch a shuttle bus from the arrivals terminal) to Baltimore's Penn Station and Washington's Union Station.

By rail
Union Station has been gloriously reconstructed, and Amtrak serves many cities along the eastern seaboard as well as the Midwest. It is located at 1st St and Massachusetts Ave. NE, just a few blocks from the Capitol, and is connected to the city by Metro. Greyhound and Peter

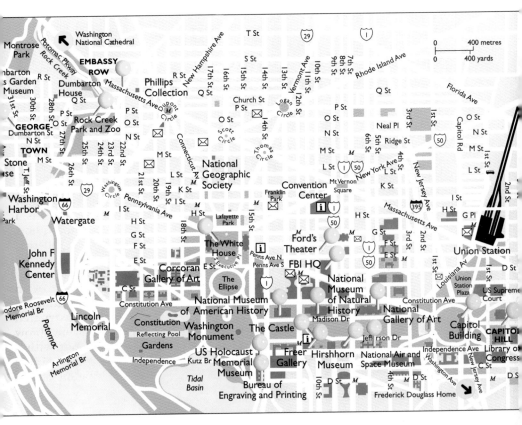

Montrose Park

Washington National Cathedral

T St

S St

EMBASSY ROW

Rhode Island Ave

New Hampshire Ave

nbarton s Garden Museum

Dumbarton House

Phillips Collection

Church St

Q St

Florida Ave

Massachusetts Ave

Dupont Circle

R St

New Hampshire Ave

17th St

16th St

15th St

14th St

13th St

Vermont Ave

12th St

11th St

10th St

9th St

8th St

7th St

O St

N St

3rd St

1st St

Capitol Rd

50

GEORGETOWN

Rock Creek Park and Zoo

Dumbarton St

Q St

P St

O St

N St

Scott Circle

Logan Circle

P St

O St

Neal Pl

Ridge St

N St

M St

L St

K St

50

Stone se

M St

Connecticut Ave

Thomas Circle

National Geographic Society

Franklin Park

Convention Center

Mt Vernon Square

New York Ave

New Jersey Ave

Massachusetts Ave

Washington Harbor

Watergate

Pennsylvania Ave

Washington Circle

Lafayette Park

H St

G St

F St

E St

The White House

Ford's Theater

FBI HQ

H St

G Pl

Union Station

John F Kennedy Center

Corcoran Gallery of Art

The Ellipse

Penns Ave N

Penns Ave S

National Museum of Natural History

National Gallery of Art

Union Station Plaza

US Supreme Court

odore Roosevelt Memorial Br

Lincoln Memorial

Constitution Ave

National Museum of American History

Madison Dr

Constitution Gardens

Reflecting Pool

Washington Monument

The Castle

Jefferson Dr

Capitol Building

CAPITOL HILL

Library of Congress

Potomac

Arlington Memorial Br

Independence

Kutz Br

US Holocaust Memorial Museum

Tidal Basin

Freer Gallery

Hirshhorn Museum

National Air and Space Museum

Independence Ave

Washington Ave

New Jersey Ave

Frederick Douglass Home

Bureau of Engraving and Printing

0   400 metres

0   400 yards

Right
Cherry blossoms, Tidal Basin

Above
Lincoln Memorial

Pan buses operate from a station a few blocks north, at 1st and L Sts NE.

By car
Arriving in DC by car can be complicated for drivers unfamiliar with the city's grid system, criss-crossed in all directions by large avenues. The Beltway (I-495) rings the city; I-95 skirts the centre via I-495. From points north on I-95, follow signs to Downtown Washington via the Baltimore-Washington Parkway and Rte 50. From points south on I-95, follow I-395 to the National Mall. From points west, I-66 brings you across the Potomac to near the Lincoln Memorial.

Public transport
Because driving is so confusing, you may want to park your car at your hotel and use the excellent Metrorail subway system, one of the cleanest and safest you'll see anywhere. Fares vary according to distance travelled and time of day; check the fare to your destination from well-lit signs in the station, and buy a farecard from machines. Be sure to hold on to it to exit the system. A Metrorail One Day Pass costing $5 gives unlimited travel from 0930 to closing time (around midnight) on weekdays, and all day otherwise; pick it up at Metro Center station. Metrobuses fill in where the subway does not; the only route you're likely to use is the 30 line (any of buses 30, 32, 34 or 36), which runs from the Capitol Building along Pennsylvania Ave. to Foggy Bottom-GWU metro station, on through Georgetown and north to the National Cathedral.

Sights

Bureau of Engraving and Printing $ *14th and C Sts SW (metro: Smithsonian); tel: (202) 874-3019; open Mon–Fri 0900–1400, except Christmas–New Year.*

Bureau of Engraving and Printing◆
Jaws drop at the sight of millions of dollars a day being printed at the Bureau of Engraving and Printing. Some $100 billion is printed here annually, and tours lead you through glass-enclosed hallways past the engraving, cutting and printing rooms. Stacks of bills in uncut sheets line the walls – so near and yet so far – but you can buy shredded bills in canisters at the gift shop. Postage stamps are also printed here, but are not included in the tour. From May to Aug a same-day timed ticket system operates: call for free tickets early in the day, and return at the time assigned.

Capitol Building $
1st St between Independence and Constitution Aves (metro: Capitol South); tel: (202) 225-6827; open Mon–Fri and some weekends 0900–1630. A 20-min guided tour starts daily from the Rotunda 0900–1545.

Library of Congress $
1st St and Independence Ave. SE (metro: Capitol South) tel: (202) 707-5000; open Mon–Fri 0830–2130, Sat 0830–1800.

US Supreme Court $
1st St and Maryland Ave. NE (metro: Capitol South); tel: (202) 479-3030; open Mon–Fri 0900–1630. Lectures are given every hour on the half-hour Mon–Fri 0930–1530 when not in session.

Folger Shakespeare Library $ *201 E Capitol St SE (metro: Capitol South); tel: (202) 544-4600; open Mon–Sat 1000–1600.*

Eastern Market $
200 block of 7th St SE (metro: Eastern Market); tel: (202) 546-2698; open Sat and Sun early morning to mid-afternoon.

Capitol Building✦✦✦

All four city districts converge on the Capitol Building, seat of the US government, and the nerve centre of all that is Washington. The building's physical beauty is one obvious attraction (its white dome is particularly striking at night); another is that you can witness Congress in session. Free tours are offered, but because of the magnificent art works, the grandeur of the halls and the historic associations, you may want to linger and look around on your own. To get a Congressional pass and watch the proceedings, Americans can apply to their senator or representative several weeks in advance, or if it's a slow day, find their relevant person and pick one up on the spot. Foreign visitors may obtain House passes at the gallery check-in desk on the third floor, and Senate passes at the Senate appointment desk on the first floor, all subject to availability. *The Washington Post* records when Senators and Representatives are sitting. The dome is currently undergoing extensive repairs, but the building will remain open.

Capitol Hill✦✦

Behind the Capitol are a number of other important buildings, and the neighbourhood itself is charming to stroll about. The **Library of Congress✦** is a research library created in 1800 to serve Congress, and now holds close to 100 million books and documents. A room in the James Madison building (there are three library buildings in the complex) contains the Gutenberg Bible and Martin Luther King's 'I Have a Dream' speech. The **US Supreme Court✦** building a block away has displays and a film outlining procedures in the nation's highest court. Court hearings may be watched on a first come, first served basis, but public seating is limited. Also in the area is the surprisingly good **Folger Shakespeare Library✦**, with a re-creation of Shakespeare's original Elizabethan theatre and one of the world's greatest collections of Shakespeare and Renaissance material. Not to be missed if you're in the area on a weekend morning is the lively **Eastern Market✦✦**, a covered market of fresh produce, meats, cheese, flowers and bric-à-brac, whose exuberance spills on to the street.

Right
The Capitol by night

The Castle: Smithsonian Institution Visitors Center *10th St and Jefferson Dr. at the Mall, SW; tel: (202) 357-2700; open daily 1000–1730.*

Woodrow Wilson House $$ *2340 S St NW (metro: Dupont Circle); tel: (202) 387-4062; open Tue–Sun 1000–1600.*

Islamic Mosque and Cultural Center $ *2551 Massachusetts Ave. NW (metro: Dupont Circle); tel: (202) 332-8343. open daily except Fri 1000–1700. All limbs must be covered, women must cover their heads and shoes must be removed.*

Below
Embassy Row

The Castle⁺

Of all the distinctive architectural styles on the Mall, perhaps the most eye-grabbing is the original Smithsonian Institution museum, known simply as the Castle for its neo-Romanesque burgundy-brick design. The building dates from the 1850s, and today serves as the Smithsonian's administration and information centre.

Embassy Row⁺⁺

Massachusetts Ave. northwest of Dupont Circle has the highest concentration of embassies in the city, hence its nickname. Many of these are in fine 19th-century mansions, while others are purpose-built in distinctive designs reflecting that country's style. A few other sites command attention along the avenue. The **Woodrow Wilson House**⁺, just off Massachusetts Ave. at 24th and S Sts, is a sturdy town house to which President Wilson retired in 1921. It is now a museum containing the personal memorabilia of one of the country's greatest leaders. Further to the northwest, the minaret and tiled courtyard of the beautiful **Islamic Mosque and Cultural Center**⁺ strongly evoke the Middle East. The edifice stands at a slight angle since Islam stipulates its temples must face Mecca. Across Rock Creek Park, and beyond the British Embassy (notable for its statue of Winston Churchill out front saluting with a 'V') stands the Vice President's Mansion, which is closed to the public.

FBI Headquarters $
935 Pennsylvania Ave. NW; tel: (202) 324-3447; open Mon–Fri 0845–1615.

Ford's Theater $ *511 10th St NW (metro: Metro Center or Gallery Place-Chinatown); tel: (202) 426-5924; open daily 0900–1700.*

Frederick Douglass home $ *1411 W St SE (metro: Anacostia, then bus B2); tel: (202) 426-5960; open daily spring–summer 0900–1700; fall–winter 0900–1600. This area is predominantly black and a little doubtful, but safe enough during the day; consider driving.*

FBI Headquarters*

One of the city's most popular attractions is the off-beat FBI Headquarters, which chronicles the role of America's top domestic crime-fighting organisation through the 20th century. Aside from busting hardened criminals like Al Capone, the FBI has involved itself in the investigation of Cold War and Vietnam War protesters, as well as developing techniques for DNA analysis, high-tech pistols, and bullet-proof vests. The hour-long tour concludes with a firearms demonstration.

Ford's Theater**

The pretty Ford's Theater was the site of President Abraham Lincoln's assassination on 14 April 1865, just days after the end of the Civil War. His assassin, John Wilkes Booth, an actor at the theatre, conceived his act as a savage parting shot for the Confederacy. Booth entered the President's unguarded box above the stage, fired a single shot, jumped down on to the stage and escaped out of the back of the theatre. Lincoln died several hours later in Petersen House across the street, also open to the public (same hours), which contains the bed (and bloodstained pillowcase) on which Lincoln died. A museum underneath Ford's Theater has more information on the assassination. The theatre is in active use, restored in the 1960s, with all the 19th-century trappings retained.

Frederick Douglass home*

One off-the-track site that's worth the trip into southeast Washington is the Frederick Douglass home. Douglass, a self-educated African-American who was one of the great figures in the emancipation of slavery, became a successful businessman, and his home has been restored to its mid-19th-century appearance. A trip here is a lesson in racial relations in America and also in DC history.

Right
The Islamic Mosque and Cultural Center

The Freer Gallery $
12th St and Jefferson Dr. SW at the Mall (metro: Smithsonian); tel: (202) 357-1300; open daily 1000–1730.

The Sackler Gallery $
11th St and Independence Ave. at the Mall (metro: Smithsonian); tel: (202) 357-1300; open daily 1000–1730.

The National Museum of African Art $ 10th St and Independence Ave. at the Mall (metro: Smithsonian); tel: (202) 357-1300; open daily 1000–1730.

The Freer Gallery, The Sackler Gallery and The National Museum of African Art✦✦

African and Asian art is gathered in abundance at these three connected museums by the Castle on the Mall. The **Freer Gallery✦✦** is actually the Smithsonian's first art gallery, featuring the collection of 1920s industrialist James Freer. In addition to Chinese porcelain and Japanese calligraphy scrolls, the Freer contains one of the world's largest collections of paintings by the American James McNeil Whistler.

As if symbolically to link the continents, two conjoining museums were built in 1987 beneath the Freer Gallery, extending behind the Castle in a three-level underground gallery. The **Sackler Gallery✦✦** features precious manuscripts and objects from ancient China and the Middle East, including jade and bronze from as far back as 3000 BC. The **National Museum of African Art✦✦** covers a broad range of sculptures, paintings and crafts from numerous countries on the African continent, including several beautiful ivory carvings.

Above
Georgetown

Opposite
The National Museum of
African Art

Dumbarton Oaks $
31st and R Sts NW
(bus 30, 32, 34, 36, or D2);
tel: (202) 339-6401; open
Tue–Sun 1400–1700.

Georgetown✦✦

Georgetown dates from the 1750s, a city before Washington, DC, was even conceived, and amassed its wealth as a port handling goods such as tobacco and timber from Virginia and Maryland, and highly desired imports from Europe. There are many late 19th-century buildings, and Georgetown's urban mansions and cobblestone streets make a perfect backdrop for strolling, window-shopping and dining. The intersection of Wisconsin Ave. and M St is its axis, and a prime commercial centre, but to appreciate the neighbourhood you'll want to explore the back streets and byways.

The Chesapeake and Ohio (C&O) Canal, built for inland trade in the mid-1800s, runs parallel to M St and the river; the towpath between 29th and 31st Sts is particularly atmospheric, and from June to Sept you can take a short ride on a mule-drawn flat-bottomed canal barge ($$). North of M St, streets such as N St and O St provide ample opportunities for gawking at the gorgeous homes of Washington's rich and powerful, and lead up to the pretty campus of Georgetown University at 37th and O Sts. This is the nation's first Catholic university, founded in 1789; its neo-Gothic Healy Hall dominates the local skyline.

Dumbarton Oaks✦✦, a lovely mansion and garden at 31st and R Sts, was the setting for the 1944 Dumbarton Oaks Conference, where discussions between the US, UK, USSR and China eventually led to the formation of the United Nations. The mansion houses a superb collection of Byzantine coins and artefacts, as well as Mayan and Aztec figurines and gold carvings.

Great Falls Park♦♦♦

The fall line of the Potomac River is about 15 miles upstream from Georgetown, a dramatic, rocky narrowing through which the river shoots with extraordinary velocity – the kind of wild river scenery you would expect to find in the West. The falls are part of the Chesapeake and Ohio Canal National Historical Park, straddling both the Maryland and Virginia sides of the river. The canal passes alongside the northern bank on the Maryland side, offering a glimpse into an intriguing part of America's industrial 19th century, the building of an inland waterways system to transport goods from rural Maryland and Ohio to Washington, DC. The mechanically ingenious lift-lock system can be seen in action as mule-drawn barges ply the conduit (Apr–Oct only). Cross the bridge on to Olmsted Island for superb views of the falls.

Hirshhorn Museum♦

This cylindrical structure on the Mall holds some excellent 19th- and 20th-century works gathered by the financier Joseph Hirshhorn. Romantic- and Impressionist-era paintings and sculptures by the likes of Renoir, Degas and Rodin are complemented by a rich gathering of works by such contemporary luminaries as Picasso, Matisse, Pollock, Bacon and O'Keeffe. The grounds of the museum, and a sunken garden across the street, form an open-air sculpture garden full of intriguing modern works.

National Air and Space Museum♦♦♦

The most popular Smithsonian museum is the National Air and Space Museum, at the southeastern corner of the Mall near the Capitol building. It can't fail to impress visitors of all ages, children especially, with its incredible array of real air- and space-craft. Planes hang majestically from the ceiling of the huge central hall, while rockets stand proud along the walls. Notable entries include the first plane to fly solo trans-Atlantic (by Charles Lindbergh), the first glider plane to fly around the world non-stop, the original Saturn V rocket and several (decommissioned) American and Soviet nuclear warheads. The museum galleries chronicle the history of aviation from the Wright Brothers through to the Space Shuttle. Tickets for the spectacular IMAX cinema must be bought up to several hours in advance.

Above
The Hirshhorn Museum

Opposite
The National Air and
Space Museum

The Mall and its monuments✦✦✦

The National Mall is the physical and cultural centre of Washington, a vast expanse of grass and footpaths lined on all sides by wonderful museums and many of the city's most recognisable monuments. Aside from spending hours, or even days upon end in the museums and galleries, the Mall is a wonderful place to relax, with a wintertime ice-skating rink by the National Museum of Natural History, and a children's funfair-type carousel ride by the Castle in the warm months. The chief monuments are covered below, while museums appear elsewhere in the text, with reference to their Mall location.

Unmissable wherever you stand, the 555ft Washington Monument is one of the city's most recognisable symbols. On clear days views from the top of the obelisk spread all the way to the Blue Ridge Mountains.

Behind the Washington Monument, the long, narrow Reflecting Pool stretches several hundred metres to the Lincoln Memorial, an impressive Grecian-style columned monument to one of the US's greatest presidents. A statue of a seated Abraham Lincoln lurks inside, and the steps have hosted countless national celebrations and demonstrations, most remarkable of which was Martin Luther King Jr's electrifying 'I Have a Dream' speech in 1963 – an appropriate setting at the feet of the man who risked the nation's unity in order to abolish slavery.

Lincoln's gaze falls kindly on the particularly moving Vietnam Veterans' Memorial, just north of the Reflecting Pool. The black granite V-shaped memorial carries more than 58,000 names of those who died or remain missing in the Vietnam War, and is well visited by relatives of the dead. Across the pool, the Korean War Veterans' Memorial is made up of stainless steel sculptures of ground troops.

South of the Reflecting Pool, the Tidal Basin is famous for its Japanese cherry blossom trees, especially enticing during early April when they explode in soft pink. You can rent paddleboats on the water in warm weather, or visit the graceful domed Jefferson Memorial along its southern edge. The design reflects Thomas Jefferson's fascination with classical architecture, and is similar to his home at Monticello, near Charlottesville, Virginia.

The National Gallery of Art $ *The Mall between 3rd and 7th Sts NW (metro: Smithsonian or Archives-Navy Memorial); tel: (202) 727-4315; open daily 1000–1730.*

The National Museum of American History $ *12th St and Constitution Ave. NW at the Mall (metro: Smithsonian or Federal Triangle); tel: (202) 357-1300; open daily summer 1000–1830; winter 1000–1730.*

The National Museum of Natural History $ *10th St and Constitution Ave. NW at the Mall (metro: Smithsonian or Federal Triangle); tel: (202) 357-1300; open daily 1000–1730.*

National Zoo $ *3001 Connecticut Ave. NW (metro: Woodley Park-Zoo or Cleveland Park); tel: (202) 673-4800; open daily 0900–1730.*

The National Gallery of Art✦✦✦

Along the north side of the Mall, the first buildings west of the Capitol are the two wings of the marvellous National Gallery of Art, which exists thanks to the generosity of industrialist Andrew Mellon. The original, gold-domed West Wing houses an excellent collection of paintings and sculptures from the Italian Renaissance, 17th–18th-century Flanders and the Netherlands, and Romantic-era France, Spain, Britain and the USA, with numerous renowned works by the likes of Raphael, Rembrandt, Rubens, Monet, Gauguin and Van Gogh. An underground walkway connects it to the super-modern East Wing which focuses on contemporary art, including works by Picasso, Lichtenstein and Warhol, and a steady stream of visiting exhibitions. The building itself is something to marvel at.

The National Museum of American History✦✦✦

One of the finest and most popular of the Smithsonian's museums is the National Museum of American History, with a constantly changing gathering of important events in America's history. Its greatest strength is that it doesn't try to glamorise: exhibits include rich displays on, for example, the so-called Great Migration of African Americans northward after the Civil War, and the altered lives of Navajo and Zuni Indians in New Mexico today. Exhibits are designed to be both visually appealing and educational, and any layman can gain much from the displays on Thomas Edison's development of electricity or the building of the Hoover Dam. Other sections are pure fun, such as turn-of-the-century locomotives, the banquet gowns of recent First Ladies, and the original Star-Spangled Banner flag.

The National Museum of Natural History✦✦

The National Museum of Natural History is a wonderful array of the planet's physical being. Highlights include reconstructed skeletons of dinosaurs such as a bron tosaurus and a pterodactyl, an elaborate collection of precious gems, including the notorious Hope Diamond (largest in the world), displays on the lives of native American peoples such as Eskimos and Plains Indians, and the creepy crawly Insect Zoo, with live tarantulas, scorpions, and lots more.

Rock Creek Park and the National Zoo✦✦

Rock Creek Park is quite remarkable, a forest right in the city, extending from the Potomac River right out into suburban Maryland. Deer roam through the park and large birds such as blue herons come to feed from the gurgling stream. The National Zoo, a local favourite, is carved into a slope in part of the park, and displays a wide range of species in commendably natural settings. Unfortunately, the zoo's two giant pandas – its pride and joy – have died, but a new pair is being sought. A century ago, the Rock Creek valley was filled with mills, but only one of these survives. Pierce Mill is not open to the public, but

US Holocaust Memorial Museum
$ 100 Raoul Wallenburg Pl. SW, near 14th St and Independence Ave. (metro: Smithsonian); tel: (202) 488-0400; open daily 1000–1730. Timed tickets are required, and you may well have to show up early to get tickets for later in the day.

Washington National Cathedral $ Wisconsin Ave. and Massachusetts Ave. NW (bus 30, 32, 34, 36, or N2); tel: (202) 364-6616; open daily 1000–1630 (extended in summer).

the stone house makes a nice setting for a picnic; by car, take Rock Creek Parkway to Beach Drive to the junction with Tilden St NW.

US Holocaust Memorial Museum✦✦✦

The harrowing story of the Nazi genocide is told at the US Holocaust Memorial Museum through photographs, artefacts, film, videotaped histories, and memorial pieces. Since its completion in 1993, this has become one of the most popular museums in the city, aimed at presenting a thorough documentation of the horror. Exploring its many exhibits can take up to half a day or more. Particularly moving is the Tower of Faces, an actual barrack building from Auschwitz, and cases full of human hair, glasses and shoes of the victims.

Washington National Cathedral✦

Occupying one of the highest points in the city, the Washington National Cathedral bears a stunning similarity to many of Europe's finest cathedrals. Twentieth-century craftsmen used 14th- and 15th-century skills to build and adorn this Gothic house of worship for the Episcopal church, which also (typically for this city) honours events and personalities in US history. It was completed only in 1990 and is the world's sixth largest cathedral, noteworthy as much for its size as for its exceptional attention to the use of space: rather than stuffing the building with ornamental excess, the designers allowed smoother surfaces to complement the airy interior. The observation tower offers splendid views of the city, and the lovely gardens on the south side make a soothing respite from the summer heat.

Right
Washington National Cathedral

The White House $
*1600 Pennsylvania Ave.
NW (metro: Farragut North,
McPherson Sq. or Metro
Center); tours run only
Tue–Sat 1000–1200.* Pick
up free tickets at the
White House Visitor
Center – these disappear
as early as 0830 – and call
ahead to verify opening
information.

**White House Visitor
Center** *1450 Pennsylvania
Ave. NW, tel: (202) 456-
7041.*

The White House**

It is an undeniable thrill to stand inside perhaps the most famous house in the world, the home of all US presidents since John Adams (the second president, after George Washington, who served in Philadelphia). However, only a small part of the ground floor can be visited, and since it is the official residence of the US President, tours may be subject to change or cancellation and you don't get to see the most important parts. The White House Visitor Center a block away is worth seeing in its own right, with historical exhibits and displays of photographs about the White House down the years. Leafy Lafayette Square opposite the mansion is a gathering point for low-key protesters of all kinds.

Entertainment

John F Kennedy Center for the Performing Arts *Virginia and New Hampshire Aves NW (metro: Foggy Bottom-GWU), tel: (202) 467-4600.*

National Theater *1321 Pennsylvania Ave. NW (metro: Metro Center); tel: (202) 628-6161 or (1-800) 233-3123.*

Warner Theater *1299 Pennsylvania Ave. NW (metro: Metro Center); tel: (202) 783-4000.*

Ford's Theater *511 10th St NW (metro: Metro Center); tel: (202) 347-4833.*

Blues Alley *Rear of 1073 Wisconsin Ave. NW; tel: (202) 337-4141.*

The Brickseller *1523 22nd St NW; tel: (202) 293-1885.*

Washington has a buzzing concert and theatre life. Listings of current shows, drama and concerts are given in *The Washington Post* and *Washington City Paper*. World-class orchestral, opera and dance performances take place at the **John F Kennedy Center for the Performing Arts**. The National Symphony Orchestra's season runs from Sept to May. There are also frequent concerts at the National Gallery of Art and at many of the Smithsonian museums.

There is no theatre district *per se*, but you can catch Broadway shows at the modern **National Theater**, or the beautifully remodelled **Warner Theater** nearby. An exceptionally atmospheric venue for performance is the reconstructed **Ford's Theater** (*see page 47*).

Despite its rather stodgy image, DC can provide the needed excitement for a night at the pubs and clubs. Georgetown (particularly Wisconsin Ave. and M St) and Adams Morgan (18th St between Columbia Rd and U St) are vigorous neighbourhoods with plenty of hotspots. DC has an unusually good collection of jazz and blues clubs, such as **Blues Alley**, a long-established, upscale yet intimate jazz club in Georgetown, presenting the top names. Anyone with a taste for good beer should head to the **Brickseller**, a large but cosy pub near Dupont Circle with a menu of over 800 brews from around the world.

Left
The White House at night

Right
Cherry blossom time at the Capitol

National Cherry Blossom Festival, a week-long exultation in early April of more than 6000 Japanese cherry trees in bloom at various monuments.

Festival of American Folklife In late June/early July hundreds of thousands of people flock to the Mall for music, arts, crafts and cuisine from America's diverse ethnic groups.

Independence Day The biggest bash of the year is the Fourth of July celebration on the Mall: day-long events culminate in a free evening concert by the National Symphony Orchestra on the west steps of the Capitol, and a glorious fireworks display at night.

Power in Washington

The US government is made up of three bodies: the Executive branch, composed of the President and Vice President, along with their cabinets; the Legislative branch (Congress), a bicameral structure comprising the Senate and the House of Representatives; and the Judicial branch, or the federal court system. This overall arrangement is intended to maintain a system of 'checks and balances' on the law of the land.

The President is the only elected official of the Executive branch. His influence is largely symbolic as the nation's chief figurehead, but he does have the power to select and approve ambassadors, judges and military leaders, and his role in the law-making process is significant in that he has the power to veto any law that Congress passes. The President chooses his Vice President, and elections are held every four years, with a maximum service of two terms.

The purpose of the Legislative branch is to make laws. The Senate is comprised of two Senators from each of the 50 states, while the House of Representatives is determined by proportionate population of the state: thus California and New York have many representatives while Idaho and Alaska have few. Again, the structure is based upon the principle of checks and balances: House members represent their local constituencies, but every state, regardless of population, has an equal number of Senators. Senators are elected by residents of their state every six years, while House members are elected in their districts every two years. One irony of the federal government's location in Washington, DC, is that the city itself, with nearly 600,000 residents, has no representation in Congress.

The top of the ladder in the Judicial system is the Supreme Court, with nine judges. Other federal courts include federal district courts and US courts of appeals. Federal courts handle cases that either involve federal laws or cross state boundaries.

Apart from the obvious power manifested in these positions, Washington is loaded with lobbyists, who represent such organisations as Greenpeace or the American Medical Association, and whose role is to influence members of Congress to vote on regulations affecting their cause. In addition, the capital is home base for countless government-related organisations such as the World Bank and the International Monetary Fund, as well as deeply influential national media such as *The Washington Post*.

Government is without question the city's chief industry, followed by tourism. Because of the frequent changes in government and related changes in government-related businesses and organisations, the Washington metropolitan area has a huge population turnover; this constant change of people has much to do with the city's lack of a clear personality.

Accommodation and food

Reservation services

Capitol Reservations
Tel: (1-800) VISIT-DC or (202) 452-1270.

Washington, DC Accommodation Tel: (1-800) 554-2220 or (202) 289-2220.

Bed and Breakfast Accommodation Tel: (202) 328-3510.

Willard Inter-Continental $$$
1401 Pennsylvania Ave. NW; tel: (202) 628-9100.

Hay-Adams $$$
1 Lafayette Sq. NW; tel: (202) 638-6600.

Latham Hotel $$ 3000 M St NW; tel: (202) 726-5000.

Allen Lee Hotel $ 2224 F St NW (metro: Foggy Bottom-GWU); tel: (202) 331-1224 or (1-800) 462-0186.

Harrington Hotel $
1100 E St NW (metro: Metro Center); tel: (202) 628-8140 or (1-800) 424-8532.

Tabard Inn $$ 1739 N St NW; tel: (202) 785-1277.

Windsor Inn $–$$ 1842 16th St NW; tel: (202) 667-0300 or (1-800) 423-9111.

Kalorama Guest House $ 1854 Mintwood Pl. NW; tel: (202) 667-6369, and 2700 Cathedral Ave. NW; tel: (202) 328-0860.

Washington's role as the centre of government and of tourism in the region means there are plenty of fine hotels, but it is still important to book as early as possible. The better central hotels offer reduced rates at weekends and in July and Aug, when Congress is in recess.

The **Willard Inter-Continental** is a Washington institution, a lavish hotel near the White House. Its chief competition comes from the **Hay-Adams**, right opposite the White House and a frequent host of international politicos. The **Latham Hotel** is a comfortable hotel in Georgetown, with shopping, dining and entertainment on the doorstep.

There are at least a couple of cheaper options downtown. The **Allen Lee Hotel** is a decent budget hotel close to the monuments. The **Harrington Hotel** is a well-established basic standard near the White House and the Mall.

Washington has a nice selection of lower and mid-range B&Bs, which generally are situated in Victorian town houses, such as the **Tabard Inn**, with its own restaurant, on the cusp of Dupont Circle and Downtown. Also appealing, but a little cheaper, is the comfortable **Windsor Inn**, close to both Dupont Circle and Adams Morgan. **Kalorama Guest House** is a simple, popular B&B operating from two separate homes in Adams Morgan and Woodley Park.

As might be expected, Washington offers a culinary choice that sweeps across the international spectrum. You'll want to branch out into such international cuisines too, because there isn't too much to be said about local eats. If there is a tradition, it's imported from the shores of the Chesapeake Bay in Maryland, or from the neighbouring southern states. Adams Morgan (18th St between Columbia Rd and U St NW) is the ethnic hotspot in town, with a rich selection of Ethiopian, Mexican, French and many other fun restaurants. Georgetown (around Wisconsin Ave. and M St NW) is a long-established part of social life in DC, with everything from cheap diners to Irish pubs to fine Italian restaurants. Most of the Smithsonian museums have café/restaurants, which are good for a cheap lunch or snack; the one in the west wing of the National Gallery of Art is highly recommended.

Georgia Brown's is a well-established downtown restaurant offering gracious southern cooking such as gumbo and pork chops in a fanciful setting. **Old Ebbitt Grill**, close to the White House, is great for steak and oysters, and famous for Washington hob-nobbing. **Sequoia** has huge windows overlooking the Georgetown waterfront and Kennedy Center, and an imaginative seafood menu.

For a taste of the international, try the excellent and reasonably priced French *haute cuisine* at **Bistro Français**, also in Georgetown. For elegant Middle Eastern cuisine, the **Lebanese Taverna** near the National Zoo is unbeatable. A fun new place for exquisite Mexican

Georgia Brown's
$$$ *950 15th St NW;*
tel: (202) 393-4499.

Old Ebbitt Grill $$–$$$
675 15th St NW; tel: (202)
347-4800.

Sequoia $$ *3000 K St*
NW; tel: (202) 944-4200.

Bistro Français $$–$$$
3128 M St NW; tel: (202)
338-3830.

Lebanese Taverna $$$
2641 Connecticut Ave. NW;
tel: (202) 265-8681.

Lauriol Plaza $$ *1835*
18th St NW, tel: (202) 387-
0035.

Kramerbooks and
Afterwords $$ *1517*
Connecticut Ave. NW; tel:
(202) 387-1462.

Pizza Paradiso $ *2029 P*
St NW; tel: (202) 223-1245.

food in the Dupont Circle–Adams Morgan area is **Lauriol Plaza**.

You can satisfy mind and body in the bookstore and café at **Kramerbooks and Afterwords**, which serves salads, sandwiches, vegetarian dishes and a weekend brunch. Also good for a light lunch or dinner near Dupont Circle is **Pizza Paradiso**, widely considered to have the best single-serve pizzas in town.

Right
Georgetown

Suggested walking tour

Phillips Collection
$$ 1600 21st St NW;
tel: (202) 387-2151; open
Tue–Sat 1000–1700,
Thur 1000–2030,
Sun 1200–1900.

**Corcoran Gallery of
Art** $ 17th St and New
York Ave. NW; tel: (202)
639 1700; open Wed–Mon
1000–1700 (Thur until
2030).

Total distance: 5 miles

Time: 3 hours for fit walkers, assuming no stops. Allow at least a full day with selected quick stops. This walk can easily be split into two separate walks: one from Dupont Circle to Georgetown (1 hour), the other from Georgetown across the Mall to the Capitol (2 hours).

Route: Hop on the metro and alight at Dupont Circle station. Take the Q St exit, then turn left down Q St to 21st St, where a burgundy-brick mansion houses the **Phillips Collection** ❶, an excellent private gallery of 19th- and 20th-century paintings, including a particularly acclaimed selection of works by Renoir. Continue a block further on Q St to Massachusetts Ave., the beginning of **EMBASSY ROW** ❷. Follow Massachusetts Ave. to 22nd St for a taste of the opulence, or continue a few blocks up Massachusetts Ave. for more, but be sure to double back to 22nd St. Walk south down 22nd St, turning right on to P St to cross the bridge over **ROCK CREEK PARK** ❸ and into **GEORGETOWN** ❹.

Wander along P St to 27th St, turn left, and then turn right on to either O St, **Dumbarton St** or N St to see some of Georgetown's finest town houses. To prolong your tour of Georgetown, take a detour to **Dumbarton Oaks** ❺ at 31st and R Sts. All of these streets empty out on to Wisconsin Ave., a prime centre of shopping and nightlife. Turn left (south) on Wisconsin Ave. to M St, and spend a little while poking into shops and cafés. Take note of the **Old Stone House** ❻ at 3051 M St, the oldest structure in Georgetown, dating from the 1760s, before heading down either 31st St or Thomas Jefferson St to the river. You could break the trip here by catching any No 30 bus downtown.

The Washington harbour restaurant/office complex fronts the river, and a path from here follows along the banks of the Potomac past the **Watergate** ❼ (location of President Nixon's notorious campaign-meddling in the early 1970s) and the **John F Kennedy Center** ❽. Cross the street at the **Lincoln Memorial** ❾ and continue on past the Reflecting Pool to the **Washington Monument** ❿.

Detour: From the base of the Washington Monument you get a good view of the **WHITE HOUSE** ⓫, and a quick walk north across the **Ellipse** ⓬ brings you closer to it. Once here, jog over to the corner of 17th St and New York Ave., where the **Corcoran Gallery of Art** ⓭ is filled with a wonderful collection of American paintings, including works by Cole, Eakins, Sargent and Cassat.

From the Washington Monument it's a leisurely walk along the **MALL** ⓮ to the **CAPITOL BUILDING** ⓯.

Shopping

Washington offers some fun opportunities to stock up on speciality gifts. The gift shops in many of the museums on the Mall have wonderful items for gift-giving or personal collections; try the **Air and Space Museum** for childrens' toys, the **National Gallery of Art** for books and framed reproductions of artworks and the **National Museum of American History** for a wide assortment of quality American-themed knick-knacks.

For anything from fresh produce to flowers to oriental rugs, not to mention a lot of fun, head to **Eastern Market** (*200 block of 7th St SE; metro: Eastern Market*), on Capitol Hill, on a weekend morning. A great place to stock up gourmet food items and picnic lunches is **Dean and DeLuca** (*3276 M St NW*) in Georgetown.

Opposite
The Mall

Below
The Capitol viewed from the National Air and Space Museum

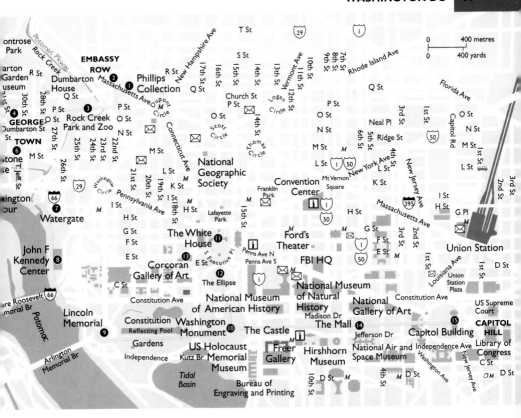

ontrose
Park

arton
Garden
useum

**EMBASSY
ROW**

T St

S St

29

1

0   400 metres
0   400 yards

R St

Dumbarton
House

**Phillips
Collection**

Church St
P St

New Hampshire Ave

17th St

16th St

15th St

14th St

13th St

Vermont Ave

12th St

11th St

10th St

9th St

8th St

7th St

Rhode Island Ave

Q St

Florida Ave

R St

Q St

30th St

28th St

29th St

31st St

P St

GEORGE
Dumbarton St

TOWN

tone
se

stone
T.Jeff.St

**Rock Creek
Park and Zoo**

P St

O St

N St

M St

L St

I St

H St

G St

F St

E St

C St

26th St

25th St

24th St

23rd St

22nd St

21st St

20th St

19th St

1 St

18th St

Connecticut Ave

Massachusetts Ave

Dupont
Circle

Scott
Circle

Thomas
Circle

Logan
Circle

O St

N St

P St

O St

N St

M St

L St

1

50

Mt Vernon
Square

Neal Pl

Ridge St

3rd St

1st St

Capitol Rd

O St

N St

M St

50

L St

3rd St

2nd St

Franklin
Park

**National
Geographic
Society**

**Convention
Center**

Massachusetts Ave

New York Ave

New Jersey Ave

395

G Pl

Union Station

ington
our

Watergate

Washington
Circle

Pennsylvania Ave

Lafayette
Park

I St

H St

G St

F St

E St

15th St

**The White
House**

**Corcoran
Gallery of Art**

The Ellipse

Penns Ave N

E St

Executive Pl

Penns Ave S

**Ford's
Theater**

FBI HQ

1

50

G St

F St

E St

3rd St

2nd St

1st St

1st St

Louisiana Ave

Union
Station
Plaza

D St

**John F
Kennedy
Center**

66

Constitution Ave

**National Museum
of American History**

**National Museum
of Natural
History**
Madison Dr

**National
Gallery of Art**

Constitution Ave

US Supreme
Court

**CAPITOL
HILL**

re Roosevelt
morial Br

Potomac

Arlington
Memorial Br

**Lincoln
Memorial**

Constitution
Reflecting Pool

Gardens

Independence

**Washington
Monument**

The Castle

US Holocaust
Kutz Br Memorial
Museum

Tidal
Basin

**Freer
Gallery**

The Mall

**Hirshhorn
Museum**

Jefferson Dr

Bureau of
Engraving and Printing

**National Air and
Space Museum**

Capitol Building

Independence Ave

Washington Ave

New Jersey Ave

**Library of
Congress**

C St

D St

Arlington and Alexandria

Ratings

Art and museums	●●●●
Gastronomy	●●●●
History	●●●●
Shopping	●●●
Children	●●
Entertainment	●●
Nature	●●
Beaches	●

The close-in northern Virginia suburbs of Arlington and Alexandria are really part of Washington, DC, and as such have numerous important monuments that merit a visit. From 1789 to 1846, the two were in fact incorporated into the district of Columbia, and today both are served by the city's Metrorail system. Arlington County is a prosperous suburb, whose chief attraction, its famous cemetery, lies across the Potomac from the Lincoln Memorial. The city of Alexandria, further downstream, actually predates Washington, and retains its cobblestoned colonial gentility, with several historic buildings and some great restaurants to visit. Alexandria was a base of George Washington, and his beautiful home at Mount Vernon sits proudly on a bluff above the Potomac, downstream. In combination with a visit to Washington, a trip across the river gives a deeper impression of the growth of both the city and the nation.

ARLINGTON NATIONAL CEMETERY*

Arlington National Cemetery $ *On the Virginia side of Memorial Bridge opposite the Lincoln Memorial (metro: Arlington Cemetery); tel: (703) 979-0690; open daily, summer 0800–1900, winter 0800–1700.*

Rising on a gentle slope across the river from the Lincoln Memorial is the vast, perfectly manicured Arlington National Cemetery, final resting place of hundreds of thousands of US servicemen and women, and of President John F Kennedy. Tombs stretch in uniform rows over 200 acres, while Kennedy's grave is given special recognition with a serene eternal flame. Nearby, stern-columned Arlington House was the home of Robert E Lee, commander of the army of Virginia during the Civil War. His mansion is preserved in period furnishings, and offers a great view of Washington from its front steps. Elsewhere, the Tomb of the Unknowns symbolises unknown soldiers from America's involvement in the terrible wars of the 20th century. The tomb is watched over 24 hours a day; try to time your visit for the hourly changing of the guard. The cemetery is closed to vehicular traffic, except for the disabled and relatives of those buried, so prepare for a long walk, or hop aboard the Tourmobile bus.

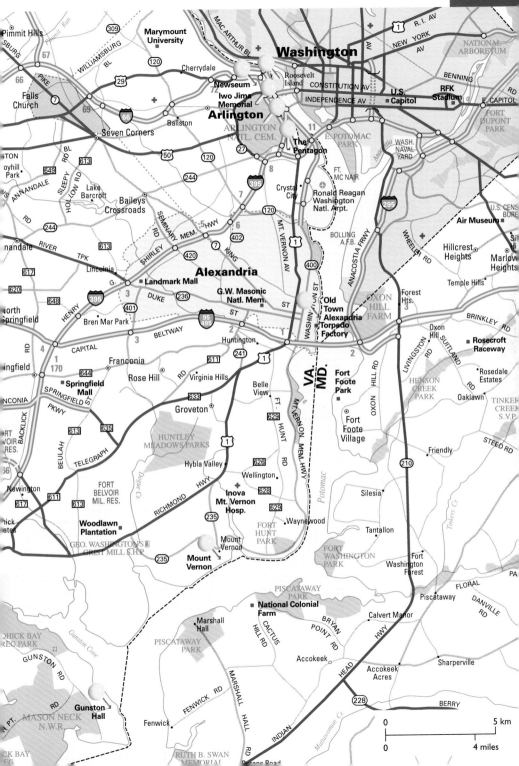

GUNSTON HALL✧

Gunston Hall $$
Rte 242 (off Rte 1 near Lorton, about 15 miles south of Alexandria); tel: (703) 550-9220 or (1-800) 811-6966; open daily 0930–1700.

A lifelong friend of George Washington, George Mason was one of the most important and yet least known of the founding fathers of the United States. He wrote the first ten amendments to the US Constitution, collectively known as the Bill of Rights. Although a member of the Constitutional Convention of 1787, Mason in fact refused to sign the Constitution because originally it had no such declaration of basic human rights, such as those of freedom of speech and freedom of religion, and did not specifically outlaw slavery. Mason's Georgian-style home, Gunston Hall, a few miles downstream from Washington's Mount Vernon in Fairfax County, is distinguished by fine interior carved woodwork, beautiful 18th-century furnishings and lush formal gardens.

IWO JIMA MEMORIAL✧

Iwo Jima Memorial $ *(See Arlington National Cemetery for details.)*

Annexed to the northern edge of Arlington National Cemetery is the evocative Marine Corps War Memorial, better known as the Iwo Jima Memorial. The capture of the Japanese island of Iwo Jima in 1945 was critical to the Americans' strategic position during World War II, and the statue, sculpted from a Pulitzer Prize-winning photograph of six US Marines planting a flag in the ground, has become one of the most enduring images of America's involvement in the war. It can be reached on foot from either Arlington Cemetery or Rosslyn metro stations.

MOUNT VERNON✧✧✧

Mount Vernon $$
George Washington Memorial Parkway; tel: (703) 780-2000; open daily Mar and Sept–Oct 0900–1700, Apr–Aug 0800–1700, Nov–Feb 0900–1600.

George Washington's home, Mount Vernon, is an enjoyable day trip from DC and essential for history buffs. (Fairfax Connector bus No 101 runs every 30 mins (rush hour) or every 60 mins (non-rush hour and weekends) from Huntington metro station, or you can get there by boat from DC on Spirit Cruises, 6th and Water Sts SW (metro: Waterfront; tel: (202) 554-8000).) It is set on 500 rolling acres of riverfront Virginia countryside, 16 miles south of Washington. The house to which the great American general and first president retired retains its simple, gracious appearance, and among the furnishings you can see are a key to the Bastille presented by General Lafayette and the bed in which Washington died in 1799. The grounds include slave quarters – ironically, many founding fathers owned slaves, despite proclamations that 'all men are created equal' – and George and Martha Washington's tombs, plus an innovative 16-sided threshing barn, built using hand-made bricks and hand-forged nails.

NEWSEUM✧✧

Newseum $ *1101 Wilson Blvd, Arlington (metro: Rosslyn); tel: (1-888) NEWSEUM; open Wed–Sun 1000–1700.*

One of the area's most exciting and entertaining new museums is the Newseum. It traces the history of news from African drumbeat messages to the development of the printing press to the growth of radio, TV and the Internet. It's fun to wander the halls loaded with press headlines announcing such events as the end of World War II or the triumphs of Muhammed Ali, and you can read the current day's news from any of 100 newspapers the world over. Interactive displays are a major feature, and children can get a kick out of playing meteorologist or news reporter.

OLD TOWN ALEXANDRIA✧✧✧

Old Town Alexandria can be reached by Metrorail to King Street station (a 20-minute walk, or take Dash bus AT2 or AT5).

Ramsay House Visitor Center *221 King St; tel: (703) 838-4200; open daily 0900–1700.*

Christ Church $ *Cameron and N Columbus Sts; tel: (703) 549-1450; open Mon–Sat 0900–1600, Sun 1400–1630.*

Gadsby's Tavern Museum $ *134 N Royal St; tel: (703) 838-4242; open Apr–Sept Tue–Sat 1000–1700, Sun 1300–1700, Oct–Mar Tue–Sat 1100–1600, Sun 1300–1600.*

Stabler-Leadbeater Apothecary Shop $ *105–107 S Fairfax St; tel: (703) 836-3713; open Mon–Sat 1000–1600, Sun 1300–1700.*

Above
Alexandria

Scottish tobacco merchants established the colonial city of Alexandria in 1749. It grew as a port competing with Georgetown upstream, before Washington was built, but is now a prominent suburb south of downtown Washington. Alexandria's historic core is locally known as Old Town, and is one of the most charming sites in the entire metropolitan area. If you've got a few days to explore Washington, reserve an afternoon and evening for Alexandria.

Alexandria's prominent citizens include George Washington and Robert E Lee. Both attended services at the lovely dark brick **Christ Church**✧, a handsome structure with a simple whitewashed interior, with a quiet graveyard containing tombs of sailors and soldiers from both North and South. One intriguing Old Town site is **Gadsby's Tavern Museum**✧, a tavern dating from 1770, with an adjoining inn built in the Federal style in 1792. There is a restaurant and tours of the building, which is decorated with period furnishings and includes a graceful second-floor ballroom,.

King Street, the Old Town's main street, swoops gently downhill to the river from Fairfax St, lined by wonderfully tidy brick and stone

Carlyle House $
121 N Fairfax St; tel:
(703) 549-2997; open
Tue–Sat 1000–1630, Sun
1200–1630.

Boyhood home of
Robert E Lee $ *607*
Oronoco St; tel: (703) 548-
8454; open Feb–mid-Dec
Mon–Sat 1000–1600, Sun
1300–1600.

town houses, mostly converted into antique shops and restaurants. Stroll down to the riverfront, where sailboats are docked at the small pier, or poke into the Torpedo Factory, which indeed manufactured torpedoes during the two World Wars, and is now an acclaimed local art gallery complex. Before leaving, take time to visit the **Stabler-Leadbeater Apothecary Shop**✦, a restored 18th-century pharmacy, **Carlyle House**✦, once the grandest manor home in the city, and the **boyhood home of Robert E Lee**✦, all of which retain the look and feel of their day.

Sons of Alexandria: George Washington and Robert E Lee

Two of the most prominent Virginians in American history both lived parts of their lives in Alexandria, and both had a significant impact on the course of the country's two most defining wars. Washington commanded the Continental Army in its decisive victory over the British during the Revolutionary War in 1781, and later served as the nation's first president before retiring to his estate at Mount Vernon. Lee, one of the country's most brilliant military figures, was offered command of the Union troops by President Abraham Lincoln at the beginning of the Civil War, but although he believed in the Union, his true loyalties lay with the South. He spurned the offer, and left the capital to lead the Army of Virginia, which became the chief military position in the Confederacy. Lee ultimately surrendered to Ulysses S Grant's Union troops at Appomattox in April 1865.

THE PENTAGON✦

The Pentagon $
Washington Blvd and
I-395 (metro: Pentagon);
tel: (703) 695-1776; open
Mon–Fri 0900–1530.

One of Arlington's more bizarre sites is the Department of Defense headquarters, the Pentagon – the largest office building in the world, a Cold War-era construction that captures the grandeur and bureaucracy of its time. Its size lies in its extraordinary girth (in a five-sided shape) rather than height, and it draws lots of tourists just for its name. The building is rather drab and unappealing, with tours including a film on its construction, plus exhibits on mundane military scenes and honours.

ROOSEVELT ISLAND✦

The wildlife preserve of Roosevelt Island lies along the Virginia shores of the Potomac. Named for Theodore Roosevelt, the 25th US president famous for his love of the wilderness and establishment of the National Park system, Roosevelt Island is a quiet place to escape from the city, seek out water life such as large birds and beavers, or sit along the banks and admire the city opposite. No cars are permitted on the island; park in the lot along George Washington Memorial Parkway and take the footbridge across, or walk from the Rosslyn metro station.

Accommodation and food in Arlington and Alexandria

Although part of Washington, DC, Alexandria has its own charm and, with its own metro station, makes an easy base from which to explore the entire city. There are two good reservations services for the area, both charging upwards of $75 per night for B&B and rooms in private homes: **Princely Bed and Breakfast of Alexandria** (*tel: (1-800) 470-5588*) and **Alexandria and Arlington Bed and Breakfast Network** (*tel: (703) 549-3415 or (1-888) 549-3415*). Old Town Alexandria is renowned for its many superb restaurants, especially their seafood.

La Bergerie $$$ *218 N Lee St, Alexandria; tel: (703) 683-1007; closed Sun.* Its marvellous French/Basque cuisine is a favourite amongst Washington's power set.

Blue Point Grill $$–$$$ *600 Franklin St, Alexandria; tel: (703) 739-0404.* Seafood in a range of styles, from New England clam chowder to Pacific Northwest salmon to Thai grilled shrimp.

The Fish Market $–$$ *105 King St, Alexandria.* A characterful place with excellent fish dishes, and not too dear.

Gadsby's Tavern $$$ *134 N Royal St, Alexandria; tel: (703) 838-4242.* Soak up colonial tavern culture where George Washington himself used to dine.

Morrison House $$–$$$ *116 S Alfred St, Alexandria; tel: (703) 838-8000.* This small Old Town hotel aims to arouse images of Alexandria's luxurious heyday.

Suggested walk

Total distance: 2 miles (less if you arrive by car instead of metro; there are several parking garages in the vicinity). Arlington, which is built for cars, is not covered in this walk.

Time: 3–4 hours with stops.

Route: From King Street metro station, walk down King St to Washington St. This 15-minute walk has no particular sites, but the brick homes, shops and restaurants lining the road are very pleasing. Turn right on to Alfred St, and you immediately come to the **Friendship Fire Engine Company ❶**, once a functioning fire station and now a museum. Turn left down Prince St, and after two blocks you come to the **Lyceum ❷**, a small museum containing photographs and maps covering the history of Alexandria. Continue down Prince St. A quick one-block detour right down Fairfax St takes you to the **Old Presbyterian Meeting House ❸**, another late 18th-century church, at which George Washington's memorial service was held.

Above
Alexandria

Back on Prince St, at the corner of S Lee St, take note of the peach-coloured **Athenaeum ❹**, once a bank and now a small art gallery. The last block of Prince St before the river is known as **Captain's Row ❺**, with the original cobblestoned street intact. Turn left on to Union St and walk one block back to King St, where the **Torpedo Factory ❻** occupies a prominent piece of land by the river. Wander through the artists' studios within, and then step out to the small pier behind it for a view of the Potomac. Take your time walking back up **King St ❼**, it is at its most quaint and enjoyable as it rolls up from the river, and is packed with antique shops, bars and restaurants. After two blocks, turn right on to Fairfax St and admire **Carlyle House ❽** before turning left up Cameron St, past **Gadsby's Tavern Museum ❾** and on to **Christ Church ❿**. From here, it's an easy walk back to the metro station, or back down to one of the many restaurants along King St.

Also worth exploring

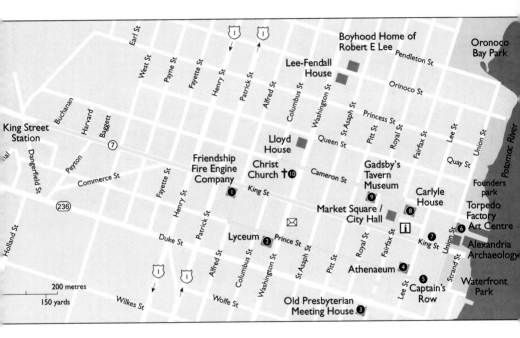

**Pope-Leighey
House at
Woodlawn Plantation**
$$ *9000 Richmond Hwy
(Rte 1 near Rte 235); open
Mar–Dec daily 0930–1600,
Jan–Feb weekends only.*

Eminent American architect Frank Lloyd Wright designed the **Pope-Leighey House❖**, near Gunston Hall, in what he termed his 'Usonian' style: simple, useful and for people of moderate means. This box-like wooden home is the only such work of his accessible to the general public. The house sits on the grounds of the **Woodlawn Plantation❖**, a graceful brick plantation home in the Georgian style, dating from 1802. Both are located at the intersection of Rtes 1 and 235 near Gunston Hall.

Right
Town Hall, Alexandria

Northern Virginia

Ratings

History	●●●●●
Gastronomy	●●●●
Shopping and crafts	●●●●
Entertainment	●●●
Museums	●●●
Nature	●●●
Children	●●
Beaches	●

As Washington, DC, grows, it increasingly swallows up northern Virginia, transforming it into a major technology centre and one of the wealthiest regions in the entire country. There are still pockets resounding with echoes of Virginia's rich history, however, such as Manassas Battlefield, site of two bloody fights during the Civil War. And beyond the suburbs, northern Virginia reveals itself as a microcosm of the entire state: head west and you are in the lovely rolling hills of northern Virginia's hunt country, spreading all the way into the foothills of the Blue Ridge Mountains. George Washington laid his hand on much of this land, living in Winchester and surveying a tiny town which now bears his name. Northern Virginia can easily be visited on a day trip from Washington, DC, but with its wealth of truly fine inns, you'll probably want to stay a night.

MANASSAS BATTLEFIELD❖❖

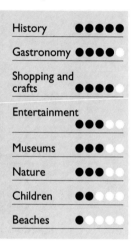

Manassas Battlefield $ *Near the intersection of I-66 and Rte 234; tel: (703) 754-1861; open daily 0830–1700.*

On 21 July 1861, troops of the inexperienced Union and Confederate armies clashed in the Civil War's first major battle, known to Southerners as the First Battle of Manassas and to the North as the Battle of Bull Run. Union troops had expected to burst through the hold and cut a direct path to Richmond, the capital of the South, but met their match in General Thomas Jackson – earning his nickname, 'Stonewall', through the Confederates' stubborn stand. What the North had expected to be a decisive victory was in fact ferocious and deadly, and set the tone for the next four years of war. The scene repeated itself on 28–30 August 1862, when 'Stonewall' Jackson again led the South to victory at Manassas, establishing a temporary upper hand in the war. Today the battlefield is set aside as a national park; walking and driving tours lead past important sites and memorials, and an excellent museum interprets the battles through displays of musketry and uniforms and a slide show.

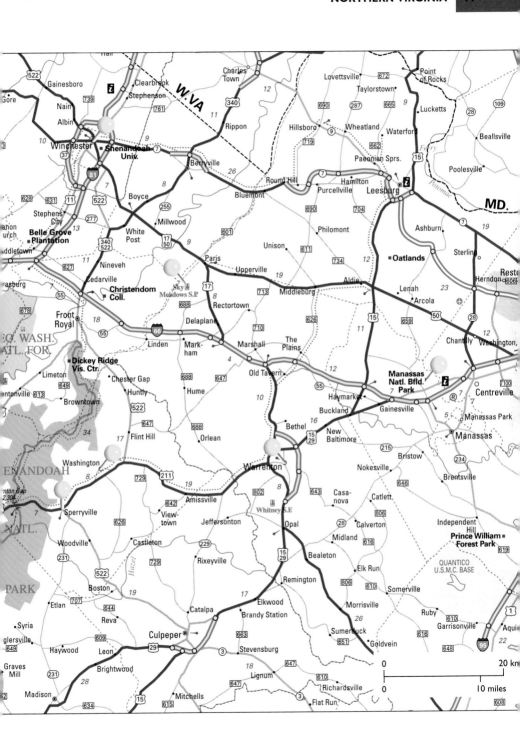

SKY MEADOWS STATE PARK**

Sky Meadows State Park Visitor Center
Rte 17 between Delaplane and Paris; tel: (540) 592-3556; open daily dawn to dusk.

If you can't make it to Shenandoah National Park, the easily accessible Sky Meadows State Park offers a gorgeous alternative, without the crowds. Draped along the gentle slopes of a quiet valley, the park takes its name from open meadows reaching upward to the forests. A leisurely walk across the fields reveals sweeping farmland below, and the visitor centre, located in a 19th-century farmhouse, holds displays on the local ecology. If you want more legwork, follow the path up into the woods, which meets the 2 200-mile-long Appalachian Trail.

Accommodation and food near Sky Meadows State Park

Three excellent inns lie to the north and east of Sky Meadows State Park.

1763 Inn $$ *10087 John Mosby Hwy; tel: (540) 592-3848 or (1-800) 669-1763.* This tranquil place, a few miles away off Rte 50 in Upperville, has a German-influenced menu; many rooms come with jacuzzi and fireplace.

The Ashby Inn and Restaurant $$–$$$ *392 Federal St, Paris; tel: (540) 592-3900, fax: (540) 592-3781; www.ashbyinn.com.* Just up the road in Paris, this is one of the finest of its kind in Virginia.

The Red Fox Inn $$ *2 E Washington St, Middleburg; tel: (540) 687-6301 or (1-800) 223-1728.* All rooms have proud four-poster beds; breakfasts are big and Virginia dinners are hearty.

WARRENTON**

Warrenton Visitor Center *183A Keith St; tel: (1-800) 820-1021. Another small tourist office is located in the New Leaf Bookstore, 43 Main St downtown.*

Old Jail Museum $ *Corner of Main and Ashby Sts; tel: (540) 347-5525; open Tue–Sun 1000–1600.*

Just beyond the grasp of Washington DC's suburbs, the town of Warrenton merits a stopover for its stately old Virginia feel. Washingtonians in fact find Warrenton an easy getaway for antique shopping and a taste of small-town Virginia. Courthouse Square is a good place to start, dominated by the heavy-set white columns of the Old Courthouse. Opposite stands the **Old Jail Museum****, a fun little place to explore, with jail buildings dating from 1808 and 1823 containing a mixed bag of Civil War weaponry, agricultural tools and a blacksmith's display. Tumble down the incline of Court St behind the Old Courthouse to view the elegant Warren Green Hotel, whose many guests over the ages have included Presidents James Monroe, Andrew Jackson and Theodore Roosevelt. Or stroll down Main Street towards the tidy red-brick Warrenton Presbyterian Church, which served as a Civil War hospital. Along the way you pass numerous antique and home décor shops, such as Sarah Belle's, at No 110.

Accommodation and food in Warrenton

There is no shortage of chain hotels and restaurants along Rte 29, but better options are available.

Black Horse Inn $$–$$$ *8393 Meetze Rd; tel: (540) 349-4020, fax: (540) 349-4242.* Refined home (though pricey) east of town, with a nice garden in which to enjoy afternoon tea.

The Depot $$ *65 S 3rd St; tel: (540) 347-1212.* Occupying Warrenton's former railroad station, it offers good American fare along with some Mediterranean specialities.

Fountain Hall $–$$ *609 S East St, Culpeper; tel: (540) 825-8200 or (1-800) 298-4748, fax: (540) 825-7716; www.fountainhall.com.* B&B in a pretty home 20 miles south in Culpeper.

Legends Restaurant and Bar $$ *67 W Lee St; tel: (540) 347-9401.* Relaxed ambience downtown.

WASHINGTON AND SPERRYVILLE✧✧

Nestling snugly in the foothills of the Blue Ridge Mountains is the utterly charming village of Washington, sometimes called Little Washington to distinguish itself from the nation's capital. Incorporated in 1749, it was laid out by (guess who?) George Washington, who was 17 at the time, and has since become a preferred destination for several renowned artists and politicians, many of whom live in the grand estates you see on the hillsides outside of town. Washington is tiny and there are no actual sites, but be sure to stroll the quiet streets, and, if you can afford it, indulge at the luxurious Inn at Little Washington.

Pint-size Sperryville, just 6 miles west along Rte 211, is quite a contrast to Washington's gentility. The residents are a mix of hard-working locals and transplanted hippies, and the place feels beguilingly rougher around the edges. Sperryville can be seen in an hour or less; inspect the shops on tiny Main St or stop into the huge Sperryville Antique Market on the eastern edge of town.

Above
Warrenton's Old Jail Museum

Accommodation and food in Washington and Sperryville

Foster Harris House $$ *189 Main St; tel: (540) 675-3757 or (1-800) 666-0153.* If the **Inn** (below) is just a bit beyond your means, this is one of at least three other good places in the immediate area. Cosy rooms and pleasant gardens overlook the foothills.

The Inn at Little Washington $$$ *Middle and Main Sts; tel: (540) 675-3800, fax: (540) 675-3100.* A masterpiece of fine dining, to go with equally sumptuous lodging. The *prix-fixe* dinners are four-course marvels, with a grand array of seasonal selections and full range of cordials and liqueurs. The Inn has been hailed by countless commentators nationwide, and the service is nothing short of impeccable. It does come with a price, of course: over $100 per person for dinner and no less than $350 for the least expensive room. Closed Tue.

WINCHESTER✧✧

ℹ Winchester-Frederick County Convention and Visitors Bureau *1360 South Pleasant Valley Rd; tel: (1-800) 662-1360; www.visitwinchesterva.com.*

🏛 George Washington's Office Museum $ *Corner of Braddock and Cork Sts; tel: (540) 662-4412; open Apr–Oct Mon–Sat 1000–1600, Sun 1200–1500.*

Stonewall Jackson's Headquarters Museum $ *415 N Braddock St; tel: (540) 667-3242; open Apr–Oct Mon–Sat 1000–1600, Sun 1200–1600; Nov–Mar Fri–Sat 1000–1600, Sun 1200–1600.*

Tucked right up into the northernmost tip of Virginia, Winchester is an intriguing little town for various reasons. George Washington spent several years in Winchester surveying the land and holding his first elected office here. His log-cabin headquarters, **George Washington's Office Museum✧**, is now a museum containing predictable personal items. More than a century later, 'Stonewall' Jackson took up residence in Winchester while leading the Confederacy through numerous Civil War operations, and his home today, **Stonewall Jackson's Headquarters Museum✧**, commemorates his feats. Of a different kind of historical significance, Winchester was also the childhood home of country music legend Patsy Cline, whose many hits in the late 1950s and early 1960s included 'Crazy' and 'I Fall to Pieces', shocking the establishment with her challenging honesty. Though scorned at the time, she has since become a favourite of the tourist authorities, who

Right
George Washington's Office Museum, Winchester

know an opportunity to make a buck when they see one. She is buried in Shenandoah Memorial Park on Rte 522 just southeast of town.

Winchester is also one of the apple capitals of America – the fruit is celebrated at the Shenandoah Apple Blossom Festival in early May, and at numerous apple harvest festivals in surrounding orchards in Sept and Oct. Beyond these attractions, the town centre is simply a pleasing place to stroll. Loudoun St downtown is a pedestrian zone that doesn't appear to have changed much since Patsy Cline's day, and there are plenty of galleries, boutiques and coffee shops in which to poke your head.

Accommodation and food near Winchester

The nicest places to stay are located outside of town.

Battletown Inn $$ *102 W Main St, Berryville; tel: (703) 955-4100*. Some 8 miles east of Winchester on Rte 7 in Berryville, offering comfortable rooms and fine country dining.

Brownstone Cottage $–$$ *161 McCarty Lane, just off Rte 50 at Rte 723 east of Winchester; tel: (540) 662-1962*. Closest non-chain accommodation to central Winchester, in a homey setting.

Hotel Strasburg $–$$ *213 S Holliday St, Strasburg; tel: (540) 465-9191 or (1-800) 348-8327, fax: (540) 465-4788*. Sitting pretty 15 miles south down either I-81 or Rte 11 in Strasburg, this feels like a grand old dame of the frontier, and has one of the best restaurants ($$) in the area.

Brewbakers $–$$ *168 N Loudoun*. Country-saloon atmosphere and similar food.

The Satisfied Mind $ *11 S Loudoun*. Eclectic used bookstore/coffee shop.

Suggested tour

Total distance: 230 miles from the intersection of Rte 50 and I-66 to Manassas Battlefield Park.

Time: 8–10 hours with selected stops. Allow 1¹/₂–2 days for more stops or if including detours.

Links: Winchester and Strasburg lie at the top of the Shenandoah Valley (*see page 79*), and Front Royal is the northernmost entrance to Shenandoah National Park (*see pages 84–5*).

Route: Coming from Washington, DC, I-66 runs directly west through the heart of northern Virginia. Take exit 57 (Rte 50 west) which soon becomes very picturesque, with long white picket fences encircling beautiful horse farms. At **Middleburg**, take note of the pretty clapboard homes lining the road, then pause at a local shop or winery before continuing on to **WINCHESTER ❶**.

Detour: SKY MEADOWS STATE PARK ❷ lies just a couple of miles south of Paris on Rte 17. This is a lovely road winding down to the former railroad junction of **Delaplane**.

Retrace your steps to Rte 50 and Winchester. From Winchester, Rte 11 south is preferable to I-81, and the town of **Strasburg** offers yet more opportunities to go antiquing, most obviously at the huge Strasburg Emporium. The town was settled in the 1700s by German immigrants (hence the name), and although the original character of the town is lost, it is still a nice place to pause or stop into the self-explanatory Stonewall Jackson Museum or Museum of American Presidents.

From Strasburg, Rte 55 leads eastward to **Front Royal**, an inland port where you can rent canoes to paddle down the easy Shenandoah River.

Detour: From Front Royal, you can travel a good third the length of Skyline Drive through the **Shenandoah National Park** before hooking up with Rte 211 at Thornton Gap, which takes you east 7 miles into **SPERRYVILLE ❸** and back to the main route. The views are wonderful along Skyline Drive; keep in mind the $10 park entrance fee.

You can also skirt the park on Rte 522 from Front Royal, a beautiful country road heading south towards Rte 211 near **WASHINGTON ❹**. Rte 211, although a four-lane highway, is soft on the eye and lightly travelled, winding its way east to **WARRENTON ❺**.

Detour: If Warrenton tickles your fancy, head south 20 miles down Rte 29 to **Culpeper**, a smaller version of the same staid brick churches and small shops.

Rte 29 north from Warrenton is no great joy to drive along, but it does lead you straight to **MANASSAS BATTLEFIELD ❻**, which itself is located just off I-66, and a quick trip back to Washington, DC.

Also worth exploring

It may come as a surprise, but Virginia is the nation's seventh largest wine-producing state, and the tradition can be traced back to Thomas Jefferson, who gained a fondness for the tipple when he served as ambassador to France. Wineries are well signposted throughout northern Virginia, and some of the many offering tours and tastings include **Prince Michel Vineyards**, off Rte 29 south of Culpeper, Farfelu Vineyard near Rte 522 in Flint Hill, **Naked Mountain Vineyard and Winery** along Rte 55 in Markham and **Piedmont Vineyards and Winery** on Rte 626 outside Middleburg.

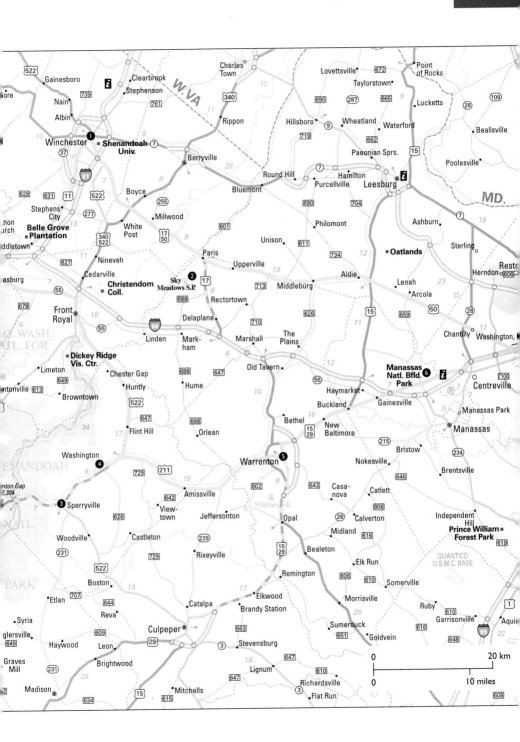

Shenandoah

Ratings

Nature and wildlife	●●●●●
History	●●●●
Gastronomy	●●●
Museums	●●●·
Shopping	●●●
Children	●●
Entertainment	●●
Beaches	●

Two distinctive geographical features lend the central portion of the Appalachian Mountains its sublime beauty and its rich historical importance. The luxuriant Shenandoah National Park (the name comes from a native American word meaning 'daughter of the stars') is one of the most visited in the nation. The mountains here are often referred to as the Blue Ridge because of their remarkable appearance: distant peaks really do look blue most days, due to the presence of a particular haze. The fertile Shenandoah Valley below was highly prized during the Civil War, and its towns today are a virtual history lesson: New Market Battlefield was the scene of a vicious battle, and towns such as Staunton and Lexington retain their proud 19th-century appearance. Numerous caves and full-season resorts provide some recreational diversion, and give this portion of the Appalachian Mountains a little something for everyone.

BATH AND HIGHLAND COUNTIES✦✦✦

ⓘ Bath County Chamber of Commerce *Rte 22, Hot Springs; tel: (1-800) 628-8092.*

Highland County Chamber of Commerce *Spruce St, Monterey; tel: (540) 468-2250.*

ⓜ Highland Maple Museum $ *Rte 220, Monterey; tel: (540) 468-2551. Call for opening hours as these change.*

Much of the western edge of Virginia is made up of sections of the expansive George Washington National Forest. The hills rise again west of the Shenandoah Valley, rubbing up against the state of West Virginia, and the area west of Staunton is a visual delight. The village of Monterey in Highland County is surrounded by sheep farms – there are in fact more sheep than people here, and all local industries are derived from the land. Just south of Monterey, the **Highland Maple Museum✦** is an old log cabin with demonstrations on how to make maple syrup. Nearby, the **Virginia Trout Company✦** gives tours of its hatchery.

Bath County gains its name, aptly enough, from the mineral springs that flow forth from its soil. It should come as no surprise, then, that the towns of Warm Springs and Hot Springs are built upon spa facilities, still in use today. The round white wooden bath houses you see near the intersection of Rtes 39 and 220 in Warm Springs are the

Virginia Trout Company $ *Rte 220, Monterey; tel: (540) 468-2280.* Call for daily tour information.

Jefferson Pools $$$ *Rte 220, Warm Springs; tel: (540) 839-5346.* Call for opening hours as these change frequently.

Jefferson Pools✦✦, one for men and one for women; for around $12–$15 you can immerse yourself in the body-temperature water. As the pools are so old Dr.they date from 1761 and 1836 respectively), they aren't in tip-top shape, so you may wish to head 5 miles south to The Homestead at Hot Springs, a lavish resort with baths that are indeed a bit hotter – but be prepared to pay for the privilege.

Accommodation and food in Bath and Highland Counties

Highland Inn $$ *Main St (Rte 220), Monterey; tel: (1-888) 466-4682.* Large white clapboard home with long porches on both storeys; a highly regarded hotel and restaurant.

The Homestead $$$ *Rte 220, Hot Springs; tel: (1-800) 838-1766; www.thehomestead.com.* Fantastic mountain resort with all the facilities and activities you could possibly think of, from the spa to golf to fine dining.

Below
George C Marshall Museum, Lexington

The Inn at Gristmill Square $$ *Rte 220, Warm Springs; tel: (540) 839-2231.* Rustic rooms and an excellent restaurant ($$) in a converted flour mill.

BRYCE RESORT✦

Bryce Resort $–$$ *Basye; tel: (1-800) 821-1444; www.bryceresort.com.* Slope-side lodges and self-catering apartments, and a good, if standard, bar and grill, all handled by the resort itself.

Set amid lovely rolling hills and low mountains, Bryce Resort offers low-key recreational activities just 2¹/₂ hours from Washington, DC. Snow machines ensure white slopes from Nov to Mar, though the skiing is not challenging. Other amenities include 18 holes of golf, tennis, horseriding and a lake for swimming and canoeing. Just down the road, Orkney Springs is a lovely former spa town with a grand hotel, no longer in use but impressive all the same.

LEXINGTON✦✦✦

❶ **Lexington Visitor Center** *106 E Washington St, tel: (540) 463-3777.*

❶ **Virginia Military Institute Museum $** *Campus of the Virginia Military Institute; tel: (540) 464-7334; open daily 0900–1700.*

George C Marshall Museum $ *Campus of the Virginia Military Institute; tel: (540) 463-7103; open daily Mar–Oct 0900–1700, Nov–Feb 0900–1600.*

Stonewall Jackson House $$ *8 E Washington St; tel: (540) 463-2552; open June–Aug Mon–Sat 0900–1800, Sun 1300–1800, Sept–May Mon–Sat 0900–1700, Sun 1300–1700.*

Lee Chapel $ *Campus of Washington and Lee University; tel: (540) 463-8768; open Mon–Sat 0900–1700, Sun 1400–1700.*

Home to two universities and several historic brick buildings, Lexington is an agreeable place to break the journey and soak up small-town Virginia. The presence of the Virginia Military Institute (VMI) has much to do with the town's identity: it supplied the Confederacy with soldiers throughout the Civil War, and remains one of the country's most prestigious military academies. The **Virginia Military Institute Museum**✦ documents its history through good, if predictable, glass cases full of uniforms and weaponry. Two of VMI's most famous sons have museums here in their honour. George C Marshall, author of the Marshall Plan to rebuild countries destroyed in World War II, graduated with the Institute's class of 1901, and the **George C Marshall Museum**✦ tells his life story. In downtown Lexington, the **Stonewall Jackson House**✦ is a plain brick house in which the celebrated commander of the Confederate Army lived for several years while he taught at VMI.

Lexington is also a lovely place to unwind. The sprawling green campus of Washington and Lee University contains the sedate **Lee Chapel**✦✦, dedicated to Robert E Lee, another Confederate general and VMI professor, who is buried underneath the building. Streets surrounding the campus are lined with beautiful old Victorian homes, and the downtown area, particularly Main St and Nelson St, is a compact series of smart red-brick and stone shopfronts with quaint boutiques and antique shops.

Accommodation and food in Lexington

Asherowe B&B $ *314 S Jefferson St; tel: (540) 463-4219.* Simple, comfortable lodgings downtown.

Lavender Hill Farm $ *1374 Big Spring Dr.; tel: (540)-464-5877 or (1-800) 446-4240.* Near Rte 60 and I-64 some 5 miles west of town, this is a working farm where you can go trout fishing or enjoy home-baked bread on the porch.

Llewellyn Lodge $–$$ *603 S Main St; tel: (540) 463-3235 or (1-800) 882-1145; www.llodge.com.* A pretty white home right in town with B&B and information on outdoor excursions.

Southern Inn Restaurant $$ *37 S Main St.* Excellent 'down home' southern cooking, and a selection of good beers and Virginia wines.

Above
General 'Stonewall' Jackson

LURAY CAVERNS✦

Luray Caverns $$$
*Rte 211 outside Luray;
tel: (540) 743-6551; open
daily 0900–1730.*

Shenandoah Caverns
Tel: (540) 477-3115.

Endless Caverns *Tel:
(540) 896-2283.*

Grand Caverns *Tel:
(540) 249-5729.*

Stunning caves pock the hills surrounding the Shenandoah Valley, the largest and most heavily advertised being Luray Caverns, outside the town of Luray. The size and the quantity of stalactites and stalagmites is spectacular, but the commercialism of the place is nothing short of ridiculous. Guided tours lead visitors along concrete footpaths, past evocative natural sculptures such as a 'gremlin' and a pair of 'fried eggs', as well as a hand-built 'pipe organ'; coloured lights heighten the beauty/kitsch. Despite the hefty admission fee, the place is always crowded, and is well and truly complemented with a plethora of gift shops and 'family-style' restaurants. If this all sounds like too much, other (albeit less dramatic) caves in the area with fewer visitors include **Shenandoah Caverns✦**, off I-81 near Mount Jackson, **Endless Caverns✦**, off Rte 11 south of New Market, and **Grand Caverns✦**, off Rte 340 north of Waynesboro.

NATURAL BRIDGE✦✦

The 90ft-span of this natural stone bridge is part of Rte 11, but you may scarcely notice it until you view it from the bank of Cedar Creek 215ft below. The setting is beautifully rural, but the lure of tourist dollars means an extravagant hotel, a silly wax museum and a hefty admission fee to see the archway. Despite these annoyances, the bridge is quite spectacular, and a path beneath it leads along the creek to some deep-pocket caverns. George Washington's initials are carved into the arch, and the land was once owned by Thomas Jefferson.

Accommodation and food near Natural Bridge

Natural Bridge Inn and Conference Center $$ *Rte 11 and Rte 130; tel: (1-800) 533-1410.* Grandiose hotel with a decent restaurant, capitalising on the location.

NEW MARKET BATTLEFIELD❖❖

New Market Battlefield Military Museum $$ *Tel: (540) 740-8065; open mid-Mar–Nov daily.*

Hall of Valor $$ *Tel: (540) 740-3101; open daily 0900–1700.*

A trip through the Shenandoah Valley is a retracing of both Confederate and Union troop movements during the Civil War. Its rich soil and the long, flat north–south passage it offered through the mountains of western Virginia rendered it highly coveted land. Several battles were waged here through the course of the war, the worst and most deadly at New Market in 1864. Among those killed were Confederate cadets – some as young as 14 – from the Virginia Military Institute (VMI) in Lexington.

The site is marked today with two excellent museums. The **New Market Battlefield Military Museum**❖❖ contains a chronological display of thousands of artefacts from the War such as General Custer's spurs and 'Stonewall' Jackson's bible. The nearby **Hall of Valor**❖❖ commemorates those killed at New Market and provides a detailed history of the battle through films and display cases. After the museums, a tour guide takes you out on to the battlefield, including a farmhouse and slave quarters that sat right in the crossfire.

Accommodation in New Market

Cross Roads Inn $ *9222 John Sevier Road (Rte 211); tel: (540) 740-4157, fax: (540) 740-4255.* Comfortable B&B on the eastern edge of town with a large yard, views of the hills and home-made strudel.

Above
The Grand Caverns

SHENANDOAH NATIONAL PARK◆◆◆

**🛈 Shenandoah
National Park**

Shenandoah National Park
is open year-round, though
Skyline Drive may be
closed at times because of
bad weather conditions.
Admission to the park is
$10 per vehicle or $3 per
person on foot; no bicycles
permitted. All park
entrances are staffed with
helpful rangers, who give
out maps and information.
There are regular visitor
centres at Dickey Ridge
(Milepost 4) and Big
Meadows (Milepost 51),
both open daily
0900–1700. For general
park information, call *(540)
999-3500*. For information
on hiring horses, call *(540)
999-2210*.

**◖ Aramark
Shenandoah
National Park Lodges**
*$–$$ Box 727, Luray, VA
22835; tel: (1-800) 999-
4714; www.visitshenandoah.
com.*

Opposite
Frozen waterfall, Shenandoah
National Park

Straddling the eastern ridge of the Blue Ridge Mountains, Shenandoah National Park extends for about 80 miles northeast to southwest, from Front Royal to Waynesboro. Skyline Drive rides the ridges all the way along it, linking up with the Blue Ridge Highway which continues all the way down to Great Smoky Mountains National Park in North Carolina. Stunning viewpoints grace both sides of the road, so you can take the drive without getting out, but this defeats the purpose of being in the mountains. There are some 500 miles of trails here, and the brochure given out at the park entrance gives tips on hikes – anything from quick jaunts to see a view or waterfall to longer circuits taking several hours or even days. The Appalachian Trail, which extends over 2200 miles from Georgia to Maine, winds through the park, marked with a white blaze.

Skyland and Big Meadows, separate administrative centres near the midpoint of Skyline Drive, both have facilities for visitors. A pair of short walks are suggested in this area. Just north of Skyland, the 1.5-mile hike up to Stony Man Mountain reveals wonderful vistas of 40-mile-long Massanutten Mountain and the Shenandoah Valley – especially beautiful at sunset. Just south of Big Meadows, an easy 0.7-mile path runs down to Dark Hollow Falls, a grand series of falls dropping over 70ft into a shady pool below.

Accommodation and food in Shenandoah National Park

All accommodation in the park is handled by **Aramark Shenandoah National Park Lodges** and includes campsites, standard hotel accommodation and pleasantly rustic cabins at Skyland Lodge (Milepost 41), Big Meadows (Milepost 51) and Lewis Mountain (Milepost 57). Lodges are usually open early Apr–Nov, cabins May–late Oct; it is imperative to book well in advance. There are dining facilities, all acceptable but none exceptional, every 20 miles or so along Skyline Drive, and you can pick up groceries at Skyland, Big Meadows and Loft Mountain (all Apr–Oct only).

Shenandoah wildlife

Shenandoah National Park is home to a wide range of wildlife, including an estimated 500 black bears. There are two species of poisonous snake: the copperhead and rattlesnake. Less fearsome creatures include Virginia white-tail deer, red and grey foxes, skunks, bobcats, raccoons, groundhogs and chipmunks. The birds most commonly seen, especially from Skyline Drive, are the turkey vulture and black vulture. The turkey vulture, or buzzard, has a wingspan up to 6ft and a red head; the smaller black vulture has a pale patch on the underside of each wing. Wild turkeys, the largest of the park's bird species, are frequently seen too, especially in the northern section. More than 1000 species of plant life are found in the park, including 18 types of orchid. Picking flowers is forbidden. Most of the park's trees are deciduous, predominantly oak and hickory, and a lush carpet of fern often lies underneath.

STAUNTON✦✦✦

ⓘ Staunton-Augusta Travel Information Center *1250 Richmond Rd (at the Museum of American Frontier Culture); tel: (1-800) 332-5219.*

ⓜ Woodrow Wilson Birthplace and Museum *$$ 18–24 N Coalter St; tel: (540) 885-0897; open Mar–Oct daily 0900–1700, Nov–Feb Mon–Sat 1000–1600, Sun 1200–1600.*

Although sometimes overlooked by tourists, the unassuming city of Staunton (pronounced 'Stanton') comes as a wonderful little surprise. The town is hilly, exceedingly clean and an authentically enchanting place to visit, having preserved its character without pandering to tourists.

Staunton has been fairly wealthy since its role as an important railroad junction around the time of the Civil War. Although today it serves only one daily Amtrak train (the Washington–Chicago 'Cardinal' route), the small train station is a destination in itself for its simple elegance, and, with the handsome brick warehouse buildings opposite, forms part of the so-called Wharf District, once a bustling commercial area now converted to boutiques and restaurants.

Beverley Street is Staunton's main drag, a marvellous throwback of three-storey buildings in various 19th-century architectural styles. Just beyond this central business district, the hills rise steeply and Staunton's fine array of Victorian and *ante-bellum* family homes line the streets. One of these homes was the birthplace of President Woodrow Wilson, in 1856. Today the **Woodrow Wilson Birthplace and Museum**✦ chronicles the life of one of the United States' greatest

**Museum of
American Frontier
Culture $$** *Near
intersection of I-66 and I-81;
tel: (540) 332-7850; open
daily mid-Mar–Nov
0900–1700, Dec–mid-Mar
1000–1600.*

presidents, including a tour of his home and displays on his many achievements, along with his favoured Pierce-Arrow limousine.

On the eastern edge of town, the open-air **Museum of American Frontier Culture**❖❖ displays farmhouses relocated here from Germany, England and Ireland, in order to present the life of the earliest settlers in this region. Costumed guides demonstrate how immigrants from these countries lived in the 1700s, and how they had forged a new American identity by the 1800s. With farm animals, a blacksmith's shop and knowledgeable interpreters, this is especially good for children.

Accommodation and food in Staunton

Belle Grae Inn $–$$ *515 W Frederick St; tel: (540) 886-5151 or (1-800) 541-5151; fax: (540) 886-6641.* A neighbourhood of its own, occupying several Victorian homes with gracious rooms and suites, and a good restaurant.

Sampson Eagon Inn $–$$ *238 E Beverley St; tel: (540) 886-8200 or (1-800) 597-9722.* Perfectly situated just off-centre, across the street from the Woodrow Wilson birthplace in an *ante-bellum* home, tastefully furnished, and offering a gourmet breakfast. Book early, as it's small.

Stonewall Jackson Hotel $ *28 S Market St; tel: (540) 885-1581.* Once one of the grandest hotels in the South, now a mere shadow of its former self, but the faded lobby and ballroom exude a past era. Very cheap, and with few amenities, so don't expect much.

Depot Grille $$ *42 Middlebrooke Ave.; tel: (540) 885-7332.* Just down from the Pullman in the Wharf District, with a similar menu and equally good setting, plus a grand long bar.

The Pampered Palate Café $ *26 E Beverley St; tel: (540) 886-9463.* Good coffee and pastries in this central café, along with simple, filling breakfasts and lunches.

The Pullman $$ *36 Middlebrooke Ave.; tel: (540) 885-6612.* Located in the classy old railroad station, and offering prime rib, local rainbow trout and Virginia wines, plus an old-fashioned ice-cream bar.

Suggested tour

Total distance: 205 miles from Front Royal to Strasburg via Waynesboro and Staunton. Add 152 miles for the detour to Bath and Highland Counties.

Left
Staunton Museum of American
Frontier Culture

Time: 6 hours actual driving time, 9 hours including the detour. Allow 2 full days for the route, up to 3 full days including the detour.

Links: Skyline Drive can be approached from Washington, DC, via Front Royal (off I-66) or Thornton Gap (Rte 211). The latter is more interesting as it takes in some of the sights of northern Virginia (*see pages 70–7*). Charlottesville (*see pages 93–4*) also makes a good launching pad to Skyline Drive via I-64. Rte 11 and I-81 both run through the Shenandoah Valley to Roanoke (*see pages 97–8*).

Route: This is an elongated circular route, and has two real highlights: the roads themselves. Most sites mentioned in this chapter can be reached by **Skyline Drive** in the Shenandoah National Park and by Rte 11, which traverses the Shenandoah Valley.

Enter the **SHENANDOAH NATIONAL PARK** ❶ at either Front Royal or Thornton Gap. Skyline Drive takes about 3 hours, as speed limits are set at 35 mph. Be sure to stop for at least a short hike; see the Shenandoah National Park section (*page 84*) for details. Exit Skyline Drive near Waynesboro, and take I-64, a short hop over to **STAUNTON** ❷.

Detour: The beautiful mountain scenery and cute towns of the **George Washington National Forest** ❸ west of Staunton are worth a trip in themselves, and all the roads through here are designated 'Virginia scenic byways'; see the Bath and Highland Counties section for details. From Staunton, follow Rte 250 west to **Monterey** ❹, then Rte 220 south to **Warm Springs** and **Hot Springs** ❺. From Warm Springs, Rte 39 east takes you to Goshen, linking up with Rte 42 north; at Buffalo Gap head east on Rte 254 back to Staunton.

🏛 Virginia Quilt Museum $ *301 S Main St, Harrisonburg; tel: (540) 433-3818; open Mon and Thur–Sat 1000–1600, Sun 1300–1600.*

Shenandoah Valley Folk Art and Heritage Center $$ *High St, Dayton; tel: (540) 879-2681; open Mon and Wed–Sat 1000–1600, Sun 1300–1600.*

The quick way up the Shenandoah Valley is I-81, but the prettier way is along Rte 11 which runs parallel. The next large town north of Staunton is **Harrisonburg** ❻, a mildly interesting place with a couple of museums on folk art traditions. The **Virginia Quilt Museum** on Main St has a select collection of quilts, pronouncing the 'role of quilting in the cultural life of society', while the **Shenandoah Valley Folk Art and Heritage Center**, off Rte 42 just south in the town of **Dayton** ❼, holds a solid collection of ceramic pots, needlework, basketry and painted chests from the region.

Rte 211 continues through **NEW MARKET** ❽ and on past a string of pretty one-street towns such as Mt Jackson, Woodstock and Toms Brook. Just before Mt Jackson, signs point you to **Meem's Bottom Bridge** on Rte 720, one of the last remaining covered bridges in the state. The valley peters out at **Strasburg** and **Winchester**, which are covered in the Northern Virginia route (*see pages 74 and 76*).

Also worth exploring: West Virginia

The border between Virginia and West Virginia is formed by mountains that become increasingly rugged the further west you go. The **Monongahela National Forest** in West Virginia is splendid and sparsely populated, and offers fabulous opportunities for hiking, skiing

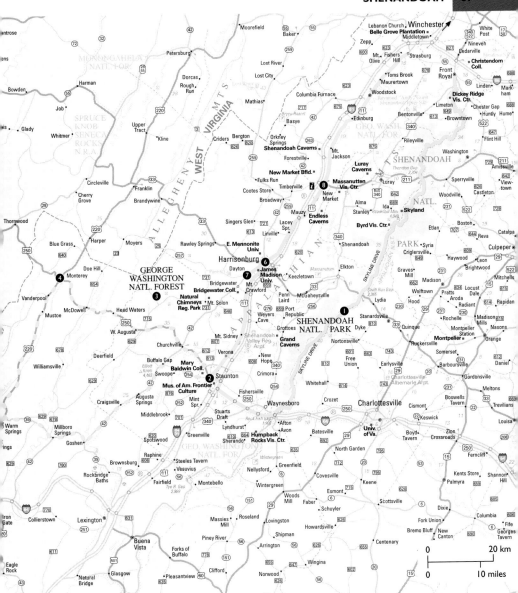

and whitewater rafting. Rte 55 from Strasburg and Rte 33 from Harrisonburg link up at the stunning cliffs of **Seneca Rocks**, a 1½-hour drive. Nearby **Spruce Knob** is the highest peak in the state, and you can drive to the top. Rte 39 from Lexington and Rte 250 from Staunton both link up with Rte 28 in West Virginia, from which Rte 66 leads you to the historic mining town of **Cass** and the excellent ski resort at **Snowshoe**, both roughly 1½–2 hours away.

The Piedmont

Ratings

Art and museums	●●●●
Gastronomy	●●●●
History	●●●●
Nature	●●●●
Shopping	●●●
Children	●●
Entertainment	●●
Beaches	●

The charming small cities of Virginia's Piedmont region offer a richly mixed bag of historical and architectural delights, with the beautiful low Blue Ridge Mountains as a backdrop. Well-heeled Charlottesville is a major draw, not least for Thomas Jefferson's extraordinary home at Monticello nearby, as well as the beautiful campus of the University of Virginia. Cities such as Lynchburg and Roanoke, once dynamic industrial centres, have gentrified historical cores and are surprisingly lively. Driving through the rolling countryside is pure joy: grand estates of old Virginia mingle with a plethora of good wineries throughout the region, and most towns retain traces of the 19th century in Main Street shopfronts, churches, and courthouses. One of the real highlights, though, is the tiny settlement at Appomattox, site of the meeting between Generals Grant and Lee that brought an end to the Civil War.

APPOMATTOX✧✧✧

This quiet little community, set amid the brooding landscape of central Virginia, was the scene of one of the most significant events in the history of the United States – the end of the Civil War. Here, on 9 April 1865, General Robert E Lee surrendered the Army of Northern Virginia to General Ulysses S Grant, commander of the Union forces.

Appomattox Court House National Historical Park✧✧, three miles from the modern town of

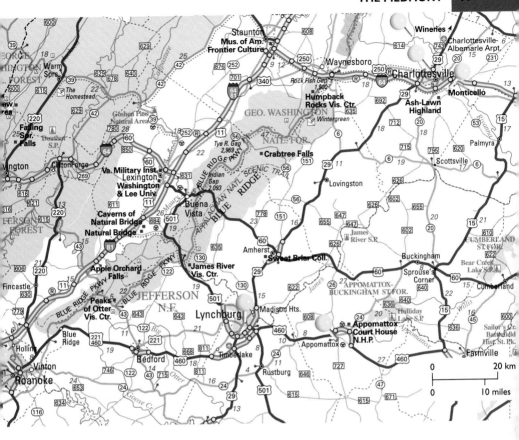

Appommattox Court House National Historical Park $ *Rte 24, north of Appomattox; tel: (804) 352-8987; open daily 0900–1730.*

Appomattox (pronounced 'AP-po-MAT-tux'), encompasses the original village, which has been restored to its 1865 appearance after falling into disrepair at the end of the century. This was only a tiny place at the time, with a court house, jail, tavern, store, law office, and a few homes; many still stand or have been rebuilt, and can be visited on a self-guided tour. The courthouse contains the visitor centre and museum, but the momentous document signing actually took place in a private home, the McLean House, which has been reconstructed. Appomattox is really very small, but there is something haunting to the village and the gently rolling countryside around that makes it a must-see in the region.

Accommodation and food in Appomattox

Babcock House Bed and Breakfast Inn $–$$ *106 Oakleigh Ave. (Rte 6); tel: (804) 352-7532 or (1-800) 689-6208, fax: (1-800) 752-7329.* Nice accommodation, and the comfortable restaurant serves the usual Virginia favourites.

Left
Appomattox Court House

Appomattox: the end of the war

The terrible war between North and South raged for four years, at a price of over 600,000 lives, and yet it all ended with a mere whimper. Lee's Army of Virginia, the last major force in the now-decimated Confederacy, lost battles at Richmond (capital of the South) and Petersburg on 1–2 April 1865, and fled westward to reach a supply train near Lynchburg. The troops were exhausted and practically starving, however, and Grant's healthy forces cut them off on 9 April. Lee realised he had no chance, and surrendered his men at Appomattox, the nearest town with a courthouse. Though minor skirmishes flared up in a few more Southern states for another two months, the agreement between Lee and Grant effectively began the long period of reconciliation.

Right
Charlottesville Fife and Drum
Honor Guard

CHARLOTTESVILLE***

Charlottesville/ Albemarle Convention and Visitors Bureau *Rte 20 south of centre; tel: (804) 977-1783.*

Rotunda $ *University of Virginia campus; tel: (804) 924-3239; open daily 1000–1600.*

The small city of Charlottesville has a spirit thoroughly dominated by the University of Virginia and its founder, Thomas Jefferson. The campus is one of the most beautiful of its kind, a stately collection of dignified red brick buildings, smooth green lawns and carefully placed trees all designed by Jefferson himself. The robust **Rotunda**** stands at its centre, with a gleaming white dome and columns modelled on the Pantheon in Rome. A small museum in the basement recalls Jefferson's special pride in this institution, still today considered one of America's finest. From here you can also join a campus tour, but you need only stand on the back steps of the Rotunda to admire the truly beautiful quadrangle, a long stretch of lawn colonnaded by low brick buildings still used today as dormitories for professors and students.

Several blocks down Main St to the east, Charlottesville's centre-most area is a pedestrianised street of shops and restaurants known as the Downtown Mall. With several notable old buildings, it's a pleasant place to stroll, or stop for ice cream or coffee. Two blocks north, at 5th and Jefferson Sts, the Albemarle County Court House includes an 1820s chapel that was shared by Baptists, Episcopalians, Methodists and Presbyterians, when worshippers included Presidents Jefferson, Monroe and Madison.

Accommodation and food in Charlottesville

1817 Historic Bed and Breakfast $–$$ *1211 W Main St; tel: (804) 979-7353 or (1-800) 730-7443.* This B&B has a pretty interior and is right near the UVA campus, but also amid bland surrounding streets.

200 South Street $–$$ *200 South St; tel: (804) 979-0200.* This gracious Southern B&B is right downtown, but the immediate neighbourhood is a bit drab.

The Clifton Inn $$–$$$ *Clifton Inn Drive, near intersection of Rtes 250 and 729 east of Charlottesville; tel: (1-888) 971-1800.* This award-winning country inn outside Charlottesville has an elegant dining room and 'romantic getaway' packages.

English Inn $ *2000 Morton Dr.; tel: (804) 971-9900 or (1-800) 986-5400.* This pleasant enough hotel is north of the centre, with a pool, sauna and fitness room.

Hardware Store Restaurant $ *316 E Main St; tel: (804) 977-1518.* A century ago this really was a hardware store and some of the old ironmongery and advertising signs are still on display. A good place for lunch or a simple dinner, with seafood, chicken and huge deli sandwiches.

Métropolitain $$$ *214 Water St; tel: (804) 977-1043.* Considered

Charlottesville's best restaurant, though you wouldn't know it from first glance: the décor is deceivingly simple. The changing menu often includes the likes of Chilean sea bass and roast leg of lamb. Dinner only, reservations recommended.

Michie Tavern $$ *Rte 53 near Monticello; tel: (804) 977-1234.* Lunchtime-only tavern appearing just as it did in Jefferson's day, located at the base of the road up to Monticello.

Tastings $$ *5th and Market Sts; tel: (804) 293-3663.* Combination wine bar/wine store/restaurant, with entrées such as crab cakes and lightly grilled meats.

Below
Michie Tavern, Charlottesville

LYNCHBURG ❖❖

Lynchburg Visitors Center 216 12th St; tel: (804) 847-1811.

Old Court House $ 901 Court St; tel: (804) 847-1459; open daily 1000–1600.

Anne Spencer House and Garden $ 1313 Pierce St; tel: (804) 845-1313; open daily by appointment.

Below
Lynchburg City Cemetery

Settled in 1727, Lynchburg sprawls across seven steep hills above the James River. The city began as a ferry crossing and developed as a tobacco town; for more than a century tobacco was processed, auctioned and made into cigarettes and plugs for chewing. During the Civil War, the city was a major Confederate storage depot and a burial place for the war dead. Several streets are designated historic districts, and the city today has echoes of its former importance with several museums and a prettified centre.

The **Old Court House❖** downtown dates from 1855 and contains a decent museum on the city's history. The Community Market to the east was a favourite of Thomas Jefferson, and is still the place to come for fresh produce and home-made crafts. A few streets up, the **Anne Spencer House and Garden❖** was once the home of this noted poet who was part of the Harlem Renaissance, and is the only black woman and Virginian included in the *Norton Anthology of Modern American and British Poetry*. In recognition of its position at a strategic crossroads, the **City Cemetery❖** at 4th and Taylor Sts contains the graves of men who fought in the Revolutionary War, but the most poignant part is the Confederate section with the graves of 2700 soldiers from 14 states who died in the Civil War.

Accommodation and food in Lynchburg

Lynchburg Mansion Inn $$ 405 Madison St; tel: (804) 528-5400 or (1-800) 352-1199. Near the centre, this grand Georgian mansion has all the trappings.

Madison Bed and Breakfast $–$$ 413 Madison St; tel: (804) 528-1503 or (1-800) 828-6422. This beautiful Victorian home dates from the 1880s, and is filled with antiques.

Jazz St Grill $$ 3225 Old Forest Rd; tel: (804) 385-0100. Located south of the centre, this is a local favourite for its New Orleans-inspired cuisine.

Percival's Isle Java Tavern $ 1208 Main St; tel: (804) 847-3059. This café/restaurant is centrally located and has good coffee, plus pizzas, sandwiches and a few dinner entrées such as tuna steak.

MONTICELLO❖❖❖

ℹ️ **Monticello Visitor Center** *Rte 20 south of centre (in the same building as the Charlottesville/Albemarle Convention and Visitors Bureau); tel: (804) 984-9822.*

🏛️ **Monticello $$$** *Rte 53 (off Rte 20); tel: (804) 984-9822; www.monticello.org; open daily Mar–Oct 0800–1700, Nov–Feb 0900–1630.*

Most visitors to Charlottesville come specifically to see the stately, though eccentric, home designed by Thomas Jefferson, third president of the United States. Maintained and preserved as a national monument to Jefferson, Monticello is located on a hilltop just southeast of Charlottesville, and commands a fine view of the central Virginia countryside. If you can't make it here, you can always see the house on the back of any 5-cent coin, but a visit gives good insight into the mind of a squire who has become a revered American icon. Virginians still refer to him as 'Mr Jefferson', an indication of the esteem in which he is held in these parts, even though he has been in the news in recent years due to evidently substantiated rumours that he bore offspring with one of his slaves.

Not content to be merely a seminal figure in American politics, Jefferson was also a fine architect, astronomer, horticulturalist and inventor. Among the quirks inside are a two-storey grandfather clock, a telescope and a gadget holding two pens which allowed Jefferson to make automatic copies of the more than 20,000 letters he wrote. The grounds are equally fascinating, and include an orchard, a vineyard, a 1000ft-long kitchen garden, the foundations of servants' quarters and Jefferson's grave.

Above
Roanoke's Art Museum of Western Virginia

ROANOKE ✦✦

ℹ **Roanoke Valley Convention and Visitor's Bureau** *114 Market Place; tel: (540) 342-6025 or (1-800) 635-5535; www.visitroanokeva.com.*

🏛 **Science Museum of Western Virginia** *$$ Center in the Square, 1 Market St; tel: (540) 342-5710; open Tue–Sat 1000–1700, Sun 1300–1700.*

Below
Hotel Roanoke

A 19th-century industrial centre which flourished with the growth of railroads and trade through the Shenandoah Valley, Roanoke today is a surprisingly urbane city with enough attractions to keep you busy for a few hours at least. It was settled by German, Welsh and Scottish immigrants in the mid-18th century, but didn't come into its own until over a hundred years later. A slight European tinge pervades, from the site of an ochre-coloured neo-classical church, to the very German-looking Hotel Roanoke in the centre, to the presence of a daily farmers' market in town. The central area has the feel of the important industrial centre it once was, and the nearby railroad tracks seem to assert its continued sense of purpose.

Roanoke is also blessed with some very good museums, three of which are gathered under one roof at the Center in the Square, a restored and converted 1914 warehouse. The **Science Museum of Western Virginia** has interactive displays and a planetarium, making it a big hit with children, while the **Art Museum of Western**

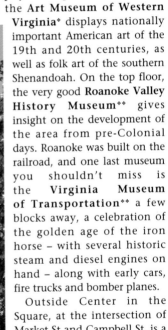

Virginia displays nationally important American art of the 19th and 20th centuries, as well as folk art of the southern Shenandoah. On the top floor, the very good **Roanoke Valley History Museum** gives insight on the development of the area from pre-Colonial days. Roanoke was built on the railroad, and one last museum you shouldn't miss is the **Virginia Museum of Transportation** a few blocks away, a celebration of the golden age of the iron horse – with several historic steam and diesel engines on hand – along with early cars, fire trucks and bomber planes.

Outside Center in the Square, at the intersection of Market St and Campbell St, is a daily open-air farmers' market, in operation since 1882. Campbell St is a trendy stretch of arty shops and international restaurants, and is good for a stroll and a meal.

Accommodation and food in Roanoke

Art Museum of Western Virginia $ *Center in the Square, 1 Market St; tel: (540) 342-5798; open Tue–Sat 1000–1700, Sun 1300–1700.*

Roanoke Valley History Museum $ *Center in the Square, 1 Market St; tel: (540) 342-5770; open Tue–Sat 1000–1700, Sun 1300–1700.*

Virginia Museum of Transportation $ *303 Norfolk Ave.; tel: (703) 342-5670; open Mon–Sat 1000–1700, Sun 1200–1700.*

Hotel Roanoke $$ *110 Shenandoah Ave.; tel: (540) 985-5900, fax: (540) 853-8290.* The city's granddaddy, this large historic hotel commands a presence on a downtown hillside, and has a very good restaurant as well.

Jefferson Lodge $ *616 S Jefferson St; tel: (540) 342-2951.* A reasonably priced motel within walking distance of the centre.

Mary Bladon House $–$$ *381 Washington Ave.; tel: (540) 344-5361.* Bed and breakfast accommodation right downtown.

Awful Arthur's $–$$ *108 Campbell Ave.; tel: (540) 344-2997.* Extensive raw bar and fresh seafood, and live entertainment Wed and Thur evenings.

Carlos Brazilian International Cuisine $$ *312 Market St; tel: (540) 345-7661.* Popular restaurant representing a good dose of many cuisines, including, indeed, Brazilian.

Star City Diner $ *118 Campbell Ave.; tel: (540) 344-4321.* Fun, family-oriented place, open late.

WINERIES*

In the past few decades, the Charlottesville area has become a mini east coast Napa Valley. Dozens of wineries have tours and wine tastings, amid splendid settings. These are some of the best:

Barboursville Vineyards *Rte 777, Barboursville, 17 miles northeast of Charlottesville off Rte 20; tel: (804) 832-3824; open Mon–Sat 1000–1700, Sun 1100–1700.* As a little bonus to the pretty setting, the grounds contain the ruins of a manor house which burned down in 1884 – and it's not hard to see that Thomas Jefferson designed it.

Horton Cellars *6399 Spotswood Trail, Gordonsville, 20 miles northeast of Charlottesville off Hwy 33 West; tel: (804) 832-7440; open daily 1100–1700 (weekends only during Mar).* Daily tastings in this stone winery, one of the largest in the state.

Jefferson Vineyards *Near Monticello on Rte 53; tel: (804) 977-3042; open daily 1100–1700.* Here you can stand on the site where Jefferson planted the colony's first vines, in one of the area's most accessible vineyards.

Oakencroft Winery *Barracks Rd (Rte 654), 4 miles west of Charlottesville; tel: (804) 296-4188; open Jan–Feb by appointment only; Mar weekends only 1100–1700; Apr–Dec daily 1100–1700.* Charlottesville's nearest vineyard is said to be one of Virginia's most picturesque.

White Hall Vineyards *Sugar Ridge Rd, Whitehall, 10 miles northwest of Charlottesville off Rte 810; tel: (804) 823-8615; open Mar–mid-Dec Wed–Sun 1100–1700.* Generally considered the best in the area.

Suggested tour

Virginia's Explore Park $ *Blue Ridge Parkway, Mile Post 115; open Apr–Oct Sat–Mon only 0900–1700.*

Total distance: 270 miles.

Time: 8 hours without stops. Allow 2 full days to enjoy the Blue Ridge Parkway, Roanoke and/or Lynchburg and Appomattox, as well as time to drive slowly and take in the scenery.

Links: The suggested tour for Shenandoah could be combined with this to give a lengthier tour of Western Virginia, or it might be a good follow-on from tours of the Arlington or Richmond regions.

Route: The quickest drive from **CHARLOTTESVILLE ❶** to Roanoke is I-64 west to I-81 south, which runs through Staunton and Lexington on the way (*see pages 81–7*). But by far the prettier route is on the **Blue Ridge Parkway**, an extension of the Shenandoah National Park's Skyline Drive, and just as scenic, with grand mountain views and some good opportunities for hikes. **Virginia's Explore Park**, at Mile Post 115 near Roanoke, is a living history museum featuring a settlement from the 1800s, with summertime costumed interpreters, a Native American village and bluegrass musicians. Take I-64 or the quieter Rte 250 west from Charlottesville to the Parkway, which winds all the way down to **ROANOKE ❷**, 120 miles south.

Below
University of Virginia, Charlottesville

From Roanoke, Rte 460 provides a lovely drive through the low hills of the Piedmont to the small, stately town of **Bedford**, whose sites include a Greek-Revival church and a stern City Hall with a local museum. Rte 460 continues on to the fun little city of **LYNCHBURG** ❸, but be sure to save time to visit the engrossing **APPOMATTOX Court House National Historical Park** ❹, near the junction of Rtes 460 and 24. There are a couple of little walks you can do here, as well as a self-guided driving tour that traces Lee's retreat.

From Appomattox back to Charlottesville it's an enjoyable drive along a few back roads: take Rte 24 east 20 miles to Rte 60 east. Turn right,

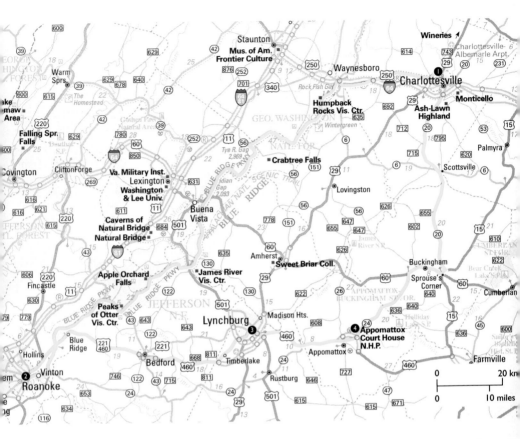

and at Sprouse's Corner, turn left on to Rte 15 north. After one mile turn left again on to Rte 20 north, which takes you through the charming streets and grand old homes of **Scottsville** before rolling past beautiful country estates and on into Charlottesville.

Also worth exploring

Ash-Lawn Highland **$$** Rte 795 near Rte 53; tel: (804) 293-9539; open daily Mar–Oct 0900–1800, Nov–Feb 1000–1700.

Montpelier **$$** Rte 20, Orange; tel: (540) 672-2728; open daily Mar–Oct 0900–1700, Nov–Feb 1000–1600.

If you're on the trail of the American presidents, **Ash-Lawn Highland** is an easy trip from Charlottesville and complements a visit to **MONTICELLO**. It's because of Thomas Jefferson, in fact, that James Monroe, 5th US president, moved to this plantation home nearby in 1793. The house contains Monroe's furnishings and the grounds make a great spot for a picnic. To complete the troika, the man who served between Jefferson and Monroe also had a home in these parts. Twenty-five miles northeast of Charlottesville, James Madison's enormous estate of **Montpelier** lords over Orange County.

Richmond

Ratings

Art and museums	●●●●●
History	●●●●●
Entertainment	●●●●
Gastronomy	●●●
Children	●●
Shopping	●●
Beaches	●
Nature	●

The state capital is relatively small; the city's population hovers around the 200,000 mark. Both Virginia Beach and Norfolk have more citizens. But that middling size seems out of proportion to Richmond's rich and turbulent history, its distinctive old neighbourhoods, outstanding cultural institutions, notable personalities, eye-catching architecture, imposing memorials, buzzing nightlife and recreational and entertainment amenities.

Named because of a similarity between the James River bend and a curve on the Thames at Richmond, England, the city's most fateful four years began in 1861, when the Ordinance of Secession was passed, leading to Richmond's prominence as capital of the Confederate States of America – and subsequently as the rebel forces' chief armaments supplier, hospital city, military target and ultimate scene of devastating conflagration. Today, at the beginning of a new century, modern progress and an enduring air of Southern civility co-exist as prevalent attributes.

Below
Richmond State Capitol

Arriving and departing

Richmond is located at the junction of the I-95 and I-64 motorways, making it a central hub for quick, moderate-distance automobile access to and from points beyond – Washington, DC (105 miles), for instance – as well as coastal locales and the Shenandoah National Park vicinity.

You can also get here via an **Amtrak** rail service. The **Richmond National Airport** lies ten miles east of the city centre, off I-64. **Groome Transportation** provides service between the airport and downtown locales (*tel: (804) 222-7222*).

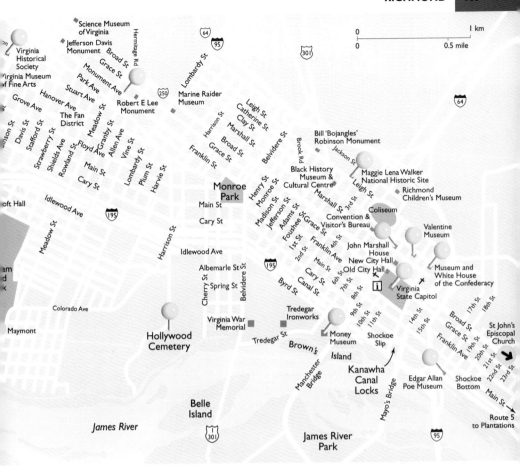

Science Museum of Virginia
Jefferson Davis Monument
Hermitage Rd
Broad St
Grace St
Monument Ave
Park Ave
Virginia Historical Society
Virginia Museum of Fine Arts
Stuart Ave
Grove Ave
Hanover Ave
The Fan District
Robert E Lee Monument
Lombardy St
Marine Raider Museum
Leigh St
Catherine St
Clay St
Marshall St
Broad St
Grace St
Franklin St
Bill 'Bojangles' Robinson Monument
Jackson St
Maggie Lena Walker National Historic Site
Richmond Children's Museum
Davis St
Stafford St
Strawberry St
Shields Ave
Rowland St
Floyd Ave
Granby St
Meadow St
Allen Ave
Vine St
Plum St
Harvie St
Main St
Cary St
Black History Museum & Cultural Centre
Henry St
Monroe St
Madison St
Jefferson St
Adams St
Foushee St
Grace St
Franklin Ave
1st St
2nd St
3rd St
Leigh St
Marshall St
Coliseum
Convention & Visitor's Bureau
John Marshall House
New City Hall
Old City Hall
Valentine Museum
Museum and White House of the Confederacy
Monroe Park
Main St
Cary St
Idlewood Ave
Idlewood Ave
Albemarle St
Spring St
Byrd St
Cary St
Canal St
Main St
4th St
5th St
6th St
7th St
8th St
9th St
10th St
11th St
Virginia State Capitol
14th St
15th St
16th St
17th St
18th St
Broad St
Grace St
Franklin Ave
19th St
20th St
21st St
22nd St
23rd St
St John's Episcopal Church
oft Hall
Idlewood Ave
Meadow St
Harrison St
Cherry St
Belvidere St
Colorado Ave
Maymont
Hollywood Cemetery
Virginia War Memorial
Tredegar Ironworks
Tredegar St
Brown's
Island
Money Museum
Shockoe Slip
Kanawha Canal Locks
Edgar Allan Poe Museum
Shockoe Bottom
Main St
Manchester Bridge
Mayo's Bridge
Belle Island
James River
James River Park
Route 5 to Plantations
0   1 km
0   0.5 mile

Getting around

ℹ Metropolitan Richmond Convention and Visitors Bureau *550 E Marshall St; tel: (800) 370-9004 or (804) 782-7777; www.richmondva.org.*

Three Visitor Centers can be found at key locations:

- *north of the city at Exit 78 off the I-95/I-64 interchange; tel: (804) 358-5511;*

- *at the airport; tel: (804) 236-3260;*

- *downtown on the Virginia State Capitol grounds; tel: (804) 648-3146.*

The Downtown Expressway (Rte 195) slices east–west through the city. Streets are laid out in a simple grid pattern. Parking facilities are plentiful, and buses operated by the **Greater Richmond Transit Company** (*tel: (804) 358-4782*) cover city-wide routes. For inexpensive self-guided sightseeing, board any of the GRTC trams at downtown stops; their routes bring you close to shopping disticts, restaurants, museums, theatres and nightclubs. Guided walking tours are available, too. For high-altitude orientation, take in panoramic views from the free-admittance observation deck atop **New City Hall** on Broad St.

Right
Monument to George Washington standing beside the Capitol

Sights

Agecroft Hall $
4305 Sulgrave Rd; open Tue–Sat 1000–1600, Sun 1230–1500.

Edgar Allan Poe Museum $ *1914 Main St; open Tue–Sat 1000–1630, Sun–Mon 1200–1630.*

Hollywood Cemetery $ *Cherry and Albemarle Sts; open daily 0800–1800.*

John Marshall House $ *818 E Marshall St; open Apr–Sept 1000–1700 Tue–Sat, 1000–1630 rest of year.*

Maggie Lena Walker National Historic Site $ *110 E Leigh St; open Wed–Sun 0900–1700.*

Agecroft Hall*
This 15th-century timbered English Tudor manor house stood in Lancashire prior to being dismantled in the late 1920s. Shipped overseas, its best parts were reassembled west of downtown, at Windsor Farms alongside the James River. Featuring the original hand-carved oak panelling and leaded- and stained-glass windows, the mansion also contains furnishings from the Tudor and early Stuart periods, plus tapestries, massive fireplaces, ornate plaster ceilings, British military artefacts and a two-storey Great Hall, with woodlands and formal gardens on the 23-acre estate. An all-British museum shop is on the premises.

Edgar Allan Poe Museum**
Five buildings, most notably the 1737 Old Stone House (Richmond's oldest dwelling), chronicle the melancholy writer's life and literary output. The Memorial Building displays memorabilia, manuscripts and first editions; the carriage house's gallery features James Carling's illustrations inspired by one of Poe's eeriest poems, *The Raven*.

Hollywood Cemetery*
Burial place of US Presidents James Monroe and John Tyler, Confederacy President Jefferson Davis, twenty-two Confederate generals and six Virginia governors. A granite pyramid memorialises the 18,000 Confederate soldiers also interred here. The cemetery covers bluffs overlooking the James River.

John Marshall House*
Built in the late 18th century for Thomas Jefferson's cousin and Revolutionary War veteran who was chief justice of the US Supreme Court from 1801 to 1835. The house retains its wide-plank pine floors, woodwork and panelling, augmented by period antiques and Marshall's personal belongings.

Maggie Lena Walker National Historic Site*
Being physically impaired, black and a woman were social hindrances in 1903. Even so, Mrs Walker became the USA's first female bank president upon establishing the St Luke Penny Savings Bank (since renamed the Consolidated Bank & Trust). A leading force in Richmond's African-American community, she also published a newspaper and founded a department store. The house in which she lived from 1904 until her death in 1934 is maintained by the National Park Service.

Maymont $ 1700
Hampton St; open
June–Aug Tue–Sat
1000–1700, Sun
1200–1700, Sept–May
Tue–Sun 1200–1700;
grounds open daily Apr–Oct
1000–1900, Nov–Mar
1000–1700.

Monument Avenue
Begins in town at Lombardy
St; ends at Horsepen
Rd/Glenside Dr. on
Richmond's western
outskirts.

Maymont✦✦

A 33-room Romanesque-Revival mansion dominates Major and Mrs John Henry Dooley's 100-acre James River country estate. The grounds include Japanese and Italian gardens, a herb garden, arboretum, children's farm and a nature centre with a 26,000-gallon terraced river aquarium, plus wildlife habitats for native Virginian black bears, bison, elk, bobcats and birds of prey. Gilded Age goodies inside the turreted manse include stained-glass windows, Oriental carpets, Tiffany vases, porcelain, tapestries, sculptures and an art-nouveau swan-shaped master bed.

Monument Avenue✦✦✦

Laid out in Parisian style in 1890 with its centre strip shaded by oaks and maples, this brick-paved boulevard is regarded as one of the USA's most beautiful urban thoroughfares. Its easternmost mile features a block-by-block 'parade' of six statues, including a 60ft-high bronze Robert E Lee astride his horse 'Traveller'. Additional statues honour other Civil War military leaders as well as naval officer Matthew Fontaine Maury (inventor of the electric torpedo), Jefferson Davis and Richmond-born tennis champion Arthur Ashe, Jr. Churches, upmarket apartment houses, slate-roofed mansions and magnolia trees line both sides of the boulevard.

Right
Museum of the Confederacy

Money Museum $
701 E Byrd St; open
Mon–Fri 0930–1530.

**Museum of the
Confederacy and
White House of the
Confederacy $** 1201 E
Clay St; tel: (804) 649-1861;
open Mon–Sat 1000–1700,
Sun 1200–1700.

**St John's Episcopal
Church $** 2401 Broad St;
guided tours Mon–Sat
1000–1530, Sun
1300–1530; re-enactments
late May–early Sept Sun
1400.

Valentine Museum $
105 E Clay St; tel: (804)
649-0711; open Mon–Sat
1000–1700, Sun
1200–1700.

Money Museum*

The history of currency is traced in the Federal Reserve Bank of Richmond's lobby. Displays include items used for bartering, rare old bills, gold and silver ingots and an uncut sheet of 12 $100,000 gold certificates.

Museum of the Confederacy and White House of the Confederacy***

Founded in 1890, this is the nation's largest museum devoted to Confederate artefacts, documents, weapons, paintings, photographs, soldiers' diaries and battlefield sketches. Uniforms and equipment belonging to military leaders 'Jeb' Stuart and 'Stonewall' Jackson are displayed, along with a replica of Lee's field headquarters and more than 500 military and governmental flags. Also on view is *The Last Meeting of Lee and Jackson*, a 15ft-high canvas painted in 1869 by E B D Julio as a memorial to the South's lost cause.

Jefferson Davis and his family lived in the 1818 Victorian mansion next door to the museum throughout his four years as the Confederacy chief executive. Among the 11 furnished period rooms open to the public are the dining room (used for cabinet meetings), library, Davis's office and upstairs bedrooms.

St John's Episcopal Church**

Built in 1741, Richmond's oldest church was the meeting place of the Second Virginia Convention in March 1775, attended by such influential Virginians as George Washington and Thomas Jefferson. Rising to support a bill authorising the training of a militia to fight against Great Britain, delegate Patrick Henry delivered his famously stirring speech, concluding with: 'Is life so dear, or peace so sweet, as to be purchased at the price of chains or slavery? Forbid it, almighty God! I know now what course others may take; but as for me, give me liberty, or give me death!'

The surrounding burial ground contains the graves of a signatory of the Declaration of Independence, two Virginia governors and actress Elizabeth Arnold, Edgar Allan Poe's mother.

Valentine Museum**

A repository of Richmond's urban and social history, decorative and industrial arts, architecture and racial inter-relationships. Vintage photographs of the city are displayed, and a gallery is devoted to the South's largest costume and textile collection. 'The Valentine' incorporates the 1812 Federal-style Wickham House, featuring a freestanding circular staircase, carved ornamentation and rare neo-classical wall paintings, along with humble quarters for domestic servants and slaves.

🏛 **Virginia Historical Society** $ *428 N Blvd; open Mon–Sat 1000–1700, Sun 1300– 1700.*

Virginia Museum of Fine Arts $ *2800 Grove Ave.; tel: (804) 353-4241; open Tue–Sun 1100–1700, Thur 1100–2000.*

Virginia State Capitol $ *Capitol Sq., 9th and Grace Sts; open for guided tours Apr–Nov daily 0900– 1700, Dec–Mar Mon–Sat 0900–1700, Sun 1300–1700.*

Opposite
Richmond by night

Virginia Historical Society✦✦✦

A vast permanent exhibit, *The Story of Virginia, an American Experience*, covers Old Dominion history from earliest settlement and Virginia's colonial era through the Civil War, World Wars I and II and present times. Items related to native son George Washington are extensive, among them the diary he kept during his first year as US President. The museum's neo-classical building opened in 1913 as Battle Abbey, a shrine to Virginians who died during the Civil War.

Virginia Museum of Fine Arts✦✦✦

Renowned for its Fabergé collection of more than 300 *objets d'art*, including five jewel-encrusted Easter eggs crafted for Russian Tsars Alexander III and Nicholas II. In addition, the museum excels in its exhibits of Greek, Egyptian, Tibetan and South American antiquities and contemporary American art, as well as the Mellon collection of French Impressionist and post-Impressionist paintings. Also notable are a life-size marble statue of the Roman emperor Caligula and six Gobelin tapestries embroidered with episodes from Cervantes' *Don Quixote*.

Virginia State Capitol✦✦✦

His admiration for the Maison Carré – a Roman temple in Nîmes, France – led to Thomas Jefferson's neo-classical design for the Capitol, in continuous use since 1788. Twin colonnaded wings were added between 1904 and 1906. Beneath the skylit central rotunda stands Jean Antoine Houdon's life-size statue of George Washington, surrounded overhead by busts of seven other Virginia-born US presidents.

Entertainment and recreation

◆ **Carpenter Center for the Performing Arts** *600 E Grace St; tel: (804) 782-3900.*

Theater Virginia *2800 Grove Ave.; tel: (804) 367-0831.*

Theater IV *114 W Broad St; tel: (804) 344-8040.*

Landmark Theater *Laurel and Main Sts; tel: (804) 780-4213.*

Coliseum *601 E Leigh St; tel: (804) 262-8100.*

The Thursday 'Weekend' section of the *Richmond Times-Dispatch* has what's-on listings for shows, concerts and nightclub offerings. Listings and reviews also appear in the hip, free *Style Weekly* tabloid.

Downtown, the 2060-seat **Carpenter Center for the Performing Arts**, originally a 1920s' Moorish-style Loew's cinema, now hosts Broadway road shows and is home to the Richmond Symphony, Richmond Ballet and Virginia Opera.

Theater Virginia, in the **Virginia Museum of Fine Arts**, is a professional theatre staging five shows (musicals, comedies, dramas and classical productions) each fall to spring season. The 1911 Empire Theater has become **Theater IV**, housing the US's second-largest children's theatre and a resident professional company presenting off-Broadway plays. National touring companies appear at the 3300-seat **Landmark**, locally nicknamed 'The Mosque' because of its exotic resemblance to an Islamic temple. Big-name showbiz

Richmond's historic neighbourhoods

Exploring them with a watchful eye will deepen your appreciation of the city's diversity and preservationist zeal.

Church Hill, east of downtown, covers 2 square miles on high ground above the river. Along the brick sidewalks of this oldest Richmond neighbourhood stand some 200 18th- and 19th-century houses; many feature cast-iron ornamentation. **St John's Church** of Patrick Henry renown is in Church Hill, as is the **Richmond National Battlefield Park Visitor Center** (see *Richmond Battlefields, pages 114–21*).

The **Fan District**, so called because its streets 'fan' out from Virginia Commonwealth University, lays claim to being the US's largest intact Victorian neighbourhood, comprising styles ranging from traditional brownstones to elegant townhouses in softly muted yellows, pinks and blues.

Shockoe Slip and **Shockoe Bottom** are side-by-side riverside districts. The 'Slip' was formerly Richmond's commercial trading centre, hence its recycled warehouses and cobblestone streets, plus Italianate brick and iron front buildings now housing shops and galleries in a half-square-mile area. Shockoe Bottom's resurgence, long hindered by James River flooding, accelerated upon completion of a floodwall. Once the city's main business and tobacco-factory district, Shockoe Bottom includes 17th St's **Farmers' Market**, in existence since 1775.

Jackson Ward became a thriving African-American cultural and entrepreneurial centre following the Civil War. Northwest of downtown, this neighbourhood features the nation's second greatest usage of architectural cast iron after New Orleans. Watch for the **Bojangles Monument**, where Leigh St and Chamberlayne Ave. intersect; it commemorates local legend Bill 'Bojangles' Robinson, Shirley Temple's tap-dancing co-star in the 1935 movie *The Little Colonel*.

Monroe Ward, on Richmond's west side, encompasses some of the city's finest 19th-century residences, with opulent domestic architecture ranging from French Renaissance to Greek Revival.

Court End, named after its proximity to federal courts of the late 1700s and early 1800s, radiates from Capitol Square. Nine National Historic Landmarks can be found amidst these elegant old residences, including the **State Capitol** and the 1813 **Governor's Mansion**, the **Valentine Museum/Wickham House** and the **Museum and White House of the Confederacy**.

Dogwood Dell *Blvd and Idlewild Ave.; tel:* (804) 780-8683.

Paramount's Kings Dominion $$$ *Exit 98 off I-95, Doswell; tel:* (804) 876-5000; *www.pkdthrills.com.*

Colonial Downs *Exit 214 off I-64, New Kent County.*

The Diamond *3001 N Blvd; tel:* (804) 359-4444.

University of Richmond Stadium *Douglas Ave. and McCloy St; tel:* (804) 282-6776.

Richmond Raft Co. *Tel:* (804) 222-7238.

Adventure Challenge *Tel:* (804) 276-7600.

Jefferson Hotel $$–$$$ *Franklin and Adams Sts; tel:* (800) 424-8014 or (804) 768-8000.

Linden Row Inn $$ *100 E Franklin St; tel:* (800) 348-7424 or (804) 648-7504.

Berkeley Hotel $$ *12th and Cary Sts; tel:* (888) 780-1300 or (804) 780-1300.

Richmond Marriott $$–$$$ *500 E Broad St; tel:* (800) 228-9290 or (804) 643-3400.

Emmanuel Hutzler House $$ *2036 Monument Ave.; tel:* (804) 353-6900.

Mr Patrick Henry's Inn $–$$ *2300–02 E Broad St; tel:* (800) 932-2654 or (804) 644-1322.

Right
Tobacco Company Restaurant, Shockoe Bottom

stars and bands (also sports events) pack them in at Richmond's **Coliseum**.

If you're visiting during summertime, join the audience at William Byrd Park's **Dogwood Dell** amphitheatre for the free-admittance Festival of Arts ballets, plays and musical performances.

Paramount's Kings Dominion is a multi-attraction 400-acre theme park, 20 miles north of Richmond, including a suspended hair-raiser of a rollercoaster, Volcano, the Blast Coaster and the 16-acre WaterWorks, with a wave pool and water slides. Music from Paramount movies enhances an ice-skating show, and laser beams and fireworks light up evening skies.

Fans of *pari-mutuel* thoroughbred racing head 25 miles east of downtown to **Colonial Downs**.

Shockoe Bottom and Shockoe Slip are Richmond's 'in' nightlife destinations for discos, comedy clubs and sundry drinking places.

Venues for spectator sports include **The Diamond**, where the Richmond Braves play AAA-level minor-league baseball. Pro soccer's Richmond Kickers host opposing squads at the **University of Richmond Stadium**.

For active-participation right downtown, whitewater rafting on the James River is provided by **Richmond Raft Co. Adventure Challenge** runs James River kayaking trips.

Right
Canal walk in Downtown
Richmond

Richmond's thickest concentrations of recommendable restaurants are in Shockoe Slip, Shockoe Bottom and the Fan district.

Annabel Lee $$$ *4400 E Main St; tel: (804) 644-5700.* Enjoy lunch, brunch or dinner while cruising aboard a paddle-wheeler riverboat.

The Frog & The Redneck $$ *1423 E Cary St; tel: (804) 648-3764.* This Shockoe Slip bistro serves such regional fare as Virginia ham and Chesapeake Bay crabcakes.

Havana '59 $$ *16 N 17th St; tel: (804) 649-2822.* Also in Shockoe Bottom; Cuban atmosphere, music, food and drink.

Joe's Inn $ *205 N Shields Ave.; tel: (804) 355-2282.* This Fan storefront restaurant serves heaping-big breakfasts and Italian-accentuated lunches and dinners.

Millie's Diner $$–$$$ *2603 Main St; tel: (804) 643-5512.* A retro 1950s diner turned into a fine little Shockoe Bottom restaurant with an eclectic menu.

Nonesuch Place $$ *1721 E Franklin St; tel: (804) 644-0832.* In Shockoe Bottom; a good choice for Southern cooking.

Accommodation and food

The Metropolitan CVB and the Visitor Centers are reliable sources of lodging listings in various price ranges, but making reservations is your affair. Most of the familiar US chains operate at least one hotel or motel in the metro area. Holiday Inn, for instance, has ten properties and six Days Inns.

For a convenient location and gracious opulence which includes the Palm Court with a Thomas Jefferson statue beneath a stained-glass skylight, opt for what's been a landmark since 1895: the **Jefferson Hotel**. A row of Greek-Revival townhouses dating from 1847 comprises the 71-room **Linden Row Inn**. Opened in 1988, the **Berkeley Hotel** is in Shockoe Slip and offers complimentary valet parking. Five blocks from historic Court End attractions, the **Richmond Marriott** is also close to the Jackson Ward and Monroe Ward neighbourhoods.

Several in-town bed and breakfasts emanate Southern charm and hospitality. One is the Italian Renaissance-style **Emmanuel Hutzler House**. Another, a Greek-Revival beauty in historic Church Hill, is **Mr Patrick Henry's Inn**.

Suggested walks

Monument Avenue

Total distance: Viewing the monuments entails a 1.4-mile walk. Backtracking by way of Main St or Grove or Stuart Ave. in the Fan district adds another 1.8 miles. Opting for a return via Grove Ave. enables you to visit the **VIRGINIA MUSEUM OF FINE ARTS**. Walking west along Stuart Ave. brings you to the **VIRGINIA HISTORICAL SOCIETY**.

Time: Depending upon your preferred pace, allow approximately 2–3 hours, at most a full morning or afternoon.

Sam Miller's Warehouse $$–$$$ *1210 E Cary St; tel: (804) 643-1301.* Excellent Chesapeake Bay seafood in this 'Slip' stalwart.

Strawberry Street Café *$–$$ 421 N Strawberry St; tel: (804) 353-6860.* Top choice in 'The Fan', a laid-back eatery and wine bar with its salad bar stashed inside an old-fashioned clawfoot bathtub.

The Tobacco Company *$$ 12th and Cary Sts; tel: (804) 782-9431.* Another 'Slip' favourite, in a former 1860s tobacco warehouse, specialising in contemporary American cuisine.

Route: Monument Ave's eastern end begins at the Lombardy St intersection, where you'll see the first Confederate hero statue, honouring General J E B Stuart. The equestrian Robert E Lee monument stands tall at the next crossroads. Jefferson Davis, president of the Confederacy, merits an especially elaborate memorial. His sculpted likeness stands amidst 13 Doric columns representing the 11 states that seceded and two others sending delegates to the Confederate Congress. Next, at the Monument Ave./Blvd intersection, you'll see the statue of Thomas 'Stonewall' Jackson atop his horse Little Sorrel. Tennis champion Arthur Ashe, Jr, is honoured with a statue, erected in 1995 at the corner of Monument Ave. and Roseneath Rd.

River walk

Total distance: Walking a bit more than 3 miles provides an overview of Richmond's portion of the US's first extensive canal system.

Time: Allow half a day for easygoing sightseeing.

Route: At **Shockoe Slip** ❶, head down 12th St to Byrd St to the **Kanawha Canal Locks**, constructed in 1854. From there, a combined canal/river walk extends 1.5 miles, connecting on to pedestrian bridges reaching **Brown's Island** ❷ and **Belle Isle** ❸. A 1-mile path on that island (site of a Civil War prison camp) passes waterfalls and 19th-century earthworks.

Back on shore, you can view remnants of the **Tredegar Ironworks** ❹ (*see page 117*), supplier of artillery, cannonballs and armour plate for the Confederate army and navy. Historical markers are positioned along the walkway. You can also walk 1 mile atop the **Richmond Floodwall's** concrete levee, with Canada geese and blue heron likely to be seen.

Right
Maymont, Richmond

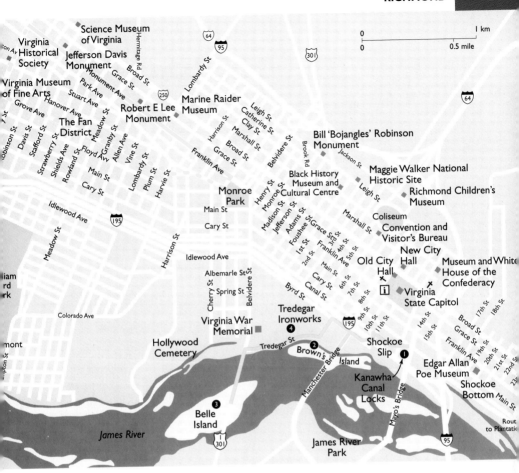

Also worth exploring

James River Plantations $ Tel: (800) 704-5423; open daily 0900–1700. Money-saving combination tickets can be purchased.

Four close-together, fully furnished exemplars of Old South aristocracy can be reached by way of a scenic 30–35-mile Rte 5 drive southeast from Richmond. **Shirley Plantation**, Virginia's oldest, was first settled in 1613; the mansion dates from 1723. The property includes brick outbuildings forming a unique Queen Anne forecourt. **Berkeley**, an early three-storey Georgian mansion (1726) filled with 18th-century antiques and heirlooms, is the birthplace of William Henry Harrison, ninth US president. **Evelynton** has been home to the Ruffin family since 1847; patriarch Edmund Ruffin fired the first shot of the Civil War at Fort Sumter. The 2500-acre property features former slave quarters and historical markers indicating 1862 wartime skirmishes. **Sherwood Forest**, surrounding a *circa* 1730, 300ft-wide mansion (the country's longest frame dwelling), was owned by two US presidents, William Harrison and John Tyler.

Richmond battlefields

Ratings

History	●●●●●
Art and museums	●● ○○○
Children	●● ○○○
Beaches	● ○○○○
Entertainment	● ○○○○
Gastronomy	● ○○○○
Nature	● ○○○○
Shopping	● ○○○○

The Confederacy's capital became the Federal forces' primary objective from the Civil War's very outset in 1861. Richmond was the South's strategic command post, medical centre, main manufacturing base and biggest supply depot for the thousands of rebel troops assigned to Robert E Lee's Army of Northern Virginia.

Overall, seven major assaults were launched against Richmond. Two, in 1862 and again in 1864, brought Union infantry and artillery within shooting range of downtown objectives. Upon evacuating their city a year later, Confederate officials authorised the burning of warehouses and supplies; fires quickly spread to the riverside commercial districts.

A visit to the Richmond National Battlefield Park puts all of that inflammatory past history into perspective. A few miles south, the smaller communities of Hopewell and Petersburg – and certainly Petersburg's nearby battlefield – also became prominent locales during the conflict that split the nation apart.

HOPEWELL**

ⓘ Hopewell Visitor Center *4100 Oaklawn Blvd; tel: (800) 863-8687 or (804) 541-2461; www.ctg.net/hopewell.*

ⓜ Appomattox Manor $ *Cedar Ln., City Point; open daily for visitor information and guided tours, 0830–1630.*

On high ground bulging into the confluence of the James and Appomattox rivers, City Point, a compact National Historic District, looms large in Civil War annals. General Ulysses S Grant made the hamlet his command post for the Union forces' relentless siege of nearby Petersburg in 1864–5 (*see page 117*). The waterways and lengthened rail lines became supply routes for 100,000 troops manning the siege lines, with Grant's headquarters functioning as his army's logistical and communications nerve centre. President Lincoln travelled twice from Washington to join in the strategy sessions. Wayside markers are informative.

On this National Park Service property, the 25 rooms of **Appomattox Manor**** accommodated Grant's staff. Nearby, the general's rebuilt log headquarters cabin stands on its original site; peer inside to see his blue uniform coat, adorned with three-star epaulets, slung over a chair.

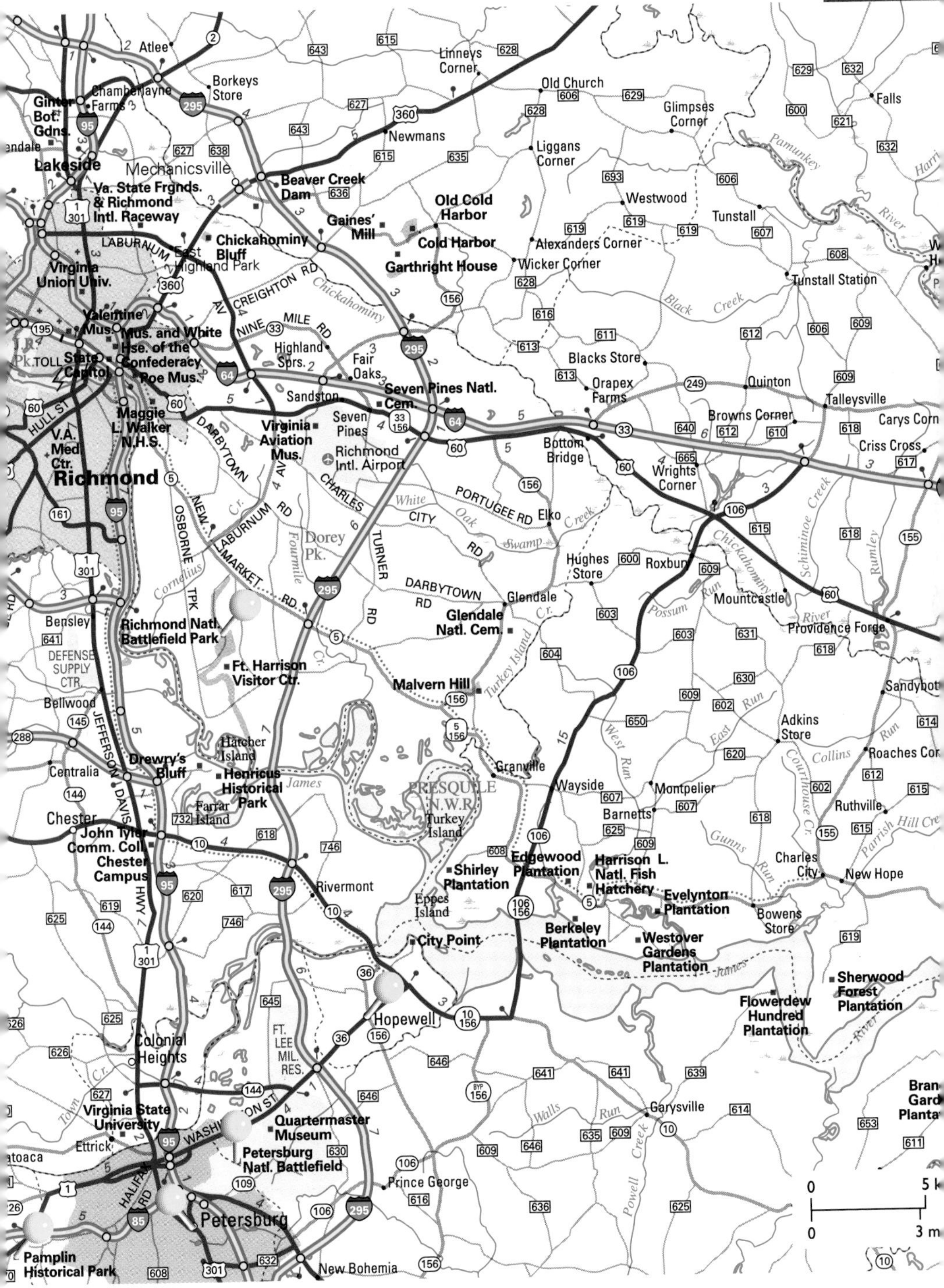

Atlee
Borkeys Store
Linneys Corner
Old Church
Falls
Ginter Bot. Gdns.
Chamberlayne Farms
Glimpses Corner
Newmans
Liggans Corner
Lakeside
Mechanicsville
Beaver Creek Dam
Pamunkey River
Va. State Frgnds. & Richmond Intl. Raceway
Old Cold Harbor
Westwood
Tunstall
Gaines' Mill
Cold Harbor
Alexanders Corner
Chickahominy Bluff
East Highland Park
Wicker Corner
Virginia Union Univ.
Garthright House
Tunstall Station
LABURNUM AV
CREIGHTON RD
Chickahominy
Black Creek
NINE MILE RD
Valentine Mus.
Mus. and White Hse. of the Confederacy
Highland Sprs.
Blacks Store
State Capitol
Fair Oaks
Poe Mus.
Orapex Farms
Quinton
Sandston
Seven Pines Natl. Cem.
Talleysville
Seven Pines
Browns Corner
Carys Corn
Maggie L. Walker N.H.S.
Virginia Aviation Mus.
V.A. Med. Ctr.
HULL ST
DARBYTOWN RD
Richmond Intl. Airport
Bottom Bridge
Criss Cross
Wrights Corner
Richmond
CHARLES CITY RD
PORTUGEE RD
Elko
White Oak Swamp
Creek
NEW MARKET RD
LABURNUM AV
Dorey Pk.
Fourmile
TURNER RD
OSBORNE TPK
Cornelius
Hughes Store
Roxbury
Chickahominy River
Schiminoe Creek
Rumley
Glendale
Possum Run
Mountcastle
Bensley
Richmond Natl. Battlefield Park
Glendale Natl. Cem.
Turkey Island Cr.
Providence Forge
DEFENSE SUPPLY CTR.
Ft. Harrison Visitor Ctr.
Malvern Hill
Sandybot
Bellwood
JEFFERSON DAVIS HWY
Adkins Store
West Run
East Run
Collins Run
Roaches Cor
Centralia
Drewry's Bluff
Hatcher Island
Henricus Historical Park
Granville
Courthouse Cr.
Farrar Island
James
PRESQUILE N.W.R.
Wayside
Montpelier
Ruthville
Chester
Turkey Island
Barnetts
Hill Cre
John Tyler Comm. Coll. Chester Campus
Parrish
Gunns Run
Edgewood Plantation
Shirley Plantation
Harrison L. Natl. Fish Hatchery
Charles City
Rivermont
New Hope
Evelynton Plantation
Eppes Island
Berkeley Plantation
Bowens Store
City Point
Westover Gardens Plantation
James
Sherwood Forest Plantation
Flowerdew Hundred Plantation
Hopewell
River
FT. LEE MIL. RES.
Colonial Heights
Town Cr.
Virginia State University
WASHINGTON ST
Quartermaster Museum
Walls Run
Garysville
Bran Gard Planta
Ettrick
Petersburg Natl. Battlefield
Powell Creek
HALIFAX RD
Prince George
Petersburg
Pamplin Historical Park
New Bohemia
0 5 k
0 3 m

Right
Confederate cavalry hero 'Jeb' Stuart commemorated on Richmond's Monument Avenue

Accommodation and food in Hopewell

Innkeeper $ *3952 Courthouse Rd; tel: (800) 822-9899 or (804) 458-2600.* This hotel comprising 104 guest rooms is only about a 10-min drive from Hopewell centre.

Broadway Cafeteria $ *120 E City Point Rd; tel: (804) 458-1700.* Affordability and copious amounts of good self-service food makes a good choice for any of three daily meals.

Captain's Cove $$ *701 W Randolph Ave.; tel: (804) 452-1368.* Perched on a bluff with James River views, seafood and steaks dominate afternoon and evening menus.

Ginny's Café $ *222 E Broadway; tel: (804) 458-1401.* Open weekdays, antiques hanging on its walls, this café is a downtown bargain for 'home-cooked' breakfasts, lunches and dinners.

PAMPLIN HISTORICAL PARK✦✦✦

Pamplin Historical Park $ *6523 Duncan Rd; open daily 0900–1700. Café and gift shop on the premises.*

A somewhat touristy attraction but worthwhile, since it was here, on 2 April 1865, that Union infantry and cavalry regiments ended Petersburg's siege by breaking through the Confederates' formidable defence lines. A 1.1-mile system of trails winds through the battlefield, amidst some of Virginia's best-preserved Civil War earthworks, artillery emplacements and picket posts. An interpretive centre displays uniforms, firearms and campaign flags; a fibre-optics battle map and interactive video programs turn the conflict into a high-tech learning experience.

Also in the park is Tudor Hall, an 1812 plantation house used as brigade headquarters by rebel General Samuel McGowan. The National Museum of the Civil War Soldier honours the 3 million men who served during the war under northern and southern commands.

PETERSBURG❖❖❖

Petersburg Visitors Center *425 Cockade Alley; tel: (800) 368-3595 or (804) 733-2400; www.petersburg.va.org.*

Siege Museum *$ 15 W Bank St; tel: (804) 733-2404; open daily 1000–1700.*

Old Blandford Church *$ 319 S Crater Rd (Rte 301); open Mon–Sat 1000–1700, Sun 1230–1600. Annual Memorial Day services are held on 9 June at 1700.*

Quartermaster Museum *$ Lee Ave., off Rte 36; tel: (804) 734-4203; open Tue–Fri 1000–1700, Sat–Sun 1100–1700.*

Flagship Inn *$ 815 S Crater Rd; tel: (804) 861-3470.*

Heritage Motor Lodge *$ 320 Rives Rd; tel: (804) 733-3444.*

High Street Inn *$–$$ 406 High St; tel: (888) 733-0505.*

Mayfield Inn *$–$$ 3348 W Washington St; tel: (800) 538-2381 or (804) 733-0866.*

Dixie Restaurant *$ 250 N Sycamore St; tel: (804) 732-5761.*

Alexander's *$–$$ 101 Bank St; tel: (804) 733-7134.*

Le Café du Jardin *$ Sycamore and Old Sts; tel: (804) 733-7206.*

The history of this little city (population 38,400) on the Appomattox River's south bank is closely linked with the final phases of the Civil War. As a manufacturing centre and railroad junction crucial to Confederate supply and transport, Petersburg became an inevitable target, with incessant Union barrages inflicting severe destruction.

Those bombardments culminated in the longest siege in US history, spanning nearly ten months and beginning in mid-1864. The **Siege Museum**❖❖ downtown presents a tableau of citizens' endurance throughout that trying period. Petersburg-born actor Joseph Cotten narrates *The Echoes Still Remain*, a cinematic retrospective of their ordeal. A panoramic *Battle of the Crater* painting is noteworthy. The museum occupies a colonnaded Greek-Revival landmark opened in 1839 as the city's commodities exchange.

South of downtown, the 18th-century **Old Blandford Church**❖❖ was used as a makeshift field hospital. Restored as a Confederate war memorial in 1901, each of its 15 stained-glass windows, including a Cross of Jewels masterpiece, was commissioned from Louis Comfort Tiffany's New York studios. Paying respects to those who died on both the 'northern blue' and 'southern gray' sides of the conflict, America's first Memorial Day remembrance was observed here in June 1866. Some 30,000 Confederate soldiers are buried in the cemetery, where the oldest tombstone dates from 1702. Another, by contrast, marks movie-star Cotten's grave.

In the US Army's **Quartermaster Museum**❖, 3 miles east of Petersburg at Fort Lee, uniforms and random kinds of military gear from all the nation's wars are exhibited, and also such miscellanea as Union General Ulysses S Grant's saddle, World War II General George S Patton's custom-fitted Jeep, supply wagons, field kitchens, governmental flags and one of the marcher's drums used in President John F Kennedy's funeral cortège.

Accommodation and food in Petersburg

Within walking distance of the battlefield, the 135-room **Flagship Inn** is an ordinary but satisfactory motel with an outdoor swimming pool. For cheaper rates, head instead to modest **Heritage Motor Lodge**. In the city's historic district, turreted **High Street Inn** (1893) is a tastefully appointed bed and breakfast. South of downtown, **Mayfield Inn** epitomises 18th-century Georgian-style plantation architecture. Ask the owners about their bed and breakfast's history, which includes its use during the Civil War's final months. Essentially a chatty diner, downtown's **Dixie Restaurant** has been going strong for more than half a century. Greek and Italian dishes are **Alexander's** house specialties; sandwich take-outs can be ordered. **Le Café du Jardin** has sidewalk tables for light pleasant-weather meals.

PETERSBURG NATIONAL BATTLEFIELD✦✦✦

Petersburg National Battlefield
$ E Washington St (Rte 36); tel: (804) 732-3521; Visitor Center open daily all year 0800–1700; battlefield open daily dawn–dusk. A 37-mile audio-taped tour of battle sites can be rented.

Grim trench warfare was waged during the Union's Overland Campaign in June 1864 on this 1 500-acre site, which includes two forts, gun pits and miles of original earthworks. Twice-daily re-enactments and cannon firings take place during summertime (mid-June–Aug). From Battery Five a trail leads to the Federal artillery's 17,000-pound seacoast mortar, nicknamed the 'Dictator', which lobbed shells on downtown Petersburg. Prominent on a 4-mile tour route is the Crater, a depression measuring 170ft by 60ft and 30ft deep, created when members of the 48th Pennsylvania Infantry dug a 511ft-tunnel to a Confederate salient and ignited 4 tons of gunpowder. Poplar Grove National Cemetery is the burial place of 6 178 Union soldiers.

RICHMOND NATIONAL BATTLEFIELD PARK✦✦✦

Richmond National Battlefield Park
Park open daily dawn–dusk.

Tredegar Visitor Center $ Tredegar St; tel: (804) 226-1981; open daily 0900–1700. Cassette/tape units can be rented for self-guided motor touring.

The park's widespread layout, in suburban and rural countryside east and southeast of central Richmond, consists of ten major battle locales and requires an 80-mile drive if covered thoroughly. Walking trails flank well-marked remains of defensive fortifications and other visible indicators of the Union forces' Peninsula (1862) and Overland (1864) Campaigns, aimed at vanquishing the Confederate capital.

On the James riverfront downtown, a visitor centre occupies a former building of the Tredegar Ironworks, the South's largest wartime arsenal.

Sites relevant to the Seven Days' Battles of 1862 include Chickahominy Bluff, where two Confederate divisions succeeded in a flanking manoeuvre that ousted the Federals from their entrenchments. At Beaver Dam Creek, North Carolinians and Georgians encountered withering gunfire during a hopeless attack. Gaines' Mill is remembered for daring Confederate onslaughts against fortified front lines along Boatswain's Creek. Despite heavy casualties, Texas and Georgia troops broke through for a rebel victory.

Massed Federal infantry and artillery defending Malvern Hill opened close-range fire (totalling 1 392 rounds) on two enemy brigades advancing across unprotected meadows and hay fields to attempt death-defying charges up the steep ridge, at a cost of 5 000 southern casualties. A forest trail reaches the promontory's overlook.

Seven miles south of Richmond, Drewry's Bluff affords panoramas of a bend in the James River, 200ft below, protected in 1862 by clifftop batteries manned by Captain Augustus Drewry's Southside Artillery. When Union gunboats, including the famous ironclad *Monitor*, steamed upriver heading for a planned bombardment of the capital, projectiles hurled from Drewry's 8in Columbiana and 6.4in Brooke cannons repulsed the flotilla.

Microtel Inn and Suites $ *6000 Audubon Dr., Sandston; tel: (888) 771-7171 or (804) 737-3322.*

Wingate Inn $ *491 International Center Dr., Sandston; tel: (800) 228-1000 or (804) 222-1499.*

Prairie Schooner $ *8036 Mechanicsville Tpk; tel: (804) 746-2333.*

Calabash Restaurant $$ *7514 Lee David Rd, Mechanicsville; tel: (804) 746-8630.*

Seven Pines Seafood $ *307 E Williamsburg Rd, Sandston; tel: (804) 737-9636.*

Bridgette's Family Restaurant $ *2305 Willis Rd; tel: (804) 271-4949.*

General Robert E Lee's last significant field victory came in June 1864 at Cold Harbor, where his officers assembled 50,000 rebel soldiers behind 6 miles of entrenchments along ravines and tree lines. Federal attackers suffered extremely heavy casualties – more than 7000 killed and wounded, mostly during the first hour of fighting. The maze of earthwork trenches can be viewed by way of a 1.25-mile tour road and 1-mile walking trail.

Accommodation and food in or near Richmond

Few people visiting the Civil War sites plan an overnight stay in the area; lodgings in Richmond aren't that far away. If you decide otherwise, however, two attractive and inexpensive non-chain properties in the vicinity of Richmond Airport, at about midpoint along the complete battlefield drive, are the **Microtel Inn and Suites** and the **Wingate Inn**.

Mechanicsville, close to the northernmost Richmond-area battlefields, is well situated for a lunchtime stopover. Chicken pot pie and hot or cold sandwiches are staples at woodsy **Prairie Schooner**. If you're touring the battlefields in a south-to-north direction, consider early evening dinner at Mechanicsville's **Calabash Restaurant**, which provides an opportunity to try Rappahannock oysters, Chesapeake clams, Gulf shrimp or backfin crabmeat. **Seven Pines Seafood** in Sandston, to the east of Richmond, purveys sandwiches (trout, flounder, shrimp, oyster, scallop, crabcake) for a quick, cheap take-out alternative.

Toward the southern (Drewry's Bluff) portion of the battlefield route, **Bridgette's Family Restaurant** provides a something-for-everyone lunch and dinner menu.

You'll also spot fried-chicken chains, burger franchises, pizza parlours and roadside food stores – as well as pancake and waffle houses, ubiquitous throughout Virginia.

Suggested tour

Total distance: 80–120 miles, depending upon how many sites you choose to visit.

Time: Allow a full day, which includes stopover time for an unhurried lunch.

Links: Battlefield-to-battlefield driving crosses I-64 east–west, so you could merge with the Historic Triangle route (*see page 146*). You'll also cross I-295 at Mechanicsville north of Richmond. Going from that juncture to I-95 northbound provides a feasible link with the Fredericksburg area route (*see page 128*).

Route: From the Tredegar Visitor Center on Richmond's riverfront,

🏛 Flowerdew Hundred $$
Flowerdew Hundred Rd; open Apr–Dec Tue–Sat 1000–1600, Sun 1300–1600.

turn left on to 9th St, then right on Broad St. Go east through the Church Hill neighbourhood to reach signposted parkland on **Chimborazo Hill**, where more than 77,800 Confederate wounded were treated in the South's largest military hospital complex. Continue by turning right on 18th St, then right on Fairfield Ave.; follow signs for Rte 360 (Mechanicsville Tpk).

On Rte 360, watch for signs indicating **Chickahominy Bluff ❶**. After returning to Rte 360, exit on to Rte 156 (Cold Harbor Rd) to reach **Beaver Dam Creek ❷** and, after 2 miles, **Gaines' Mill ❸**, then 1 mile onward to **Cold Harbor ❹**.

From that Civil War site, go left on Old Hanover Rd, then next right on to Grapevine Rd. Where it ends, steer left on to Meadow Rd, where the **Battle of Savage Station** was waged in 1862. Meadow Rd becomes Rte 156 again after you've crossed Rte 60. Following a 12-mile drive from Savage Station, you'll see roadside signs for **Malvern Hill ❺**.

Continue south via Rte 156 across the Benjamin Harrison Bridge for Hopewell. Turn right on Rte 10 (Randolph Rd); watch for **Flowerdew Hundred**, a 17th-century working farm where in 1864 the Union Army of the Potomac crossed a 2000ft pontoon bridge assembled by its Corps of Engineers under combat conditions. A schoolhouse museum displays colonial Virginian artefacts. Continue to Appomattox St, then Cedar Ln. to reach National Park Service sites at **City Point ❻**.

From **HOPEWELL ❼**, drive 8 miles via Rte 36 to **PETERSBURG NATIONAL BATTLEFIELD PARK ❽** and 2.5 miles to **PETERSBURG ❾**. Heading north on I-95 across the Appomattox River, take Exit 64 on to Willis Rd for a 2.5-mile drive to **Drewry's Bluff ❿**. Back on I-95, drive to Richmond, thereby closing the battlefield loop. The distance from Petersburg to Richmond totals 23 miles.

Also worth exploring

Clustered in Hopewell's Crescent Hills neighbourhood, 44 prefabricated **mail-order houses** from Sears, Roebuck & Co. were erected from kits between 1926 and 1937. Most are on Oakwood and Prince George Aves. From City Point, drive west on Broadway. An illustrated brochure is available from the Visitor Center.

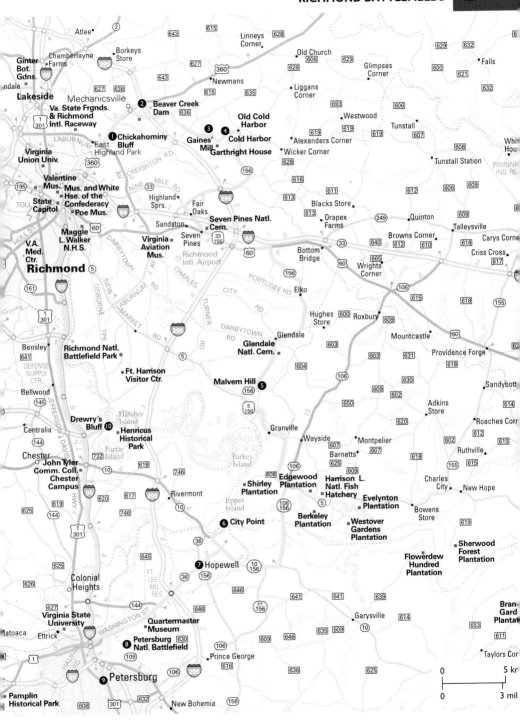

Atlee •   2

Linneys Corner   628   6

643   615

Chamberlayne Farms   Borkeys Store

Old Church   606   629   Glimpses Corner   629   632   Falls   600

Ginter Bot. Gdns.

627   628   621   632

ndale   Newmans   360

Lakeside   Mechanicsville   627   638   643   615   635   Liggans Corner

Va. State Frgnds. & Richmond Intl. Raceway   2   **Beaver Creek Dam**   636

693   •Westwood   606   Tunstall

1 301

❶ **Chickahominy Bluff**   3   4   **Old Cold Harbor**

Gaines' Mill   **Cold Harbor**   619   619   619   607   608   Whi Hou

Virginia Union Univ.   East Highland Park   360

Garthright House   Alexanders Corner   Wicker Corner   Tunstall Station   PAMUNK IND. RE.

156   628

Valentine Mus.   Mus. and White Hse. of the Confederacy   33   Highland Sprs.   Fair Oaks

616   611   612   606   609

State Capitol   Poe Mus.

613   613   Blacks Store   Orapex Farms   249   Quinton   609   E

Maggie L. Walker N.H.S.   60   Sandston

V.A. Med. Ctr.   **Virginia Aviation Mus.**   Seven Pines   **Seven Pines Natl. Cem.**   33 156

Talleysville   Browns Corner   640   612   610   618   Carys Corne

Richmond   5   60   Bottom Bridge   33   Wrights Corner   665   Criss Cross   617

Richmond Intl. Airport   60   156

161   106   615   618   155

1 301   CITY RD   Elko   PORTUGEE RD

Bensley   641   **Richmond Natl. Battlefield Park**   DARBYTOWN RD   Glendale   Hughes Store   600   Roxbury   609   Mountcastle   60   6

DEFENSE SUPPLY CTR.   **Ft. Harrison Visitor Ctr.**   **Glendale Natl. Cem.**   603   603   631   Providence Forge   618

Bellwood   145   604   106   630   Sandybott

Malvern Hill   5   156   650   609   602   Adkins Store   614

Centralia   144   **Drewry's Bluff**   ❿   **Henricus Historical Park**   Granville   620   Roaches Corr   602   612

Chester   John Tyler Comm. Coll. Chester Campus   732   Farrar Island   Wayside   607   Montpelier   607   Ruthville   155   615

Barnetts   625   609   618

620   617   Rivermont   746   608   106   **Edgewood Plantation**   **Harrison L. Natl. Fish Hatchery**   Charles City   New Hope

625   619   746   **Shirley Plantation**   5   **Evelynton Plantation**   Bowens Store

144   Eppes Island   156   ❻ **City Point**   **Berkeley Plantation**   **Westover Gardens Plantation**   619

36   645   **Sherwood Forest Plantation**

Colonial Heights   626   ❼ **Hopewell**   10   156   **Flowerdew Hundred Plantation**

FT. LEE MIL. RES.

625   627   Virginia State University   144   646   646   641   641   639

atoaca   Ettrick   **Quartermaster Museum**   Garysville   614   Bran Gard Planta   653

❽ **Petersburg Natl. Battlefield**   630   635   609   10   611

109   106   Prince George   Taylors Cor

1   ❾ **Petersburg**   106   616   636   625

❾ **Pamplin Historical Park**   608   301   632   New Bohemia   156

0   5 kr

0   3 mil

Fredericksburg area

Ratings

Gastronomy	●●●●●
History	●●●●●
Art and museums	●●●●
Shopping	●●●●
Children	●●○○○
Entertainment	●●○○○
Beaches	●○○○○
Nature	●○○○○

Settled in 1728, Fredericksburg's location in a fertile valley at the head of Rappahannock River navigation made it a prosperous tobacco-trading port. George Washington spent most of his boyhood years here, later purchasing a house on Charles Street for his mother, Mary Ball Washington. James Monroe, destined to become the fifth US president, set up his law office in Fredericksburg in 1786. A 40-block National Historic District encompasses more than 350 buildings from the 18th and early 19th centuries.

The city (current population about 19,000–20,000) became a Civil War armed camp and hospital for wounded troops of both the Confederate and Union armed forces. Some of that conflict's bloodiest battles were fought in town and nearby – especially in such western-vicinity locales as Chancellorsville, Spotsylvania and the Wilderness. All of the area's major battlefields are situated within a 17-mile radius of riverfront Fredericksburg.

FREDERICKSBURG✦✦✦

ℹ Fredericksburg Visitor Center 706 Caroline St; tel: (800) 678-4748 or (540) 373-1776; www.fredericksburgva.com. Ask about money-saving combination tickets for admittance to most-visited attractions.

Spotsylvania County Department of Tourism 4704 Southpoint Pkwy; tel: (800) 654-4118 or (540) 891-8687.

Opposite
Hugh Mercer Apothecary Shop

Get oriented at Market Square's **Fredericksburg Area Museum and Cultural Center**✦✦ in the former town hall and market house, built in 1815. Six galleries on two floors – plus the upstairs Council Chamber – trace the region's natural and social history by way of artefacts, tools, toys, furniture, paintings and photographs, Civil War weaponry, craft demonstrations, audiovisual presentations and special exhibits.

The **Hugh Mercer Apothecary Shop**✦ displays 18th-century medicinal remedies (leeches and snakeroot, for example) which patients had to endure during those pre-anaesthesia days. Dr. Mercer closed shop upon joining the Continental Army as a brigadier general in 1776. The **Rising Sun Tavern**✦ was built in 1760 for Charles Washington, George's youngest brother, and was later turned into a stagecoach stop and centre of Fredericksburg's social life. Costumed 'wenches' welcome visitors with a touristy representation of colonial tavern jollity and serve a complimentary spiced drink.

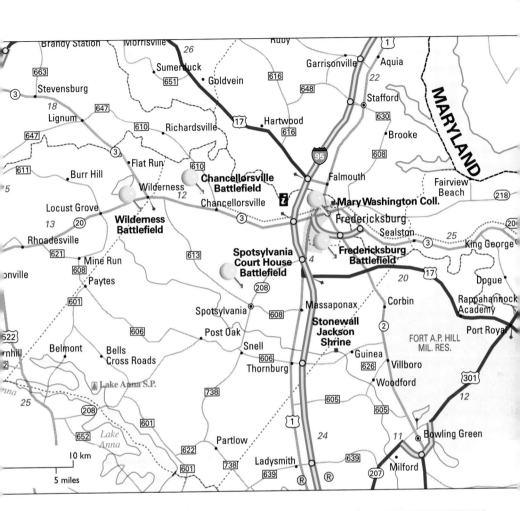

Fredericksburg, at a midpoint 50 miles north of Richmond and 50 miles south of Washington, DC, is conveniently accessible from those metro areas via the north–south I-95 motorway. From east to west, Rte 3 connects the small city with Virginia's Tidewater and Shenandoah Valley regions. An Amtrak train station is merely three blocks south of the centrally located Visitor Center.

A trolley tour of Fredericksburg's sightseeing circuit covers nearly three dozen historic attractions in 60 minutes (tel: (540) 898-0737). Ask at the Visitor Center for five fully detailed and illustrated *Walking through History* brochures, useful for self-guided touring throughout the city centre. Two of these publications enable visitors to follow the course of the Civil War's hard-fought Fredericksburg Campaign of December 1862.

Fredericksburg Area Museum and Cultural Center $ *907 Princess Anne St; tel: (540) 371-3037; open Mar–Nov Mon–Sat 1000–1700, Sun 1300–1700, rest of year Mon–Sat 1000–1600, Sun 1300–1600.*

Hugh Mercer Apothecary Shop $ *1020 Caroline St; tel: (540) 373-3362; open Mar–Nov daily 0900–1700, rest of year 1000–1600.*

Right
Kenmore Plantation

For six years, beginning in 1788, James Monroe and his wife Elizabeth lived at what is now the **James Monroe Museum and Memorial Library✤✤**, which displays Louis XVI furniture purchased in Paris while he was US minister to France – along with books, portraits, correspondence and documents highlighted by a section of President Monroe's 1823 address to Congress, which became the influentially internationalist Monroe Doctrine.

After wealthy planter Fielding Lewis married George Washington's sister Betty, they lived in the mid-Georgian brick mansion at **Kenmore Plantation and Gardens✤✤✤**, especially noted for the gorgeously sculpted plasterwork on ceilings and above the fireplaces. The English and American furnishings are authentic 18th-century period pieces. Washington bought the modest clapboard **Mary Washington House✤** for his mother upon her move from nearby Ferry Farm in 1772. She lived here until her death 17 years later. Some of her belongings are on display, and boxwoods she planted still thrive in the English-style garden. Hostesses in colonial attire conduct half-hour tours.

St George's Episcopal Church✤, a tall-steepled structure (1849), features a memorial window dedicated to Mary Washington, plus three stained-glass windows designed at Louis Comfort Tiffany's New York City studio. In 1863, General Robert E Lee's Confederate soldiers gathered here for religious revival meetings. A year later, the church became a hospital for wounded Union troops.

Rising Sun Tavern
$ *1304 Caroline St; tel: (540) 371-1494; open daily 0900–1700 (Mar–Nov), 1000–1600 rest of year.*

James Monroe Museum and Memorial Library $ *908 Charles St; tel: (540) 654-1043; open daily 0900–1700 (Mar–Nov), 1000–1600 rest of year.*

Kenmore Plantation and Gardens $ *1201 Washington Ave.; tel: (504) 373-3381; open Mon–Sat 1000–1700, Sun 1200–1700 (Mar–Dec), Mon–Sat 1000–1600, Sun 1200–1600 rest of year.*

Mary Washington House $ *1200 Charles St; tel: (540) 373-1569; open daily 0900–1700 (Mar–Nov), 1000–1600 rest of year.*

St George's Episcopal Church $ *905 Princess Anne St; open Mon–Sat 0900–1700, guided tours Mon–Fri 1000–1500.*

Numerous antique shops line both sides of downtown's Caroline St; more are on Sophia and William Sts.

Right
Tiffany stained glass in St George's Episcopal Church

Accommodation and food in Fredericksburg

Heritage Inn $
5308 Jefferson Davis Hwy; tel: (800) 787-7440 or (540) 898-1000.

Kenmore Inn $ 1200 Princess Anne St; tel: (800) 437-7622 or (540) 371-7622.

Richard Johnston Inn $ 711 Caroline St; tel: (540) 899-7606.

Fredericksburg Colonial Inn $ 1707 Princess Anne St; tel: (540) 371-5666.

Selby House $ 226 Princess Anne St; tel: (540) 373-7037.

Wytestone Suites $–$$ 4615 Southpoint Pkwy; tel: (800) 794-5005 or (540) 891-1112.

Fredericksburg KOA $ 7400 Brookside Ln.; tel: (540) 898-7252.

La Petite Auberge $–$$ 311 William St; tel: (540) 371-2727.

Le Lafayette $$ 623 Caroline St; tel: (540) 373-6895.

Sammy T's $ 801 Caroline St; tel: (540) 371-2008.

Smythe's Cottage $$ 303 Farquier St; tel: (540) 373-1645.

Brock's Riverside Grill $$ 503 Sophia St; tel: (540) 370-1820.

Claiborne's $$$ 200 Lafayette Blvd; tel: (540) 371-7080.

Virtually every US hotel or motel chain has one or more properties in the area. One alternative, a short drive from the Mary Washington College campus and Fredericksburg Battlefield, is the **Heritage Inn**. Another, centrally located in the Old Town district, is the **Kenmore Inn**, an elegant late 1700s mansion (with full breakfasts and dinners).

A pair of 18th-century Old Town row houses comprise the eight-room **Richard Johnston Inn**. Civil War-era antiques and artefacts fill the **Fredericksburg Colonial Inn**. **Selby House** also appeals to those interested in Civil War history; it's a bed and breakfast with four guest rooms in a well-appointed annex adjoining a Victorian house.

For lodgings in a contemporary setting with an indoor pool, fitness facility and full buffet breakfasts, consider **Wytestone Suites**. This all-suites hotel (each room includes a kitchenette) is adjacent to the Massaponax outlet shopping mall.

Among area campsites is **Fredericksburg KOA**.

For information and reservations pertaining to lodgings in the area's outlying Spotsylvania and Stafford counties, telephone *(800) 373-1776* or *(540) 972-8596*.

Despite its small size, Fredericksburg has an amazing number of good restaurants. **La Petite Auberge** offers traditional French dining in a cheerful garden setting. Similarly, **Le Lafayette** does classic French cuisine in 'The Chimneys' – a Georgian-style house (1771) designated a Virginia and National Historic Landmark.

Sammy T's is an inexpensive soup-and-salad establishment; pasta, burgers, vegetarian dishes and typically southern Brunswick stew; sidewalk seating in pleasant weather. Another money-saving choice for soups and salads, plus tasty desserts, is the **Downtown Café** (*324 William Street*), while **Spanky's** (*917 Caroline Street*) does sandwiches galore.

You can find 'ye olde' atmospherics at **Smythe's Cottage**, in what used to be a blacksmith shop (1840) with a brick patio out at the back, full of local memorabilia; a recommendable choice for such Virginia favourites as peanut soup and chicken pot pie.

Brock's Riverside Grill has chicken, seafood and beef specialties at dinnertime in a setting overlooking the tidal Rappahannock River, and also does take-outs.

Fredericksburg's ritziest, priciest restaurant, with a top-notch wine list, is **Claiborne's** – in the city's restored railroad depot, dating from 1910.

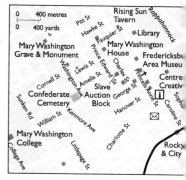

FREDERICKSBURG AND SPOTSYLVANIA NATIONAL MILITARY PARK✦✦✦

ⓘ Fredericksburg Battlefield Visitor Center $ *1013 Lafayette Blvd (Rte 1); tel: (540) 373-6122; open mid-June–mid-Aug daily 0800–1730, rest of year 0800–1700.*

Chancellorsville Battlefield Visitor Center $ *Rte 3 West; tel: (540) 786-0605; open daily 0900–1700, plus extended summer hours. Audio tapes for self-guided touring can be rented at each centre.*

ⓘ Each of the four battlefield parks has wayside exhibits, Civil War defensive earthworks, historic buildings, memorials, interpretive driving routes and walking trails in addition to picnic facilities. One admittance price provides access to all four parks. *Open daily dawn–dusk.*

From the Civil War's very beginning in 1861, northerners had an 'On to Richmond' rallying cry, anticipating a swift victory after routing defenders of that crucial 'rebel' city. However, strategically situated Fredericksburg and its field-and-stream environs – midway between the Federal and Confederate capitals – blocked any semblance of a decisive advance. Instead, opposing forces slugged it out in four epic battles over the course of the next three years. Their intense, relentless warfare resulted in estimated death tolls of 70,000 northern soldiers and 35,000 southerners. Overall, the park covers 16 sites on 8 400 acres of terrain curving beyond the city centre.

Time-travelling begins at **Fredericksburg Battlefield✦✦✦** (11–15 December 1862). Despite harassment by Confederate sharpshooters, Union divisions under General Ambrose E Burnside's command managed to enter Fredericksburg by making a pontoon-bridge crossing of the Rappahannock River from Stafford Heights – meanwhile ravaging the city with short-distance artillery barrages. Robert E Lee's 'most one-sided victory' came during the following three days. The general's 78,000-man force – infantry entrenched behind Sunken Road's stone walls (an original portion of which still exists), cannon and mortar gunners on a ridge called Marye's Heights – repulsed 14 successive Union assaults. Burnside withdrew his demoralised army, retreating back across the river after nightfall on 15 December. A walking trail extends alongside Sunken Road; 15,000 Union soldiers are buried in the Fredericksburg National Cemetery atop Marye's Heights.

Next in sequence comes **Chancellorsville Battlefield✦✦✦** (27 April–6 May 1863). Union General Joseph Hooker (Burnside's replacement) led another river-crossing, this time north of Fredericksburg. Following a ten-mile westward advance towards Chancellorsville, his 134,000 troops encountered Lee's 60,000-man Army of Northern Virginia at a strategic crossroads. In a surprise manoeuvre, 'Stonewall' Jackson's cavalry corps attacked the 6-mile Federal line's right flank, resulting in a major southern victory despite heavy casualties on both sides.

A year later, General Ulysses S Grant's armies achieved a third Union crossing of the Rappahannock, then advanced 5 miles past Chancellorsville to the junction at Wilderness Tavern, locale of **Wilderness Battlefield✦✦✦** (5–6 May 1864). Lee advanced to meet the northerners, marking history's first Lee vs Grant encounter. Two days of fierce fighting ensued in a forest's dense, tangled undergrowth – 60,000 southerners holding double that number to a stalemate.

Lee and Grant again faced off a year later, near a village court house standing at the shortest roadway route to Richmond. The

Spotsylvania Court House Battlefield✵✵✵ (8–21 May 1864) recalls two weeks of combat – including 20 hours on 12 May at a salient known as 'Bloody Angle'. Within this square-mile area, 13,000 soldiers died during the war's toughest and longest-sustained hand-to-hand fighting. Close to the court house, the Spotsylvania Confederate Cemetery contains 600 military gravesites.

Suggested tour

Total distance: 50–55 miles if you cover the four battlefields in and well beyond central Fredericksburg; 75 miles if you cover all related sites.

Time: 5–6 hours' leisurely driving – but best to plan a full day, morning to sunset.

Links: After your battlefields drive, connect with the Northern Virginia route (*see page 75*). From Fredericksburg and its immediate eastern environs, connect with the Tidewater region route (*see page 135*).

Route: From downtown's National Historic District, drive 2 miles west on Lafayette Blvd to reach the **FREDERICKSBURG BATTLEFIELD Visitor Center** and adjacent **Fredericksburg National Cemetery** ❶. Then continue west via Rte 3 for 10.5 miles; this dual carriageway passes a seemingly endless conglomeration of shopping malls, car dealerships and fast-food establishments, but eventually opens on to rolling farmland. At **CHANCELLORSVILLE BATTLEFIELD** ❷, a 10-mile roadway curves past extensive remains of Confederate trenches and earthworks. After another 6.3 miles via Rte 3 (Plank Rd) in combined rural and sparsely populated suburban countryside, you'll arrive at **WILDERNESS BATTLEFIELD** ❸, a widespread expanse of forested acreage where you might see whitetail deer scampering through the underbrush. Reach the exhibit shelter by turning on to Rte 20. While touring this battlefield, watch for the evocative memorial to the Union Army's 5th New Jersey Infantry Regiment. Follow Rte 613 (Brock Rd) off Rte 3 southward for 10.5 miles to reach the exhibit shelter at the **SPOTSYLVANIA BATTLEFIELD** ❹, where 'Bloody Angle' is clearly signposted. The relatively small **Spotsylvania Confederate Cemetery** is south of the battlefield, near the intersection of Rtes 613/628. For an 11-mile return drive to Fredericksburg, take Rte 608 east to its junction at Rte 1, which again becomes Lafayette Blvd as you approach the city's southwestern outskirts.

Also worth exploring: Lake Anna State Park

Fresh-air recreation around Lake Anna can be combined with a drive to the battlefields.

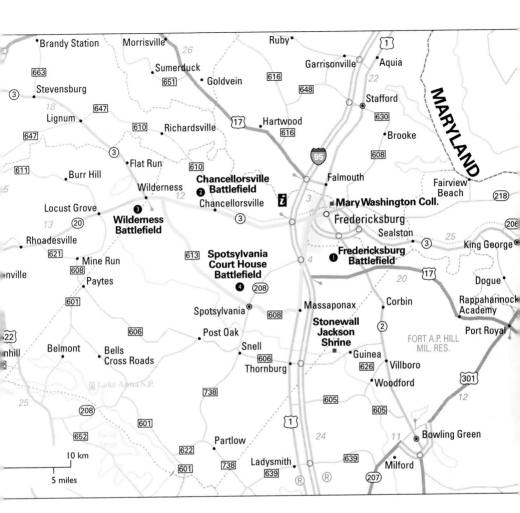

Lake Anna State Park 6800 Lawyers Rd, Spotsylvania; tel: (540) 854-5503; open daily.

Lake Anna Winery 5621 Courthouse Rd, Spotsylvania, on Rte 208; tel: (540) 895-5085; open Wed–Sat 1100–1700, Sun 1300–1900.

Lakewood $ Tel: (540) 895-5844.

This public spread surrounds one of Virginia's most popular lakes and features a sandy beach, in-season food concessions, pontoon boat rides and plenty of space for picnicking and hiking, plus nearby campsites. Eight marked trails with distances ranging from 0.3 to 2 miles wind through the wooded terrain. From Spotsylvania, follow Rte 208 (Courthouse Rd) southward via Post Oak village; turn on to Rte 601 to reach the park's entrance. For fastest, 26-mile access direct from Fredericksburg, drive south on I-95; take Exit 118 for a scenic drive through Thornburg, Snell and Post Oak via Rte 208. Country grocery stores for takeouts are reasonably numerous. **Lakewood** is a combined motel and restaurant 2 miles from the park at **Lake Anna Winery**, where you can taste Cabernet Sauvignon, Merlot, Chardonnay and Seyval.

Tidewater

Ratings

History	●●●
Nature	●●●
Beaches	●●
Gastronomy	●●
Shopping	●●
Art and museums	●
Children	●
Entertainment	●

The Potomac, Rappahannock, James and York rivers slice Virginia's low-lying coastal plain into jagged fingers of land (locals call them 'necks') poking into huge Chesapeake Bay. Each neck – indented with tidal creeks, mini-bays, inlets, coves and estuaries – comprises an ecosystem featuring nature sanctuaries. The region, in fact, is a stopover on the 'Atlantic flyway' travelled by millions of migratory birds. Because of those topographical indentations, the state's portion of bayfront shoreline (shared with Maryland) exceeds 3 300 miles. Short-distance roads connect random fishing villages and country towns.

County names – King William, Richmond, Lancaster, King and Queen, Middlesex, Gloucester, York, Northumberland, Isle of Wight – stem from English colonial settlement. The Northern Neck has American history-book significance, mainly because George Washington and Robert E Lee's birthplaces are close together on the upper part of that peninsula, where the Potomac River flows into Chesapeake Bay.

BAYSHORE NORTHERN NECK✦✦✦

ⓘ Lancaster County Visitor Center 453A N Main St, Kilmarnock; tel: (800) 579-9102 or (804) 435-6092.

ⓜ Reedville Fishermen's Museum $ 504 Main St (Rte 360); tel: (804) 453-6529; www.northernneck. com/museum; open May–Oct Wed–Mon 1030–1630, Nov–Dec and mid-Feb–Apr Fri–Mon 1030–1630.

Northumberland and Lancaster counties comprise the eastern portion of 'The Neck', with close geographic affinity to Chesapeake Bay's ecology and weather patterns. The mostly flat landscape's deepest cleft is formed by the Great Wicomico River.

In 1874, a New England ship captain named Elijah W Reed founded his namesake town of Reedville, a picturesque community with Victorian houses near the banks of Cockrell's Creek. Thanks to his foresight, citizens amassed modest fortunes by hauling in menhaden, a Chesapeake Bay fish still caught and reprocessed for crop fertiliser and protein-rich livestock feed. That endeavour's heyday is recalled in the **Reedville Fishermen's Museum**✦, with its permanent collection and rotating exhibits in the 1875 William Walker House and latter-day Covington Building. Boats and equipment used by the area's watermen to harvest fish, oysters and blue crabs are displayed outdoors.

A mile from the Rappahannock River docks in Irvington, the

Mary Washington Coll. (218)

Fredericksburg

Fred.burg &
Spot. N.M.P. (17)

tonewall
son Shrine (2)

FORT A.P. HILL
MIL. RES.

626

605 605

24 639 207

11 Bowling Green

2 721

625

301 601

kings
minion

13 Hanover

land 54

656

606

615 605

keside 13 627

Richmond

12

Sandston

nsley

23
rfield

ester 26

Colonial
Hts.

ttrick

Petersburg N.B.

Petersburg

9

703

20 km

10 miles

Naval Surface
Warfare Center
Dahlgren Div.

(205) Colonial
Beach

(205) Oak
Grove (3)

George Washington
Birthplace Natl. Mon.

Westmoreland S.P.

Robert E Lee's
Birthplace

624 36

622 Montross

624

Champlain 637
631

27 Rappahannock
N.W.R.

627 Warsaw

Tappahannock

642

Loar St. For. 360

14 620

629

King
William

14

King & Queen
Courthouse

30

West Point

33

601

30 273

R New Kent

York River S.P.

60

Chickahominy

609 602 155 615

56 623

5 Charles
City

10

Williamsburg

Brandon Gardens

613 646

21 Prince
George

625

Surry

Chippokes
Plantation S.P.

Bacon's
Castle

Christopher
Newport Univ.

Smithfield

620
628

620

Lexington Park

(4)

(5)

(235)

Coles
Point

612 Mt. Holly

202

204

Kinsale

203 624

Callao 29

607

23

Bush Mill Stream
Natural Area
Preserve

Belle Isle S.P.

610

640

602

Urbana

603

16

West Point 19

198

17

606

Heathsville 644

612

365 Burgess

Wicomico
Church

201 13

Passenger Cruises
to Tangier Island

Hughlett Point
Natural Area
Preserve

200 Kilmarnock

Irvington

12 White Stone
695

Lancaster

Saluda 33 8 3

Topping

33

3
14

17

14 Mathews

617

614 629

13 Mobjack
Bay

14

Gloucester

York

22

Gloucester Point

Colonial Natl. Hist. Park

Yorktown

21 Newport News/
Williamsburg Intl. Arpt.

60 134

Langley
A.F.B.

Poquoson

Hampton

Hampton
Univ.

17
258

664

New Pt.
Comfort

Newport
News

Reedville

Chesapeake

(Seasonal)

Bay

Busch
Gardens

Colonial
N.H.P.

FORT
EUSTIS

Isle of Wight

Historic Christ Church $ *Rte 200; open Mon–Fri 1000–1600, Sat 1300–1600, Sun 1400–1700. Episcopal services Sun 0800 (June–early Sept).*

The Tides $$$ *480 King Carter Dr., Irvington; tel: (800) 843-7166 or (804) 438-5000.*

Hope and Glory Inn $$ *634 King Carter Dr.; tel: (800) 497-8228 or (804) 438-6053.*

Windmill Point Resort $$ *Rte 695, White Stone; tel: (804) 435-1166.*

The Morris House $–$$ *826 Main St; tel: (804) 453-7016.*

Cedar Grove $–$$ *2743 Fleeton Rd; tel: (800) 497-8215 or (804) 453-3915.*

Inn at Level-fields $ *10155 Mary Ball Rd, Lancaster; tel: (800) 238-5578 or (804) 435-6887.*

Elijah's $$ *729 Main St, Reedville; tel: (804) 453-3621.*

Crazy Crab $–$$ *902 Main St, Reedville; tel: (804) 453-6789.*

Peppermints $ *858 Main St, Reedville; tel: (804) 453-6468.*

Chesapeake Café $–$$ *652 N Main St, Kilmarnock; tel: (804) 435-3250.*

Sandpiper Restaurant $–$$ *850 Rappahannock Dr., White Stone; tel: (804) 435-6176.*

cruciform **Historic Christ Church**✦ has stood virtually unchanged since its completion in 1735. Visitors can admire the marble baptismal font, Queen Anne holy table, the original Communion silver, the 'triple-decker' pulpit and 26 high-backed pews. On the north coast's Yeocomico River, Kinsale was settled in 1708, making this tiny sailing-boat haven and long-ago steamboat landing the oldest port town on Virginia's side of the Potomac.

Accommodation and food in Bayshore Northern Neck

Northern Neck's poshest and best-known waterfront resort is **The Tides**, with a superlative marina-view dining room. Irvington's bed and breakfast alternative is an 1890s elementary school impressively remade into the **Hope and Glory Inn**. Vacationers' perks at **Windmill Point Resort** include a 1-mile white-sand beach, two swimming pools, golf course and three tennis courts.

Built in 1895, **The Morris House** is a turreted Queen Anne-style Victorian bed and breakfast on Reedville's 'millionaire's row'. Another in-town bed and breakfast with water views is **Cedar Grove**. Southern graciousness also defines the 1857 **Inn at Level-fields**.

One of the area's choicest restaurants for seafood and prime cuts of beef is a former cannery in Reedville, now **Elijah's**. The laid-back **Crazy Crab** features a wraparound deck overlooking the harbour. In a pink cottage, **Peppermints** serves soups, sandwiches and ice cream.

Two amiable establishments in close-together Kilmarnock and White Stone are the **Chesapeake Café** and the **Sandpiper Restaurant**. Nearby Burgess has folksy **Rosie Lee's** (*Rte 360; tel: (804) 453-6211; $*). The aptly named **Good Eats Café** (*jct Rtes 202/203; tel: (804) 472-4385; $*) adds to the enjoyment of a stopover in Kinsale.

MIDDLE PENINSULA✦✦✦

ℹ Gloucester County Chamber of Commerce 6688 Main St, Gloucester; tel: (804) 693-2425.

Tappahannock-Essex Chamber of Commerce 205 Cross St, Tappahannock; tel: (804) 443-5431.

ⓜ Virginia Institute of Marine Science $ 1208 Greate Rd, Gloucester Point; tel: (804) 684-7000; www.vims.edu; open Mon–Fri 0800–1630.

☾ Linden House $ 11770 Tidewater Trail, Champlain; tel: (804) 443-1170.

The Inn $ 250 Virginia St, Urbanna; tel: (804) 758-4852.

🍴 Raw Bar $ 250 Virginia St, Urbanna; tel: (804) 758-4852.

After Six Restaurant $$ 250 Virginia St, Urbanna; tel: (804) 758-4852.

Lowery's $$ Church Lane, Tappahannock; tel: (804) 443-2800.

Rivahside Café $ 221 Prince St, Tappahannock; tel: (804) 443-2333.

River's Inn $$ 8109 Yacht Haven Dr., Gloucester Point; tel: (804) 642-9942.

Victoria's $ 6597 Main St, Gloucester; tel: (804) 693-2826.

Its mouth opened wide by deep-water Mobjack Bay, this chunky peninsula looks like the head of a snapping turtle. The Rappahannock and York rivers form the top-to-bottom contours. Three towns in particular – Gloucester, Tappahannock and Urbanna – have well-preserved historic districts. Urbanna's Oyster Festival, held annually during the first weekend of November, attracts upwards of 100,000 people. On the York River, Gloucester Point's **Virginia Institute of Marine Science✦** maintains eight aquariums containing saltwater fish indigenous to Virginia, plus endangered sea crabs; a 'touch tank' enables visitors to handle hermit crabs, starfish and sea

urchins. Farmers raise soya beans, wheat, barley, oats and rye on wide expanses of inland terrain; you'll also see occasional horse ranches. And you'll come upon country stores purveying takeout food, a chance to try Virginian oyster and crab-cake sandwiches.

Accommodation and food in the Middle Peninsula

Dating from the 1750s, **Linden House** in Champlain is a bed and breakfast amidst English gardens. In Urbanna's village centre, **The Inn** augments guest rooms with its daytime **Raw Bar** and **After Six Restaurant**.

Eat in or order a takeout at **Lowery's**, thriving as a family restaurant in Tappahannock since 1938. A more intimate downtown eatery is the **Rivahside Café**.

At Gloucester Point's marina, **River's Inn** cooks freshly caught Chesapeake Bay seafood.

Victoria's, in Gloucester, is a satisfying midday choice for salads, sandwiches, burgers and pizza.

In Urbanna, **The River's Edge** is a snack bar and ice-cream parlour at 217 Virginia Street. For heartier fare such as clam chowder and oyster stew, stroll to the **Virginia Street Café**, on Virginia and Pearl Streets.

UPPER NORTHERN NECK***

ⓘ Northern Neck Tourism Council
479 Main St, Warsaw; tel: (800) 393-6180 or (804) 333-1919; www.northernneck.org.

Westmoreland County Visitor's Center
Courthouse Sq., Montross; tel: (888) 783-9282 or (804) 493-8440.

ⓣ George Washington Birthplace National Monument $ Rte 204; tel: (804) 224-1732; open daily 0900–1700.

Stratford Hall Plantation $$ Rte 214; tel: (804) 493-8038; www.stratfordhall.org; open daily for guided tours 0900–1630. Actor Jason Robards narrates an introductory 13-minute film, The Lees of Stratford.

Caledon Natural Area $ Rte 218, King George County; open daily 0800–dusk.

Westmoreland State Park $ State Park Rd, off Rte 3; open daily 0800–dusk.

ⓒ The Inn at Montross $–$$ 21 Polk St, Montross; tel: (804) 493-0573.

Bushfield Manor $$ Rte 780, Mount Holly; tel: (888) 307-0404 or (804) 472-4171.

Mt Holly Steamboat Inn $$ Rte 202, Mount Holly; tel: (804) 472-3336.

Driving eastward from Fredericksburg's outskirts brings you to this rural, fertile chunk of Virginia Tidewater country. The most notable attractions are either on or near the Potomac River frontage, with southerly stretches of Maryland's coast visible across the water.

The 'Founding Father' of the USA entered this world on 22 February 1732, at his ancestral 538-acre plantation on Pope's Creek in what is now the **George Washington Birthplace National Monument***. In the Memorial House, built to replace the burned-down original, costumed guides point out furnishings and utensils typifying the period. The acreage includes a Colonial Living Farm with livestock, crops and a herb garden. *A Childhood Place* is an informative 14-minute film.

Close by, **Stratford Hall Plantation*** was home to four generations of Lees, one of the South's most illustrious families – but it's best known as the birthplace in 1807 of Robert E Lee, fated to be commissioned the Confederate army's commander-in-chief. Sloping down to the river, Stratford Hall's 1600-acre spread includes woodlands, meadows, gardens and a working farm, plus more than 2 miles of nature trails bordering the Potomac and the plantation's mill pond. The patrician, H-shaped manor house is a classic example of Colonial architecture on a grand scale. Among the furnishings are some of the Lee family's original pieces, notably infant Robert's crib.

Two nature-reserve parks, both atop Potomac cliffs, attract outdoor enthusiasts. The **Caledon Natural Area*** is summer habitat for one of the East Coast's largest concentrations of American bald eagles. In this woods-and-wetland environment, the big birds can be spotted as they forage around Boyd's Hole and Caledon Marsh. The park includes picnic facilities and 5 miles of trails winding through marshlands and an old-growth forest. Hikers exploring 1299-acre **Westmoreland State Park*** are rewarded with river panoramas from the Horsehead Cliffs, with beachfront picnic grounds on-site.

Accommodation and food in Upper Northern Neck

Several of the region's bed and breakfasts are historic and recommendable, for instance, **The Inn at Montross**, a 1790s structure with the original John Minor's Pub of 1685 downstairs; the innkeepers serve lunches and gourmet dinners. On Buckner Creek off the Potomac, neo-Georgian **Bushfield Manor** is close to Mount Holly's public golf course. Nearby, alongside the Nomini Bridge, **Mt Holly Steamboat Inn** features breakfasts and dinners on a screened patio.

At the tip of a wooded Potomac peninsula, **Coles Point Plantation** offers a marina, 110 campsites, swimming pool and restaurant.

On Stratford Hall's sprawling acreage, **The Plantation Dining Room** excels in home-style Virginia cooking for afternoon and

Coles Point Plantation $ *Rte 612 Cole's Point; tel: (804) 472-3955.*

The Plantation Dining Room $ *tel: (804) 493-9096.*

Driftwood Restaurant $–$$ *Rte 612, Cole's Point; tel: (804) 472-3892.*

Wilkerson's $$ *3900 McKinney Blvd, Colonial Beach; tel: (804) 224-7117.*

Monroe Bay Landing $$ *11 Monroe Bay Ave., Colonial Beach; tel: (804) 224-7360.*

Eckhard's $$ *Rte 3, Topping; tel: (804) 758-4060.*

Right
Flowering Dogwood

Tangier and Chesapeake Cruises $$ *468 Buzzard Point Rd, Reedville; tel: (804) 453-2628. Operates between Reedville and Tangier Island (May–mid-Oct).*

evening meals. Outrageously rich chocolate peanut-butter cake is a dessert specialty. In Cole's Point, the **Driftwood Restaurant** is a sea-food-and-steak hangout. On the Colonial Beach shorefront **Wilkerson's** seafood, steak and chicken entrées dominate the lunch, dinner and weekend buffet menus. Also pleasantly situated is **Monroe Bay Landing.** Near Montross, **Eckhard's** is a *gemütlich* German restaurant with a Bavarian accent.

Suggested tour

Total distance: 175 to 190 miles, including detours, to reach all notable points of interest.

Time: With side-road shorefront locales to entice you, allow at least one full day, but preferably two.

Links: Begin a south-to-north Tideway region tour after leaving Yorktown on the Virginia's Historic Triangle route (*see page 146*). Starting instead at uppermost Northern Neck connects you with the Fredericksburg area route (*see page 128*).

Route: From Yorktown, cross the Rte 17 toll bridge spanning the York River to reach the **MIDDLE PENINSULA** at **Gloucester Point ❶**; drive 13 miles to **Gloucester ❷** and its photogenic, early 19th-century Courthouse Square Historic District. Continuing 19 miles on Rte 17 brings you to Saluda. From there, head 4 miles north via Rtes 33/227 to reach charming little **Urbanna** ❸, a tobacco-trading port founded in 1680. Backtracking to Rte 33, drive east to Rte 3 for a 14.5-mile drive via the 2-mile-long Rappahannock River bridge to White Stone at the southern tip of **BAYSHORE NORTHERN NECK** ❹, 14.5 miles overall.

Turn left on to Rte 200 for a 2-mile drive to **Irvington** ❺. North from there, watch for signs leading to historic **Christ Church** on a side road. Then tour onward to **Kilmarnock** ❻, Lancaster County's commercial hub, and another 12 miles through Wicomico Church to Burgess, just beyond the Great Wicimico River bridge. Steer right on to Rte 360; after 6 miles, you'll be in **Reedville** ❼, port of embarkation for passenger (not car-ferry) cruises to **Tangier Island** ❽, midway between the Northern Neck and Virginia's Eastern Shore. Backtrack from Reedville to Burgess; take Rte 360 through Heathsville, Lottsburg and Callao. Reach placid **Kinsale** by meandering several miles north on Rte 621.

Detour: At Kilmarnock's crossroads, head 7.5 miles west on Rte 3 to **Lancaster** ❾. As in Gloucester, you'll come upon a Historic Courthouse District. Mary Ball, George Washington's mother, was born at a nearby Epping Forest farmstead. For an exercise break, hike the town's 2.5-mile **Hickory Hollow Nature Trail**. Find it by turning off Rte 3 on to Rte 604. A bit further from town, via Rte 354, **Belle Isle State Park** ❿ has picnicking and boating facilities. A 5-mile trail through fields and marshes ('hunting grounds' for herons and egrets) reaches the Rappahannock River. Return to Rte 3 via Rte 201, passing backwoods creeks, swamps and mill ponds.

Taking Rte 202 at Callao, travel 20.5 miles north by way of Mount Holly to **Montross** ⓫ in the **UPPER NORTHERN NECK**. Montross is 5 miles south of **Stratford Hall Plantation** – and from there it's a 9.5-mile jaunt on Rte 3 to **George Washington Birthplace National Monument** and **Westmoreland State Park** ⓬. In Oak Grove, **Ingleside Plantation Vineyards** ⓭ has been producing premium wines and sparkling wines for more than a century. From Oak Grove, go 6 miles north on Rte 205 to the Potomac resort town of **Colonial Beach** ⓮, then to the **Caledon Natural Area** ⓯ off Rte 218. On that highway, continue 29 miles west to reach the bridge leading directly into Fredericksburg.

Also worth exploring

Across the Rappahannock River from the Northern Neck, **Tappahannock** was originally called New Plymouth upon settlement in 1680. Colonial and Victorian houses and public buildings, along with antique shops and Essex County's history museum, embellish the historic district. Reach this mini-city by driving 17 miles west via Rte 360 from Callao.

608
15 **Naval Surface Warfare Center Dahlgren Div.**
MaryWashington Coll. 218
Fredericksburg
206 16
205
Fred.burg & Spot. N.M.P. 17
20
tonewall kson Shrine
FORT A.P. HILL MIL. RES
626
605 605
639 207
R
2
721
630
625
301 601
652
600 604 628
600
Kings minion
land
54
604
605
656
615 605
606
627
Lakeside 13
Richmond
Mechanicsville
Sandston
ansley
erfield
ester
Colonial Hts.
ttrick
Petersburg
703
7
602
35
602

4
(4)
Lexington Park
235
5
Colonial Beach
205
14
George Washington Birthplace Natl. Mon.
Oak Grove
13
12
Westmoreland S.P.
Robert E Lee's Birthplace
624 36
Montross 11
622
Champlain
635
637
631
624
630
625
Rappahannock N.W.R.
27
17
627
Warsaw
Tappahannock
612
Mt. Holly
202
604
202
Kinsale
203
Callao
607
612
Heathsville 644
360 **Burgess**
7
642
29
23
Bushy Mtn Natural Area Preserve
Wicomico Church
201
200
7 **Reedville**
13
8
Passenger Cruises to Tangier Island
Hughlett Point Natural Area Preserve
360
684
28
19
10 **Belle Isle S.P.**
9 **Lancaster**
14
620
629
640
602
17
200 6 **Kilmarnock**
5 **Irvington**
4 **White Stone**
695
King William
14
610
King & Queen Courthouse
Urbanna
3
603
Saluda
33
8
3
Topping
33
30
25
Chelsea Plantation
West Point
601
14
606
198
33
249
New Kent
30
33
30
273
17
614
629
14
156
600
106 609
60
3
14 **Mathews**
2 **Gloucester**
617
New Pt. Comfort
295
5
609 602 155
615
1 **Gloucester Point**
Colonial Natl. Hist. Park
Yorktown
James River Plantations
26
5
Charles City
623
56
22
Williamsburg
Busch Gardens
Colonial N.H.P.
Newport News/ Williamsburg Intl. Arpt.
21
95
Colonial
Hopewell
10
Brandon Gardens
609
Prince George
156
613 646
625
10 **Surry**
31
Chippokes Plantation S.P.
26
FORT EUSTIS
134
Poquoson
Langley A.F.B.
Bacon's Castle
31
60
Christopher Newport Univ.
Hampton
40
615
31
617
665
17 258
Hampton Univ.
Smithfield
620
620
628
620
Newport News
664
Isle of Wight
64

20 km

10 miles

Virginia's historic triangle

Ratings

Children	●●●●●
History	●●●●●
Shopping	●●●●○
Art and museums	●●●○○
Gastronomy	●●●○○
Entertainment	●●○○○
Nature	●●○○○
Beaches	●○○○○

In 1607, colonists from the London Company established the New World's first permanent English settlement, naming it Jamestown to honour King James I. The introduction of tobacco cultivation in 1612 brought a small measure of prosperity and, seven years later, America's earliest representative government – the House of Burgesses – convened here. But daily existence remained harsh and perilous; two years after the founding, only 60 of the 500 settlers had survived disease and starvation. This capital of colonial Virginia eventually moved into a planned city called Williamsburg, named after England's William III.

Yorktown, a Tidewater tobacco port founded in 1691, completes the time-line triangle. Joined by French allies, George Washington's troops defeated General Charles Cornwallis's entrapped British redcoats in 1791 for the decisive victory in America's War of Independence. Less than a century later, Yorktown was embroiled in the Civil War's land-and-sea Peninsula Campaign.

BUSCH GARDENS WILLIAMSBURG✦✦

Busch Gardens Williamsburg $$$
1 Busch Gardens Blvd off Rte 60; tel: (757) 253-3350; opening times vary seasonally, so call ahead.

Visitors to this multi-activity theme park can dine, shop and be entertained in fantasy versions of 17th-century English, Scottish, French, German and Italian villages. And they can whoop and yell on 40 thrill rides – among them Apollo's Chariot, a 'hypercoaster' that plunges 825ft at speeds exceeding 70mph.

CARTER'S GROVE✦✦

Carter's Grove $$$
Carter's Grove Rd, off Rte 60; tel: (804) 229-1000; open mid-Mar–Oct Tue–Sun 0900–1800, Nov–Dec 1000–1600.

On an 18th-century plantation estate spread over a bluff above the James River, this Georgian mansion is elegantly furnished in Colonial Revival style. Visitors can also view former pine-log slave quarters and the partially reconstructed site of Wolstenholme Towne, settled in 1619 by 220 English colonists.

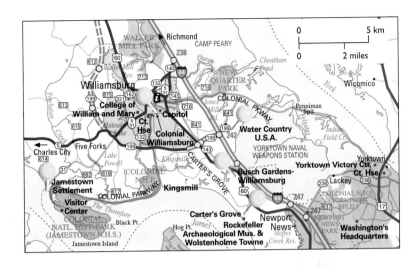

JAMESTOWN SETTLEMENT❖❖❖ AND YORKTOWN VICTORY CENTER❖❖❖

ℹ️ **Jamestown-Yorktown Foundation** *Williamsburg; tel: (888) 593-4682 or (757) 253-4838; www.historyisfun.com.*

🎫 **Jamestown Settlement $$$ and Original Site $** *Rte 31; open daily 0900–1700.*

Yorktown Victory Center $$ *Rte 238; open daily 0900–1700; mid-Jun–mid-Aug 0900–1900.*

Yorktown Battlefield $ *Colonial Pky; tel: (757) 898-3400; Visitor Center open daily 0900–1700. Save money by purchasing a combination ticket for admittance to all four locales.*

These sites draw equal attention to two of the US's epochal events, marking the beginning and end of Colonial America. Both have exhibition galleries with excellent orientation films, *Jamestown: The Beginning* and Yorktown's *A Time of Revolution.*

Jamestown's acreage includes a Powhatan Indian Village with reed-covered dwellings and crafts demonstrations, plus a re-creation of the settlers' palisaded James Fort. One hundred and four of them made it to the New World aboard three ships: the *Susan Constant,* the *Godspeed* and the *Discovery.* Full-scale replicas can be boarded.

On adjacent Jamestown Island, Colonial National Historical Park rangers point out the excavated remnants of the settlers' **Original Site**❖, with a 5-mile loop drive for self-guided touring.

Continental Army soldiers re-enact daily regimental routines – parade-ground drills, weaponry cleaning, preparation of rations, medical care – in **Yorktown Victory Center's**❖ encampment. Barnyard fowl and livestock inhabit a 1780s 'living history' farm where tobacco and corn are cultivated.

A film, *Siege of Yorktown,* is shown in the Visitor Center at **Yorktown Battlefield**❖❖❖ on the opposite (eastern) side of town from the Victory Center. A signposted 7-mile tour passes American and French siege lines, earthwork fortifications, artillery emplacements and British surrender sites. Along a separate 9-mile drive, descriptive markers indicate American and French encampment areas.

A marble Victory Monument, dedicated in 1884, stands 98ft tall in Yorktown centre.

Accommodation and food in Jamestown and Yorktown

Jamestown Beach Campsites $ *Jamestown Rd; tel: (800) 446-9228 or (757) 229-7609.* With 600 pitches and less than 1 mile from the Jamestown site. Lunch-time meals are served in Jamestown Settlement's café.

Duke of York $ *508 Water St, Yorktown; tel: (757) 898-3252.* Motel with a river view.

York River Inn $$ *209 Ambler St, Yorktown; tel: (800) 884-7003 or (757) 887-8800.* A local bed and breakfast alternative.

Nick's Seafood Pavilion $$ **Water St, Yorktown;** *tel: (757) 887-5269.* Overlooks the York River and Coleman Bridge.

Above
Yorktown Victory Center

Opposite
Jamestown Settlement's replica
of the *Discovery*

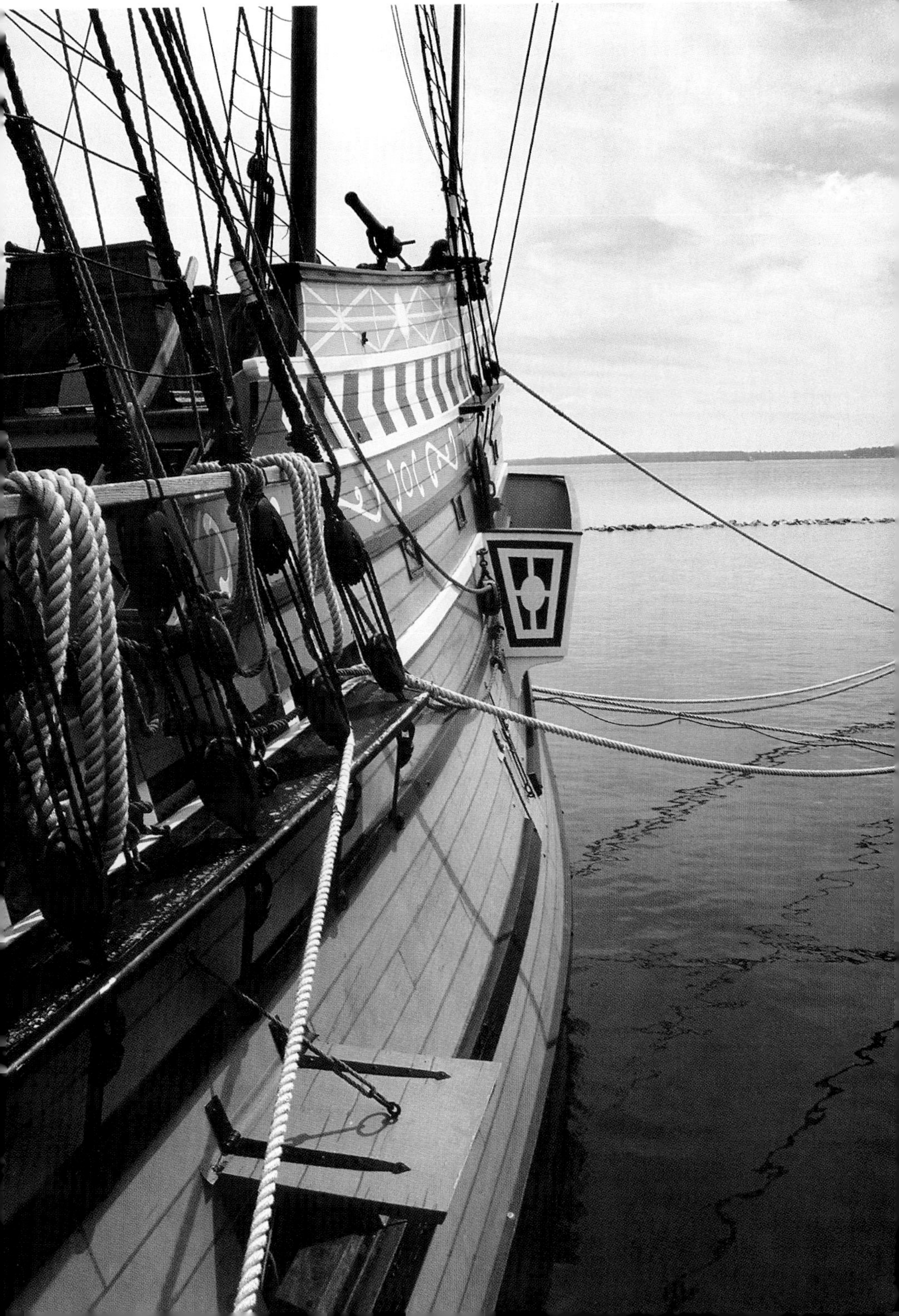

WATER COUNTRY USA✦

Water Country USA $$$ *Rte 199; tel: (757) 229-9300; open May–mid-Sept. Hours vary seasonally, so call ahead.*

Designed for swimmers and splashers of all ages. Malibu Pipeline is a two-person tube ride; families in giant inner tubes raft down Big Daddy Falls; white-water excursions surge through the Atomic Breakers; Nitro Racer, a speed slide, features a 320ft-long drop. Cow-A-Bunga is a children's play area, and aquacade shows are scheduled daily.

WILLIAMSBURG✦✦✦

Williamsburg Area Convention and Visitors Bureau *202 Penniman Rd; tel: (800) 368-6511 or (757) 253-0192; www.visit williamsburg.com.*

Two **Colonial Williamsburg Visitor Centers** provide information on admission charges, attractions and events. Take Exit 238 off I-64 to reach the main one by car (*tel: (757) 220-7645; open Sun–Thur 0830–1800, Fri–Sat 0830–1900*). A smaller facility is in town at Merchants Square (*Duke of Gloucester St; tel: (757) 229-1000; open Sun–Thur 0830–1800, Fri–Sat 0830–1900*).

Thanks to preservation and restoration projects primarily funded by zillionaire John D Rockefeller, Jr, a sizeable city-centre tract was resurrected as immensely popular colonial Williamsburg in the 1920s. Staffed by costumed 'townsfolk' and interpreters, this Historic Area emulates the appearance and lifestyles of what was Virginia's capital from 1699 to 1780. Nearly 600 buildings – government edifices, stores, artisans' workshops, taverns, an apothecary, a parish church, a courthouse, a guardhouse and gaol, a grocery, a printing office, a public hospital and residences – are 18th-century originals or faithful look-alikes. Ninety acres of gardens adhere to period landscaping concepts. In resplendent regalia, a fife and drum corps makes periodic marching appearances down Duke of Gloucester St, the mile-long main thoroughfare. Programmes of events (entertainment and otherwise) are published in a weekly *Visitor's Companion* tabloid.

Three museums are on-site, too. The Abby Aldrich Rockefeller Folk Art Center displays an outstanding assemblage of early-American folk art. Colonial-era Bassett Hall became the Rockefellers' 1930s abode, sumptuously furnished with Chippendale, Federal and Empire pieces. Artisans' works in the DeWitt Wallace Decorative Arts Gallery include the largest collection of English pottery outside the UK and the world's foremost collection of antique Virginia furniture.

Facing broad Palace Green, the Georgian-style Governor's Palace replicates the 1722 original, occupied by seven royal governors, then by Patrick Henry and Thomas Jefferson – the Virginia Commonwealth's first two governors. Visitors guided through the Capitol, where America's first representative assembly convened, learn about the heated debates and defiant speeches that preceded warfare for independence from British rule.

Granted a royal charter in 1693 (therefore America's second-oldest university after Harvard), Williamsburg's **College of William and Mary** features a harmonious campus layout complete with a lake amidst Crim Dell's wildflower refuge. The **Wren Building**, its architecture influenced by England's Sir Christopher Wren and completed in 1695, is the nation's oldest academic structure in continuous use. Three Virginia-born W&M alumni went on to become US presidents: Thomas Jefferson, James Monroe and James Tyler.

Right
Williamsburg's Capitol

Accommodation and food in Williamsburg

The **Colonial Williamsburg Foundation** arranges reservations for lodgings and restaurants situated within the Historic Area (*tel: (800) 447-8679 or (757) 229-1000*).

Four hotels are official Colonial Williamsburg properties; all share the above telephone numbers, and all offer free parking. The quartet's poshest and priciest is **Williamsburg Inn $$$** (*136 E Francis St*), a golf-and-tennis resort with a ritzy Regency dining room, indoor/outdoor swimming pools and fitness facilities. More rustic **Williamsburg Lodge $$–$$$** (*310 S England St*) has comparable amenities. On 44 wooded acres, **Williamsburg Woodlands $$** (*102 Visitor Center Dr.*) is casual and family-oriented. So is the more modest, 200-room **Governor's Inn $** (*506 N Henry St*).

Visitors can choose from a range of accommodation close to the Historic Area – hotels, motels, bed and breakfasts – including every national chain operation in every cost category. The **Williamsburg Hotel and Motel Association** provides a free reservation service (*tel: (800) 446-9244 or (757) 220-3330*).

Williamsburg Hospitality House $$ (*415 Richmond Rd; tel: (800) 932-9192 or (757) 229-4020*), comprising 297 guest rooms, is two blocks from the Historic Area and across the street from the William and Mary college campus. The **Homewood Suites Hotel $$** is a mile away (*601 Bypass Rd; tel: (888) 892-9900 or (757) 259-1199*). Camellias and magnolias embellish 10 acres of grounds at the **Governor Spottswood Motel $** (*1508 Richmond Rd; tel: (800) 368-1244 or (757) 229-6444*).

Location and ambience make **A Primrose Cottage $–$$** an especially recommendable bed and breakfast (*706 Richmond Rd; tel: (800) 522-1901 or (757) 229-6421*), and also **Governor's Trace $$** (*303 Capitol Landing Rd; tel: (800) 303-7552 or (757) 229-7552*).

Outlying campsites include **Fair Oaks Campground $** (*901 Lightfoot Rd; tel: (800) 892-0320 or (757) 565-2101*), 5 miles west of town, with pitches for RVs and tents on 50 forested acres.

Four non-smoking restaurants (**$$–$$$**) with 'ye olde' tavern atmosphere are inside the Colonial Williamsburg Historic Area. They share a reservation number (*tel: (757) 229-2141*). **Chowning's Tavern** replicates an 18th-century English ale house. Steaks and chops highlight the **King's Arms** menu. **Christiana Campbell's** focuses on seafood. **Shields** is a good choice for such traditional Virginian fare as crayfish soup, *rôtisserie*-roasted chicken, Surry County pork chops and fruit cobbler.

Eateries galore line Williamsburg's busiest thoroughfares. For Chesapeake Bay and Atlantic Ocean seafood, dine at **Berret's $$–$$$** (*199 S Boundary St; tel: (757) 253-1847*). Down-home Virginia specialties (including peanut soup and Smithfield ham) are favoured selections at the **Jefferson Restaurant $$** (*1453 Richmond Rd; tel: (757)*

229-2296). Experience plantation cooking in a non-touristy 18th-century dining room at **Old Chickahominy House $$** *(1211 Jamestown Rd; tel: (757) 229-4689)*. Close to the college, sandwiches served at the **Green Leafe Café $** *(765 Scotland St; tel: (757) 220-3405)* fit students' budgets.

Free ferryboat crossing

Right alongside Jamestown Settlement, the Colonial Parkway and Rte 31 converge at the river's edge, where the **Jamestown Scotland Ferry** takes on passengers and automobiles for its 15-minute crossing to the landing at Scotland in Surry County, long-existent farmland for cotton, peanuts and tobacco. There's no charge for what's been a state-run operation since 1945 – providing vacationers with a chance to imagine what the earliest English settlers saw and felt when they ventured upstream. Four ferryboats – the *Williamsburg, Surry, Virginia* and *Pocahontas* – make the year-round James River crossing *(for schedules, tel: (800) 823-3774; www.vdot.state.va.us/info/jt-ferry)*.

From the landing, Rte 31 leads south to Surry, a crossroads village close to **Smith's Fort** *(Smith's Fort Ln., off Rte 31)*, where in 1609 Capt John Smith constructed defensive barricades in what was then part of the New World's uncharted wilderness frontier. Now the site features an 18th-century plantation house with a boxwood and herb garden.

After driving 3 miles east from Surry, you'll reach **Chippokes Plantation State Park** *(695 Chippokes Park Rd, off Rte 10)*, its farm started by Capt William Powell – one of the Jamestown settlers – and cultivated continuously since 1619. On-site there is a plantation house containing displays of household antiques, plus a working sawmill, cropland and a Farm and Forestry Museum. The park's rambling terrain includes hiking trails and picnic grounds.

From there, continue another 3 miles to reach a side road leading to triple-chimneyed **Bacon's Castle** *(465 Bacon's Castle Trail, off Rtes 10/617)*, claimed to be among North America's oldest documented brick houses. Built in 1665 by English immigrant Arthur Allen, its name stems from a rebellion against royal colonial governor Sir William Berkeley that erupted 11 years later, when the property was seized and occupied by troops loyal to fire-brand organiser Nathaniel Bacon. The castle garden was laid out in 1680.

In sharp contrast, there is the free-admittance **Surry Nuclear Information Center** *(Hog Island Rd, off Rtes 10/650; tel: (757) 357-5410; www.vapower.com; open Mon–Fri 0900–1600)*. Outside is a game refuge, and inside the nuclear power station are interactive displays.

Surrey House $$ *(11865 Rolfe Hwy, Surry; tel: (757) 294-3389)* is a recommendable stop for Virginian lunch or dinner.

Suggested tour

Unspoiled landscape

Note that petrol stations and other public service facilities (and also unsightly billboards) are non-existent along the Colonial Parkway's entire length. The route features numerous turnings signposted with explanatory markers, and you'll travel through an unspoiled realm of forests, fern groves, marshes, creeks and ravines, plus riverside meadows at the western and eastern ends. One turning overlooks Jones Mill Pond and its flotilla of swans.

Total distance: 23 miles

Time: At most half a day, even allowing time for stopovers at noteworthy turnouts along the Colonial Parkway.

Links: Richmond (*see pages 102–13*) is 50 miles west of Williamsburg via the I-64 motorway – slightly more if you prefer following Rte 5 (the John Tyler Hwy) through Charles City by way of the James River Plantations, slightly less if you link the Richmond battlefield route (*see pages 119–20*) with the Historic Triangle.

After crossing the Coleman Bridge from Yorktown to Gloucester Point, you can begin the Tidewater region route (*see pages 135–6*) by continuing north on Rte 17.

Heading south from Williamsburg on I-64 gets you to Newport News and Hampton on the Hampton Roads route (*see pages 155–6*).

Route: The very scenic 23-mile **Colonial Parkway** curves across a narrow peninsula, between **JAMESTOWN SETTLEMENT** ❶ on the Jamestown River and **Yorktown** on the York River. At mid-point is **WILLIAMSBURG** ❷, where the three-lane parkway tunnels beneath the Colonial Williamsburg Historic Area. **Jamestown** sites are 8 miles from Williamsburg; Williamsburg to Yorktown entails 13 miles of parkway driving.

Right
Gloucester St, Williamsburg

If you start at the parkway's western (Jamestown) end, a short-distance deviation via Rte 199 and then Rte 60 southbound gets you to **BUSCH GARDENS** ❸ and **CARTER'S GROVE** ❹. From that latter site, a very scenic one-way country road meanders 6 miles north to Williamsburg.

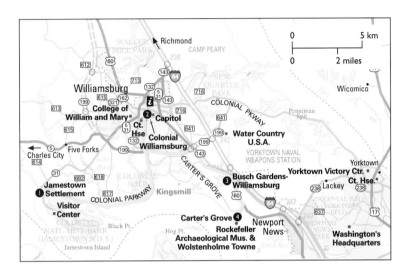

Hampton Roads

Ratings

Beaches	●●●●●
History	●●●●○
Art and museums	●●●○○
Children	●●●○○
Nature	●●●○○
Gastronomy	●●○○○
Entertainment	●○○○○
Shopping	●○○○○

Named after England's third Earl of Southampton, the general Hampton Roads area covers a sizeable expanse of waterways and heavily urbanised terrain in Virginia's southeastern corner. This is also the southernmost section of Virginian Tidewater country, where Chesapeake Bay and the Atlantic Ocean converge. Navigable sea lanes brought English settlers at the early 17th-century beginning of North American colonisation. Two and a half centuries later, a historic Hampton Roads naval engagement involved Union and Confederate 'ironclad' warships.

Present-day US Navy vessels amount to a highly visible presence, offshore and in one of the world's best-situated deepwater harbours. (In marine terminology, a 'road' is a place of safe anchorage.)

Virginia Beach is aptly named: the state's most populous city features 28 miles of fine surf-washed beachfront, plus 3 miles of oceanside boardwalk and an in-town state park – hence its popularity as a summer vacation destination.

HAMPTON✧✧

The region is served by **Norfolk International Airport**, 1.5 miles north of I-64, and by **Newport News/Williamsburg International Airport** on Newport News' northern outskirts, also accessed via the I-64 motorway. In addition, that James River city is on the **Amtrak** rail route.

Diverse elements make this an interesting little city. Among them are a fishing-boat fleet, Langley Air Force base and Fort Monroe's still active army installation, crucial Civil War connections, Hampton University's pioneering importance in educating African-Americans, 1959 space training for the first US astronauts, whale-watching excursions, recreation at Buckroe Beach and a 1920 carousel spinning in a pleasant riverfront park.

Downtown's **Virginia Air and Space Center✧✧✧** features vintage and experimental aircraft and aeronautic and space exhibits (many are interactive), including the *Apollo 12* command module and a chunk of 3-billion-year-old moon rock. Films are shown in a giant IMAX theatre.

Completed in 1834, Fort Monroe's moat-surrounded bastion remains the largest rock fortification ever built in America. In its **Casemate Museum✧✧**, Fort Monroe (*tel: (757) 727-3391; open daily*

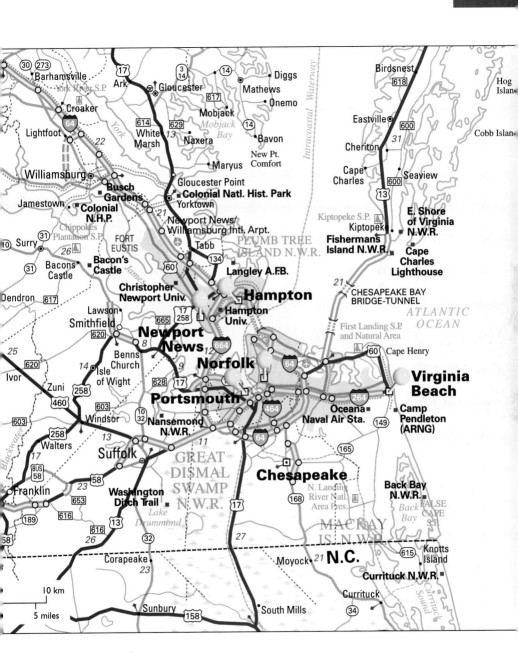

30 273
Barhamsville
York River S.P.
17 Ark
3 14 Gloucester
14
Diggs
618 Birdsnest
Hog Island

Creaker
Mathews
617
Onemo

64 Lightfoot
614
White Marsh
629
Mobjack
Mobjack Bay
14
Eastville
600
Cobb Island
31

22
Naxera 13
Bavon
Cheriton

Williamsburg
New Pt. Comfort
Maryus
Cape Charles
600
Seaview

Busch Gardens
Gloucester Point
Colonial Natl. Hist. Park
Yorktown
13

Jamestown
Colonial N.H.P.
21
Newport News/
Williamsburg Intl. Arpt.
Kiptopeke S.P.
Kiptopeke
E. Shore of Virginia N.W.R.

Chippokes Plantation S.P.
FORT EUSTIS
26
Tabb
134
PLUMB TREE ISLAND N.W.R.
Fisherman's Island N.W.R.
Cape Charles Lighthouse

10 Surry
31
Bacons Castle
Bacon's Castle
60
Langley A.F.B.
21
CHESAPEAKE BAY BRIDGE-TUNNEL

Dendron
617
Christopher Newport Univ.
Hampton
ATLANTIC OCEAN

Lawson
17 665 258
Hampton Univ.
First Landing S.P. and Natural Area

Smithfield
620
Newport News
8
664
60 Cape Henry

25
620
Benns Church
9
12
Norfolk
54

Ivor
14
Isle of Wight
258
628 17
Portsmouth
264
Virginia Beach

Zuni
460
603
Windsor
10 32
Nansemond N.W.R.
464
Oceana Naval Air Sta.
149
Camp Pendleton (ARNG)

258
Walters
13
11
54
165

17
Suffolk
GREAT DISMAL SWAMP N.W.R.
Chesapeake
685

BUS 58
Franklin
23 58
Washington Ditch Trail
17
N. Landing River Natl. Area Pres.
168
Back Bay N.W.R.

189
653
616
Lake Drummond
Back Bay
FALSE CAPE S.P.

58
616
26
32
27
MACKAY IS. N.W.R.

Corapeake
23
Moyock
21
N.C.
615
Knotts Island

10 km
Currituck N.W.R.

5 miles
Sunbury
158
South Mills
Currituck
34
Currituck Sound

ⓘ Hampton Visitor Center *710 Settlers Landing Rd; tel: (800) 800-2202 or (757) 727-1102; www.hampton.va.us/tourism.*

ⓘ Virginia Air and Space Center *$ 600 Settlers Landing Rd; tel: (757) 727-0900; www.vasc.org; open summertime Mon–Wed 0900–1700, Thur–Sun 0900–1900; rest of year daily 1000–1700.*

1030–1630; $) visitors view Civil War memorabilia and the cell where Confederate President Jefferson Davis endured two years' imprisonment after the conflict.

Accommodation and food in Hampton

Built on a grand scale in 1928, **The Chamberlin $–$$** (*2 Fenwick Rd; tel: (800) 582-8975 or (757) 723-6511*) has a superb waterside location within the military post, at the tip of Old Point Comfort.

For inventive 'fusion cuisine', dine at **Bobby's Americana $$–$$$** (*17 E Queens Way; tel: (757) 727-0545*). Marina panoramas enhance **Oyster Alley Outside Restaurant $$** (*700 Settlers Landing Rd; tel: (757) 727-9700*). Virginian home-style cooking prevails at the **Grey Goose $$** (*101A W Queens Way; tel: (757) 723-7978*).

NEWPORT NEWS✦✦

ⓘ Newport News Tourist Information Center *13560 Jefferson Ave.; tel: (888) 493-7386 or (757) 886-7777; www.newport-news.org.*

ⓜ Mariners' Museum *$$ 100 Museum Dr.; tel: (757) 596-2222; open daily 1000–1700.*

Virginia War Museum *$ 9285 Warwick Blvd; tel: (757) 247-8523; open Mon–Sat 0900–1700, Sun 1300–1700.*

Newport News Park *$ 13564 Jefferson Ave.; tel: (757) 886-7912; open daily dawn–dusk.*

Virginia Living Museum *$$ 524 J Clyde Morris Blvd; tel: (757) 595-1900; open summertime Mon–Wed, Fri–Sat 0900–1800, Thur 0900–2100, Sun 1000–1800; rest of year Mon–Sat 0900–1700, Thur 1900–2100, Sun 1300–1700.*

The Shipbuilding and Drydock Company has dominated this city's economy and James River vistas since 1886. Contrast that industriousness with the élite North End/Huntington Heights neighbourhood, art galleries and riverside Victory Arch of 1919. The beautifully situated, comprehensive **Mariners' Museum✦✦✦** is the best of its kind in America, and don't miss the equally first-class **Virginia War Museum✦✦✦**.

Outdoors, roam through the 8 065-acre **Newport News Park✦✦** (America's second-largest municipal park; bicycle rentals available) and observe diverse wildlife via woodland trails at the **Virginia Living Museum✦✦✦**.

Accommodation and food in Newport News

North of downtown, the 1896 **Boxwood Inn $–$$** (*10 Elmhurst St, Lee Hall Village; tel: (757) 888-8854*) is a B&B with meals served in its charming Blue Willow Tea Room. Some of the 101 rooms at **Mulberry Inn $** (*16890 Warwick Blvd; tel: (800) 223-0404 or (757) 887-3000*) have self-catering facilities. There are plenty of campsites in **Newport News Park $** (*tel: (800) 203-8322 or (757) 888-3333*).

'Go Italian' at **Al Fresco $$** (*11710 Jefferson Ave.; tel: (757) 873-0644*) – or Germanic at **Das Waldcafé $$** (*12529 Warwick Blvd; tel: (757) 930-1781*). **The Crab Shack $$** (*7601 River Rd; tel: (757) 245-2722*) is a seafood favourite. So is **The Train Station $$** (*2295 Harbor Rd; tel: (757) 247-7512*).

NORFOLK✦✦✦

Norfolk Convention and Visitors Bureau *232 E Main St; tel: (800) 368-3097 or (757) 664-6620; www.norfolkcvb.com.*

Norfolk Naval Base *$ Tour Office, 9079 Hampton Blvd; tel: (757) 444-7637. Phone ahead for guided tour schedules, and 'open house' visits aboard designated warships.*

Chrysler Museum of Art *$ 245 W Olney Blvd; tel: (757) 664-6200; open Tue–Sat 1000–1700, Sun 1300–1700.*

Douglas MacArthur Memorial *$ MacArthur Sq. (City Hall Ave. and Bank St); tel: (757) 441-2965; open Mon–Sat 1000–1700, Sun 1100–1700.*

Nauticus *$$ National Maritime Center, 1 Waterside Dr.; tel: (757) 664-1000; open summertime daily 1000–1700; rest of year Tue–Sat 1000–1700, Sun 1200–1700.*

Virginia Zoological Park *$ 3500 Granby St; tel: (757) 441-2706; open 1000–1700.*

Home port of the US Atlantic Fleet and the world's largest **naval base**✦, Norfolk burgeoned as a sailor's haven during the two World Wars. That's still a fact of local life, but the city has simultaneously evolved into the region's business, mercantile and cultural capital.

Following several depressed decades, downtown's resurgence began when the Waterside marketplace pavilion opened in 1983, overlooking riverfront promenades, amidst a backdrop of high-rise buildings. Then, in 1999, came the MacArthur Center, a huge, strikingly designed shopping/dining complex.

Two distinctive neighbourhoods are worth visiting: old Freemason and gentrified Ghent (named after the 1814 Treaty of Ghent, which ended the British-American War of 1812).

For high-class prestige, nothing matches Norfolk's **Chrysler Museum of Art**✦✦✦, especially renowned for its world-class glass collection, including gorgeous creations by Tiffany, Gallé and Lalique. Also well represented are 19th- and 20th-century French and American paintings and sculptures, and art-nouveau furniture. Old City Hall, an 1850 Classical-Revival landmark, houses the **Douglas MacArthur Memorial**✦✦✦, a museum devoted to the epochal life and times of five-star general Douglas MacArthur. He and his wife are entombed in the rotunda.

Massive battleship-grey metallic architecture makes **Nauticus**✦✦✦ impossible to miss on its riverfront site. Subtitled the National Maritime Center, with an upstairs Hampton Roads Naval Museum, exhibits delve into naval and aquatic lore. Open to the public, the battleship USS *Wisconsin* and a 1933 tugboat are permanently anchored at adjoining piers.

Weather permitting, head for the Norfolk Botanical Garden – noted for its 250 varieties of azaleas and interlaced with 12 miles of pathways – or the **Virginia Zoological Park**✦✦, the state's biggest and best.

Right
Nauticus museum

Accommodation and food in Norfolk

Built in 1906, in the heart of downtown, **James Madison Hotel** **$–$$** (*345 Granby St; tel: (888) 402-6682 or (757) 622-6682*) has been impressively renovated. Ghent's **Page House Inn $$** (*333 Fairfax Ave.; tel: (800) 599-7659 or (757) 625-5033*) is a resplendent B&B in an 1889 mansion.

Thanks to downtown's renaissance, you'll have no problem finding tempting restaurants. Lobster is the specialty at **Freemason Abbey $$** – originally a Presbyterian church (*209 W Freemason St; tel: (757) 622-3966*). The **Monastery $$** (*443 Granby St; tel: (757) 625-8193*) is Czech-Hungarian.

There are two top-notch eateries in the MacArthur Center: **Kincaid's $$** (*tel: (757) 622-8000*), a fish, chop and steakhouse, and **Castaldi's $$** (*tel: (757) 627-8700*) for Italian cooking.

Ghent's trendiness includes such hip favourites as the **Wild Monkey $$** (*1603 Colley Ave.; tel: (757) 627-6462*) and the art-deco **Elliot's $$** (*1421 Colley Ave.; tel: (757) 625-0259*).

On stage and screen

Norfolk's Chrysler Hall is home to the Virginia Symphony, with additional concert dates in Virginia Beach's modernistic Amphitheater, and also Hampton and Newport News. Also in Norfolk is the Harrison Opera House, a premier facility for Virginia Opera productions. The Virginia Stage Company, in residence at the historic Wells Theater, receives critical acclaim for its performances, both contemporary and Shakespearean. There's a Peninsula Community Theater in Newport News, and Hampton has its American Theater for stage shows, jazz concerts and classic films. Portsmouth's cinematic venue is unique. Light meals are served while movies are shown on the big screen in the 1945 Commodore Theater. And watch for schedules of performing arts festivals throughout this maritime region.

PORTSMOUTH✦✦✦

Portsmouth Convention and Visitors Bureau *505 Crawford St, Suite 2; tel: (800) 767-8782 or (757) 393-5327; www.ci.portsmouth.va.us.*

Naval Shipyard Museum *$ 2 High St; tel: (757) 393-8591; open Tue–Sat 1000–1700, Sun 1300–1700.*

Children's Museum of Virginia *$ 221 High St; tel: (757) 393-8393; open summertime Tue–Sat 1000–1900, Sun 1300–1700; rest of year Tue–Sat 1000–1700, Sun 1300–1700.*

Separated by deep sea lanes from Norfolk, with that city's skyline in view, Portsmouth was established in 1752. The Gosport Shipyard became the nation's largest in the 18th and 19th centuries – subsequently launching America's first battleship (USS *Texas*) in 1892 and first aircraft carrier (USS *Langley*) 30 years later.

But a Civil War 'first' is better known. Confederate shipbuilders converted the wooden frigate *Merrimac* into the CSS *Virginia* – naval warfare's earliest armour-plated vessel – destined to battle the ironclad USS *Monitor* off Newport News on 9 March 1862.

High Street is lined with restaurants, pubs and antique shops. Stroll the brick sidewalks of Olde Towne, a square-mile showpiece of Colonial, neo-Georgian, Greek Revival and Victorian domestic architecture.

Discover titbits about historic, 'seaworthy' Portsmouth in its **Naval Shipyard Museum**✦✦. Even grown-ups enjoy the **Children's Museum of Virginia**✦✦, mainly due to the amazingly sizeable Lancaster Antique Toy and Train Collection.

Accommodation and food in Portsmouth

Above
Portsmouth naval base

Opposite
Tissot's painting, *The Artists' Wives*, in the Chrysler Museum

The Victorian **Olde Towne Inn $$** (*420 Middle St; tel: (757) 397-5462*) is a centrally located bed and breakfast.

Café Europa $$ (*319 High St; tel: (757) 399-6652*) is recommendable for Portuguese-Mediterranean dishes. River-view **Jewish Mother $** (*1 High St; tel: (757) 398-3332*) is a good choice for deli sandwiches. For German food and imported beer, be seated at the **Bier Garden $–$$** (*434 High St; tel: (757) 393-6022*).

VIRGINIA BEACH✧✧✧

ⓘ City of Virginia Beach Visitors Information Center
2100 Parks Ave.; tel: (800) 446-8038 or (757) 437-4888; www.vbfun.com.

ⓘ First Landing/Seashore State Park $ *2500 Shore Dr.; tel: (757) 412-2300; open daily 0800–dusk; visitor centre open Apr–Nov 0900–1800.*

Back Bay National Wildlife Refuge/False Cape State Park $ *4005 Sandpiper Rd; tel: (757) 721-2412; open daily dawn–dusk.*

Virginia Marine Science Museum $$ *717 General Booth Blvd; tel: (757) 425-3474; open summertime daily 0900–2100; rest of year 0900–1700.*

Old Coast Guard Station Museum $ *24th St and Atlantic Ave.; tel: (757) 422-1587; open Mon–Sat 1000–1700, Sun 1200–1700; closed rest of year Mon.*

Ocean Breeze Fun Park $$–$$$ *General Booth Blvd; tel: (757) 425-1241. Call ahead for admittance prices and hours of various attractions.*

Nearly 3 million visitors flock here annually, drawn to the lengthy beachfront and boardwalk – now concrete-surfaced, with a parallel bicycle path – begun in 1888. To accommodate the throng, 'the Beach' has 11,000-plus guest rooms; 53 hotels and motels line both sides of Atlantic Avenue.

Vacation popularity inevitably breeds T-shirt shops, salt-water taffy (a sweet consisting of molasses, brown sugar and butter) stands, tacky souvenirs, miniature golf and other such stuff. But you can also go eco-tour kayaking and deep-sea fishing, feast on fresh seafood and choose from 'something-for-everyone' entertainment. This spread-out boom town's population exceeds the half-million mark.

Vast **First Landing/Seashore State Park✧✧✧**, Virginia's most-visited natural area, features salt-marsh habitats, a maritime forest, freshwater ponds where Spanish moss 'drips' from cypress trees and nearly 20 miles of scenic hiking trails. Further south, nature trails wind through oceanic barrier-island terrain in **Back Bay Natural Wildlife Refuge✧✧✧** and **False Cape State Park✧✧✧**.

The **Virginia Marine Science Museum✧✧**, the state's largest aquarium, includes sharks, sea turtles, bottlenose dolphins, harbour seals, stingrays, horseshoe crabs and river otters, along with feathered creatures. Galleries recalling shipwrecks in rough seas fill Virginia Beach's **Old Coast Guard Station Museum✧**, a life-saving station dating from 1903. For crazy contrast, **Ocean Breeze Fun Park✧** offers such pursuits as a shipwreck-themed mini-golf course, Wild Water Rapids wave pool and bungee-jumping.

Accommodation and food in Virginia Beach

The big-name chains are omnipresent along and near the boardwalk. Call either of two central-reservations services *(tel: (800) 822-3224 or (800) 766-6782)*. Independently operated hotels and motels are even more plentiful, such as **Colonial Inn $$** *(2809 Atlantic Ave.; tel: (800) 344-3342 or (757) 428-5370)* and **Thunderbird Motor Lodge $–$$** *(35th and Oceanfront; tel: (800) 633-6669 or (757) 428-3024)*. Virginia Beach's classic hotel (since 1927) is the hilltop **Cavalier $$** – with a 1970s oceanside adjunct *(42nd and Oceanfront; tel: (888) 446-8199 or (757) 425-8555)*.

For a bed and breakfast alternative, an 1895 boarding school has been turned into **Barclay Cottage $–$$** *(400 16th St; tel: (757) 422-1956)*. **First Landing/Seashore State Park $** has 233 campsites *(tel: (800) 933-7275)*.

Dozens of eateries specialising in seafood are yours for the choosing. Recommendable boardwalk-bordering restaurants include **Waterman's $$** *(415 Atlantic Ave.; tel: (757) 428-3644)* and **Laverne's $$** *(7th and Oceanfront; tel: (757) 428-6836)*.

Further south, romantic candlelight enhances **Rudee's on the Inlet $$** (*227 Mediterranean Ave.; tel: (757) 425-1777*), close to **Rockefellers $$** (*308 Mediterranean Ave.; tel: (757) 422-5654*). Untouristy **Mary's $** (*616 Virginia Beach Pkwy (17th St); tel: (757) 428-1355*) is a mile inland from the surf.

Suggested tour

Total distance: 105 to 110 miles; add a total of 45–50 miles for drives to Great Dismal Swamp and Smithfield.

Time: Not counting those side trips, non-stop motoring between Norfolk, Portsmouth, Hampton and Newport News would take less than a full day. But, of course, allow adequate 'out-of-the-car' time for stopovers.

Links: Newport News and Hampton are on the same Tidewater peninsula as the Historic Triangle's Williamsburg–Jamestown–Yorktown route (*see page 146*). From Williamsburg, exit off the Colonial Parkway on to I-64 for a 23-mile southbound drive to Newport News. From Rte 13 on Virginia's Eastern Shore (*see page 190*), you can reach the Hampton Roads conurbation via an engineering wonder: the 17.6-mile Chesapeake Bay Bridge-Tunnel; toll payment required.

● Isle of Wight Visitors Center *130 Main St, Smithfield; tel: (800) 365-9339 or (757) 357-5182. Available: Old Town walking-tour brochures.*

Route: With **NORFOLK ●** as your starting point, drive east along Waterside Drive. Follow Rte 264W signs to **PORTSMOUTH ●** via the Downtown Tunnel; after 3 miles, you'll reach Crawford St, then Water St (alongside the Elizabeth River) in the downtown district, where High St is the main thoroughfare. Then backtrack to Norfolk.

Drive 20–22 miles east from Norfolk to **VIRGINIA BEACH ●** by way of Rte 264/44. Watch on your right for 68ft Mount Trashmore, a solid-waste landfill site transformed into a recreational park with lakes and playgrounds. The otherwise featureless expressway becomes residential 22nd St, leading straight to oceanfront Atlantic Ave.

Depart Virginia Beach by driving north on Atlantic Ave. to its 89th St terminus; turn on to Rte 60, curving past **First Landing/Seashore State Park**. Three miles beyond, you'll cross a bridge spanning northside Virginia Beach's Lynnhaven Inlet – you will be in Norfolk's Ocean View district after another 8 miles.

Rte 60 meets Rte 64 for access through the Hampton Roads Bridge-Tunnel to **HAMPTON ●**. Loop via Rte 258 through Hampton's Phoebus neighbourhood to reach Fort Monroe and its **Casemate Museum**. Hampton's other stellar attraction, the **Virginia Air and Space Center**, is right downtown.

From Hampton, drive 8–9 miles west on Rte 258 (Mercury Blvd, lined

Above
Virginia Beach

with shopping malls, fast-food places and petrol stations) to **NEWPORT NEWS** ❺, where James River shipbuilding works come into view. Turn right on to Jefferson Blvd to reach the **Mariners' Museum** and – further north – **Newport News Park**. Return to Hampton via Rte 64 and from there back into Norfolk via that highway's bridge-tunnel.

Detour: From Newport News, cross the James River Bridge to arrive in Isle of Wight County. Reaching Rte 10, drive 5.5 miles to **Smithfield**, one of Virginia's most photogenic communities with its Colonial, Federal and Victorian architecture, and home of Smithfield hams, famous state-wide. Fifteen houses and four public buildings are of 18th-century vintage; fourteen predate the Revolutionary War.

Also worth exploring

🏛 **Great Dismal Swamp National Wildlife Refuge $**
Headquarters at 3100 Desert Rd, Suffolk, VA; tel: (757) 968-3705; open daily sunrise–sunset.

Despite its less than alluring name, the **Great Dismal Swamp** is a national wildlife refuge of considerable scope (223,000 acres, partially extending into North Carolina) and unspoiled beauty, reached by driving a short distance south beyond metro Norfolk–Portsmouth. Wildlife inhabitants include black bears, wildcats, foxes, whitetailed deer and otters, plus more than 200 species of birds. Woodlands consist of bald cypress, juniper, black gum, red maple and yellow poplar trees. Nature trails and an interpretive boardwalk extend to centrally situated Lake Drummond, surrounded by an eerie forest of gnarled, moss-draped cypresses.

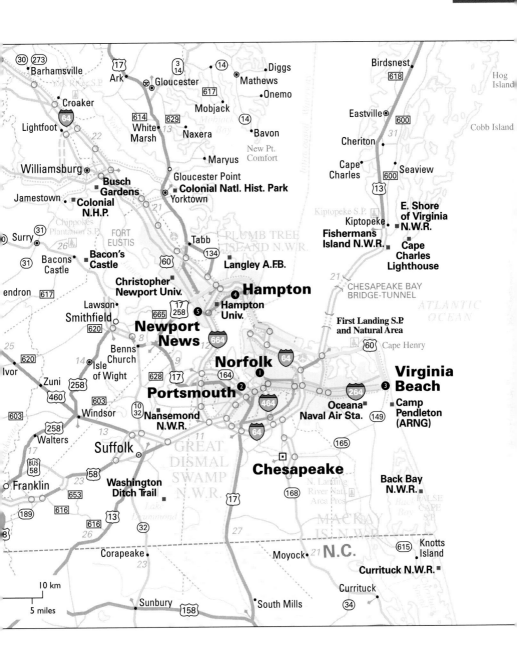

Baltimore

Ratings

Art and museums	●●●●●
Children	●●●●
Entertainment	●●●●
Gastronomy	●●●●
History	●●●●
Shopping	●●
Beaches	●○○○
Nature	●○○○

The Port of Baltimore's Colonial-era prominence and development as a rail-to-shipping centre made the city a major industrial centre, and in turn America's second largest port of entry for immigrants. These factors have given Baltimore the lively, vibrant and somewhat gritty blue-collar and ethnic character that visitors find so appealing today.

On a steady rise from its port's decline, Baltimore has re-invented its waterfront around the centrepiece of the newly restored USS *Constellation*, a 19th-century sailing ship. Once-dilapidated docks have been transformed into the brand new and beautiful Inner Harbor, its sturdy brick warehouses and sparkling new buildings filled with museums, trendy shops, entertainment stages and dozens of places to eat and drink. In the neighbourhoods around it, old ethnic enclaves remain, now studded with dining places. Today's Baltimore is fun, upbeat, historic and filled with activity.

Arriving and departing

ⓘ Baltimore Area Visitors Center *On the Inner Harbor opposite Constellation Pier; tel: (410) 837-INFO(4636) or (800) 282-6632; www.baltimore.org.*

⇄ Baltimore-Washington International Airport *Tel: (410) 859-7100.*

Amtrak *Tel: (800) 872-7245.*

Maryland Area Rail Commuter (MARC) *Tel: (800) 325-RAIL.*

Baltimore is linked to Washington by I-295, the Baltimore–Washington Parkway, and to Wilmington (Delaware) and Washington by I-95, which passes through the city. Rte 2 joins it with Annapolis to the south. The Baltimore Beltway, I-695, surrounds the city, with easy access to the centre from each exit.

Baltimore-Washington International Airport (BWI) is 10 miles south of the city centre, served by most major carriers, including budget-stretching Southwest Airlines.

Amtrak and Maryland Area Rail Commuter (MARC) connect the airport with Baltimore's Penn Station, a 20-minute ride. Mass Transit Administration (MTA) bus No 17 connects downtown Baltimore and the airport. More expensive, but convenient for those with luggage, BWI Airport Shuttle and Baltimore Airport Shuttle link Inner Harbor hotels to the airport. Frequent Amtrak trains connect Baltimore and BWI Airport to both New York and Washington, DC, while MARC runs between Baltimore and Washington, a 1-hour trip.

**Mass Transit
Administration
(MTA)**
Tel: (410) 539-5000.

BWI Airport Shuttle
Tel: (800) 258-3826.

**Baltimore Airport
Shuttle** Tel: (410) 821-5837.

Right
Washington Monument

Getting around

**Many of downtown
Baltimore's streets
are designated by a
compass point. The
north–south division is
Baltimore St, while
Charles St separates east
from west.**

Nearly everyone begins a Baltimore visit at the Inner Harbor, where many of the museums are located. To its north is the elegant old neighbourhood of Mount Vernon, dominated by the tall monument to George Washington. East of the harbour is Little Italy, south of which is lively Fells Point. Rising from the opposite side of Inner Harbor is historic Federal Hill, with more museums at its base. Most places visitors want to see are in or close to these areas.

While in Baltimore, you will certainly want to explore at least one of its old neighbourhoods, residential sections that retain their distinct flavours and their commercial cores, with shops, restaurants, churches and community spirit.

The many well-marked car parks may be crowded during weekdays. Commuter Rail stations at Beltway exits have Park-and-Ride lots, but if you are staying in the city, your hotel will have moderately priced or free parking.

Ed Kane's Water Taxi *Tel: (410) 563-3901 or (800) 658-8947; Nov–Mar daily, 1100–1800, Apr–Oct 1100–2100, Fri–Sat 1100–2400, May–early Sept 1000–2300, Fri–Sat 1000–2400.* In summer, boats run every 15–20 minutes.

Harbor Shuttle *Tel: (410) 675-2900.* Boats connect the Inner Harbor, Fells Point and Canton, with free shuttles to Fort McHenry and Little Italy, year-round, less frequently in winter.

Public transport

MTA bus and rail travel often involves several transfers, but MARC's bus and Metro map lists major attractions and hotels, with their best connections. You need the exact change, but for more than two rides in a day, buy the $3 day pass. To signal a stop, push the yellow stripe on the wall.

Water taxis and shuttles offer a cheap, fast, year-round service with 17 stops near major sights. Day passes include multiple reboarding, trolley connections to Fort McHenry, and discounts to attractions.

Tours

Clipper City **$$** *Next to Science Center; tel: (410) 539-6277; www.sailingship.com; Mon–Sat 1200 and 1500, Sun 1500 and 1800.* This schooner offers 2-hour and longer sailing tours.

Harbor Belle **$–$$$** *Henderson's Wharf, Fell St, Fells Point; tel: (410) 764-3928; cruises run Fri 1730, Sat 1915, Sun 1045.* This replica paddle-wheel steamboat offers buffet dinner on Sat and champagne brunch on Sun.

Harbor City Tours **$$** *Tel: (410) 254-TOUR(8687).* A 90-minute bus tour leaves Harborplace four times daily or will pick up at downtown hotels. Tours are witty, lively, good on history and include on-and-off reboarding; a combination ticket adds a 1-hour narrated harbour cruise.

Mount Vernon Walking Tour *Tel: (410) 605-0462.* An exploration of the sites and history of the neighbourhood's two most famous romances: Jerome Bonaparte and Betsy Patterson, and the Duke and Duchess of Windsor.

Nighthawk **$$** *Thames St, Fells Point; tel: (410) 276-7447; daily.* Sailing cruises.

Right
Inner Harbor

Sights

American Visionary Arts Museum $$ 800 Key Hwy, under Federal Hill; tel: (410) 244-1900; www.avam.org; open Tue–Sun 1000–1800.

B & O Railroad Museum $$ 901 W Pratt St, at Poppleton St; tel: (410) 752-2490; www.borail.org; open daily 1000–1700; weekend excursion trains ($) depart 1130, 1230, 1430, 1530.

Baltimore Maritime Museum $$ Pier III, E Pratt St, on the Inner Harbor; tel: (410) 396-3453; ships usually open daily 1000–1800, longer summer hours, weekends only in winter. Maritime attractions have joined as **National Historic Seaport of Baltimore** and sell combined admission passes with water transportation.

Baltimore Museum of Art $$ Art Museum Dr., Charles St at 31st St; tel: (410) 396-7100; open Wed–Fri 1100–1700, Sat-Sun 1100–1800. Free on Thur.

Baltimore Museum of Industry $ 1415 Key Hwy; tel: (410) 727-4808; open Tue–Fri 1200–1700, Sat 1000–1700, shorter winter hours.

Baltimore Zoo $ Druid Hill Park; tel: (410) 366-5466; open daily 1000–1600, later summer weekends.

American Visionary Arts Museum**

The artworks in this museum are by untrained or self-taught artists, uninfluenced by any formal traditions. They range from brilliant to bizarre, and the materials used can be surprising.

B & O Railroad Museum**

The roundhouse of America's first passenger railway station contains many beautifully restored historic steam and diesel locomotives, passenger cars and freight wagons. Visitors are welcome to climb aboard, and excursion trains run on weekends.

Baltimore Maritime Museum**

The floating collection includes the US Coastguard cutter *Taney*, the only ship surviving from the Japanese attack on Pearl Harbor in 1941. The record-holding US submarine *Torsk* (11,884 dives) was the last warship to sink an enemy vessel in World War II. Lightship *Chesapeake*, commissioned in 1939, served as a floating lighthouse in the Chesapeake Bay.

Baltimore Museum of Art***

The museum's displays rotate through its premier 85,000-piece permanent collection. The Matisse, Picasso and Cézanne paintings are outstanding, as are collections of ancient mosaics, African folk arts and eight galleries of Old Masters.

Baltimore Museum of Industry**

The museum is located in an 1870 oyster cannery complete with belt-driven machine shop and giant pressure cooker. Baltimore's garment, printing and other major industries are represented with displays and demonstrations of actual working machinery. Children enjoy hands-on experiences and the 1906 steam tugboat moored outside.

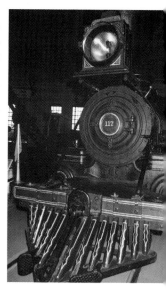

Baltimore Zoo**

In Druid Hill Park, the zoo includes among its realistic habitats an African Watering Hole, home to rhinoceros, zebra and gazelle. Siberian tigers are among the rare species. Hands-on activities earned it ratings as America's best zoo experience for children.

Basilica of the Assumption
Cathedral and Mulberry Sts; tel: (410) 727-3564; open 0700–1700 Mon– Fri, 0700–1830 Sat–Sun. Tours are given after the 1045 Sunday mass (about 1200).

Evergreen House $$
4545 N Charles St, Johns Hopkins University; tel: (410) 516-0341; open Mon–Fri 1000–1600, weekends 1300–1600; tours hourly until 1500.

Federal Hill *Off Light St, across Inner Harbor from the World Trade Center.*

Fells Point is
reached by Water Taxi from Inner Harbor or by following Caroline St south from Little Italy.

Flag House and 1812 Museum $ *844 E Pratt St, at Albemarle St; tel: (410) 837-1793; www.flaghouse.org; open Tue–Sat 1000–1600.*

Basilica of the Assumption*
The first Roman Catholic cathedral in the United States was designed by Benjamin Latrobe, and is considered one of the world's top examples of neo-classical building.

Evergreen House**
This 48-room Italianate mansion contains collections of Japanese netsuke, Tiffany glass, Chinese porcelain and post-Impressionist paintings. You can also tour the gardens and spacious grounds.

Federal Hill*
These gentrified old row houses, with antique shops, restaurants and the boisterous Cross Street Market, are a National Historic District. The best view of the Inner Harbor and city skyline is from the park at its northern end.

Fells Point***
Dating from the 1700s, Fells Point is an early maritime community, with homes of merchants, carpenters and shipwrights built close to the busy harbour. This lively neighbourhood of shops, antique stores, pubs and restaurants is a weekend favourite of young people and students, and shoppers at the markets on Broadway.

Flag House and 1812 Museum**
Built in 1793 and furnished to that period, this was the home of Mary Pickersgill, maker of the 9-by-13m (30-by-42ft) flag that survived the British bombardment of Fort McHenry during the War of 1812.

The Star-Spangled Banner

Francis Scott Key was on board a British ship negotiating the release of an American doctor, when the British fleet attempted to take Baltimore. Throughout the night of steady rocket fire he waited, until 'by the dawn's early light' he saw the huge American flag that Mary Pickersgill had sewn still 'gallantly streaming' over Fort McHenry. So moved was he by the sight of its 'broad stripes and bright stars' that he wrote a verse describing it which later became the national anthem, 'The Star-Spangled Banner'.

Opposite
B & O Railroad Museum

Above
Baltimore Museum of Industry

Fort McHenry National Monument $ *E Fort Ave.; tel: (410) 962-4290, open daily June–Aug 0800–2000, Sept–May 0800–1700.* Grounds, earthworks and the Visitors' Center are free. Water-taxi tickets include free shuttle to the fort.

Hampden *W 36th St, just west of Johns Hopkins University campus, is Hampden's central street.*

Homewood House *$$ 3400 N Charles St, Johns Hopkins University; tel: (410) 516-5589; open Tue–Sat 1100–1600, Sun 1200–1600, last tour 1530.*

Little Italy *Follow Pratt St east from Inner Harbor for two blocks, and Little Italy is just south, between Pratt St and Eastern Ave.*

Maryland Historical Society Museum and Library $ *201 W Monument St; tel: (410) 685-375; open Tue–Fri 1000–1700, Sat 0900–1700, Sun 1100–1700.*

Fort McHenry National Monument*
During the War of 1812, this 1790 brick fort withstood the British bombardment of Baltimore. The Visitors' Center has a film and exhibits, and inside the fort are officers' quarters, guardrooms, the powder magazine, earthworks and cannons. On summer weekends, uniformed actors re-enact life in the garrison.

Hampden*
Many visitors miss this neighbourhood away from the city centre that is like the Baltimore of several decades ago. Women there will call you 'Hon' (short for honey), and the laid-back pace is epitomised at the Café Hon (*see page 167*), the neighbouring Hometown Girl shop and in the not-too-old merchandise of Hampden's antique shops.

Homewood House**
Notable for the exceptional craftsmanship of its interior ornamentation and period furnishing, this is an outstanding example of Federal architecture, built in 1801.

Little Italy**
Baltimore's lively Italian community is filled with restaurants, two parish churches, colourful festivals and a Bocce Court on Stiles St. St Anthony's Festival in mid-June and Columbus Day in early October are especially active times.

Maryland Historical Society Museum and Library***
This packed museum includes the Radcliffe Maritime Museum, a Children's Gallery and Civil War and War of 1812 rooms. The original manuscript of 'The Star-Spangled Banner' is here, and its star attractions are the collections of American decorative arts and 19th-century American silver.

Above
Maryland Historical Society Museum

Maryland Science Center $$ *601 Light St; tel: (410) 685-2370; open summer Mon–Thur 0930–1800, Fri–Sun 0930–2000, winter 1000–1700, weekends 1000–1800.*

Mount Vernon *Charles and Monument Sts, north of Inner Harbor.*

National Aquarium in Baltimore $$$ *Pier 3, 561 E Pratt St; tel: (410) 576-3800; www.aqua.org; opening hours vary, usually summer 0900–1800 (later on weekends), Sept–June 1000–1700. Purchase a timed ticket early in the day.*

Port Discovery $$ *35 Market Pl.; tel: (410) 727-8120; open Tue–Sun 1000–1730.*

Below
National Aquarium
dolphin show

Maryland Science Center✦✦

Explore the Chesapeake Bay environments, the Hubble Space Telescope and space research, electricity and other sciences through hands-on exhibits and hourly live demonstrations (*weekdays 1030–1330, weekends 1030–1730*). The IMAX Theater and the Davis Planetarium also have regular shows.

Mount Vernon✦✦✦

Once the centre of Baltimore's high society, Mount Vernon is a well-kept mecca for arts and culture. Museums, fine shops, galleries and 'Restaurant Row' cluster around the genteel parks at the foot of the Washington Monument, and it is the best place to get a feel for the Baltimore of a century ago.

National Aquarium in Baltimore✦✦✦

The aquarium is a centre for education about the marine environment and conservation, and exhibits thousands of creatures – over 600 species of fish, birds, reptiles, amphibians and marine mammals. Stars include a giant octopus, electric eels, an Atlantic coral reef, a 16ft anaconda and a rain forest alive with sloths, parrots, monkeys, frogs and fishes. Dolphins perform in the Marine Mammal Pavilion, at daily 25-minute shows.

Port Discovery✦✦✦

Port Discovery is an exciting new interactive activity and learning museum for children aged 5 to 13, who will love crawling into a giant kitchen sink to learn about environmental issues or starring in a show in the TV studio.

Robert Long House
$ 812 S Ann St, Fells Point; tel: (410) 675-6750; tours Thur 1000, 1300 and 1500.

USS Constellation $$
Pier I, Constellation Dock at 301 E Pratt St; tel: (410) 539-1797; www.constellation.org; open for tours May–mid-Oct daily 1000–1800, off-season 1000–1600. May be open July–Aug evening hours.

Walters Art Gallery $$
600 N Charles St; tel: (410) 547-9000; www.thewalters.org; open Tue–Fri 1000–1600, Sat–Sun 1100–1700.

Washington Monument
$ N Charles St at Mount Vernon Pl; tel: (410) 837-4636; open Mon–Sat 1000–1700, Sun 1200–1700.

Westminster Hall Burying Ground and Catacombs Fayette and Greene Sts; tel: (410) 706-2072. There are free tours on the first and third Fri and Sat of each month (by reservation Apr–Nov).

World Trade Center $
Inner Harbor; open Mon–Sat 1000–1700, Sun 1200–1700.

Robert Long House✦✦
The city's oldest urban residence dates from 1765. Headquarters of Baltimore's Preservation Society, the restored brick house is furnished with period antiques as befits an 18th-century merchant's home.

USS Constellation✦✦✦
On the waterfront this is the star attraction. Its 1999 restoration yielded new information on the sailing ship's age and history, which included capturing slave-trade ships off Africa and carrying famine-relief supplies to Ireland.

Walters Art Gallery✦✦✦
The gallery's 30,000 objects cover five millennia of fine and applied art, ranging from ancient Egyptian sculpture and decorative arts to Fabergé eggs and Asian arts.

Washington Monument✦
This was the first architectural monument in the United States honouring George Washington. Climb its 228 steps for a view of the skyline and rooftops of Mount Vernon or see the small museum at its base.

Westminster Hall Burying Ground and Catacombs✦
The burial place of the writer Edgar Allen Poe, whose monument is in the corner plot, is among Baltimore's oldest cemeteries, with rare underground crypts, at an 1852 Presbyterian church.

World Trade Center✦
From the top of the 423ft tower of the world's tallest pentagonal building, you can get a long view of the city and a short view of Baltimore's history.

Festivals and events

Waterfront Festival Tel: (888) 225-8466. In late April there is food, boat rides and entertainment at Inner Harbor.

Independence Day Several days of activities celebrate 4 July, with a fireworks display at Inner Harbor.

Star-Spangled Banner Weekend Tel: (410) 962-4290. In early Sept Fort McHenry has re-enactments, ending with Sat fireworks.

Fells Point Fun Festival Tel: (410) 675-6756. In early Oct, this is a big street fair with crafts, music and lots of food.

Thanksgiving Parade Tel: (410) 837-4636. In late November, the parade has equestrian units, marching bands, clowns and floats.

Accommodation and food

Abercrombie Badger Bed and Breakfast $$ *58 West Biddle St; tel: (410) 244-7227 or (888) 9BADGER, fax: (410) 244-8415, www.badger-inn.com.* Directly opposite Meyerhoff Symphony Hall, these are elegantly decorated lodgings, ranging from cosy singles to large rooms with sitting areas and four-poster beds.

The Admiral Fell Inn $$ *888 South Broadway, Fells Point; tel: (410) 522-7377.* This quietly elegant inn overlooks the harbour. Room furnishings often include antique wooden seamen's chests. Outstanding breakfast buffet, and accommodating staff.

The Inn at Henderson's Wharf $$ *1000 Fell St, Fells Point; tel: (410) 522-7777 or (800) 522-2088.* On the waterfront, this inn has 38 well-furnished rooms.

Mr Mole Bed and Breakfast $$ *1601 Bolton St; tel: (410) 728-1179, fax: 410-728-3379, www.MrMoleBB.com.* Fine antiques and collections, and the Aussie innkeeper, make this stunningly decorated town house in Bolton Hill one of a kind. Two suites can each accommodate three guests – good for families.

Restaurants gather in neighbourhoods, with most near the waterfront, Little Italy, Fells Point and along Charles Street in Mount Vernon.

Amicci's $ *231 High St, Little Italy; tel: (410) 528-1096.* Its checked tablecloths and the warm, kindly atmosphere epitomise traditional family Italian restaurants.

Bertha's $$ *734 S Broadway; tel: (410) 327-5795.* The mussels are famous, although it serves other dishes. Sunday brunch (*1130–1400; $*) offers country sausages or creamed oysters. Mrs McKinnon's Scottish afternoon tea (*Mon–Sat 1500–1700; $*) is by reservation.

Café Hon $ *1002 W 36th St, in Hampden; tel: (410) 243-1230.* This is a relaxed restaurant with home-style favourites, including lasagna, meatloaf and good crabcakes. Specials might be fried chicken (Tue) or fish and chips (Fri).

Ciao Bella $$ *236 S High St, Little Italy; tel: (410) 685-7733.* A traditional Italian menu includes excellent veal, with polished service and ambience.

Fat Lulu's $$ *1818 Maryland Ave.; tel: (410) 685-4665.* Cajun and Creole food is served up with jazz and blues.

Hamilton's $$ *888 S Broadway, Fells Point; tel: (410) 552-2195.* One of the city's finest restaurants serves well-presented, creative dishes where superb flavour is the bottom line. Starters may include frogs' legs or *foie gras* and main dishes might feature pheasant.

Louie's Café \$\$ *518 N Charles St; tel: (410) 230-2998.* The stunning interior is matched by an innovative menu featuring venison, catfish, and mahi-mahi baked in coconut milk. Live jazz at dinner and weekend brunch.

Obrycki's \$\$–\$\$\$ *1727 E Pratt St; tel: (410) 732-6399.* Baltimoreans' favourite waterfront crab house since the 1940s specialises in hard-shelled crabs, crabcakes or delicious Crab Imperial. Closed in winter.

Women's Industrial Exchange Tea Room \$ *333 N Charles St; tel: (410) 685-4388; open Mon–Fri 0700–1400.* The Tea Room serves traditional breakfast and lunch dishes, and is known for chicken salad and devilled eggs. No credit cards.

Vaccaro's \$ *222 Abermarle St; tel: (410) 685-4905; open 0700–2400.* The restaurants in Little Italy get their desserts from this café; expect a wait on weekend evenings.

Wayne's Bar-B-Que \$\$ *Harborplace Pavilion, 301 Light St; tel: (410) 539-3810.* Barbecue and good beers are combined with country music.

Entertainment

Baltimore Opera Company *Lyric Opera House, 140 W Mount Royal Ave.; tel: (410) 494-2712.*

Baltimore Symphony Orchestra *Joseph Meyerhoff Symphony Hall, 12121 Cathedral St; tel: (410) 783-8000.*

Pier 6 Concert Pavilion *Pier 6, Pratt St; tel: (410) 837-4636; summer.*

Inner Harbor Ice Rink *Rash Field, past Science Center; open late Nov–early Mar weekdays 1200–1400, 1600–1800, 1900–2100, Sat 1000–1800, 1900–2200, Sun 1200–1700, 1900–2100.*

Opposite
Inner Harbor

Baltimore is known for the broad range of its cultural life. **Baltimore Opera Company** presents grand opera starring international artists, with projected English translation. The **Baltimore Symphony Orchestra** has a steady schedule of top popular and classical performers such as Yo-Yo Ma, Pinchas Zukerman and Itzhak Perlman. The Inner Harbor has several venues for performances, in all price ranges, many free, including **Pier 6 Concert Pavilion**, a tent-theatre for rock, blues, country and jazz.

Inner Harbor Ice Rink offers public skating and free entertainment, including lunch-hour concerts, skating parties and inexpensive public lessons.

Shopping

Fells Point is filled with artists' studios, craft shops and antique shops. **Bay and Country Crafts** (*1635 Lancaster St*) specialises in Chesapeake Bay crafts, including carved wooden duck decoys. **Elzeard Pottery** (*602 South Ann St*) and **The Silver Store** (*1640 Thames St*) sell handmade pottery and sterling silver jewellery respectively. Some shops close winter weekdays.

North Charles St in Mount Vernon has art and craft galleries and **Women's Industrial Exchange** (*333 N Charles St*) where they sell homely handwork, such as knitted mittens and baby gifts. **Antiques Row** (*N Howard and W Reed Sts*) has several shops with silver,

Baltimore is known for its noisy, busy neighbourhood markets, where many locals do their daily shopping. The largest (140 vendors) is **Lexington Market**, on W Lexington St. **Cross St Market** is on Federal Hill and two are on Broadway in Fells Point. These are excellent places to eat lunch or find picnic foods.

Victoriana and pricey furniture. **The Antique Warehouse** (*1300 Jackson St; open Tue–Sun*) on Federal Hill is a multi-dealer market of antiques and collectibles.

Harborplace Pavilion and The Gallery, connected by a skywalk, or Market Center, on Franklin and Liberty Sts, are shopping malls with chain stores and boutiques.

Suggested walk

Total distance: About 2 miles, a mile or so more including the detour.

Time: Allow at least a couple of hours to take in the sights, and a full day if you want to spend some time visiting the attractions.

Route: Begin at the Visitors' Center at Inner Harbor and follow the **Waterfront Promenade** past USS *CONSTELLATION* ❶ to the NATIONAL AQUARIUM ❷. Crossing the footbridge, you will come to the Coastguard cutter *Taney*, the submarine *Torsk* and the lightship *Chesapeake*, all part of the **BALTIMORE MARITIME MUSEUM** ❸.

Turning your back on the harbour for a moment, walk to Pratt St and turn left. You will pass I M Pei's pentagonal **WORLD TRADE CENTER** ❹ and **The Gallery** ❺, a modern complex of shops and eateries. Continue to Charles St and turn right.

Detour: Instead of turning left on Pratt St, turn right, crossing the wide street to find **FLAG HOUSE** ❻, on your left, and the several blocks of **LITTLE ITALY** ❼ extending to your right. Return along Pratt St.

Charles St is lined with impressive buildings, the first of which is the half-timbered German Renaissance-style **Hansa Haus** ❽, built for the North German Lloyd Steamship Company. As you climb the hill, you will pass several ornate stone-worked façades and doorways. At Saratoga St is **St Paul's Episcopal Church** ❾, a brick Romanesque building with Tiffany stained-glass windows.

As Charles St splits to accommodate Washington Place, the **WALTERS ART GALLERY** ❿ is on the left. Ahead is the **WASHINGTON MONUMENT** ⓫. This area is called Mount Vernon, in honour of Washington's Virginia plantation. At the monument, look to the right, down **East Monument St**, to see **Brownstone Row** ⓬. The statue in the park is of the New Englander who endowed **Peabody Conservatory** ⓭, to your right; it is worth stepping inside to see the magnificent library. Opposite the conservatory is the **Mount Vernon Place United Methodist Church** ⓮, a masterpiece of Victorian Gothic in coloured sandstone.

On the other side of the monument, on **West Monument St**, are some of Baltimore's most elegant town houses, separated by a tranquil park. At the far end of the park, turn right on to **Cathedral St** and walk one block to **Madison St**, turning left. At the corner of **Park Ave.** is the **Presbyterian church** ⓯, which has Baltimore's highest spire and a remarkable plaster-work interior, with a fan-vaulted ceiling similar to that of Henry VII's chapel in London's Westminster Abbey.

Turn left on **Park Ave.** and continue to West Monument St, where a left turn brings you past the **MARYLAND HISTORICAL SOCIETY** ⓰, in the 1847 Enoch Pratt House. Opposite, the **Episcopal church** has a fine wrought-iron chancel gate and a Tiffany stained-glass window. At Cathedral St, turn right to reach the neo-classical **BASILICA OF THE ASSUMPTION** ⓱, and opposite, the art-deco **Enoch Pratt Free Library** ⓲.

Two blocks further downhill, Saratoga St angles to the left, returning you to Charles St. Turn right and follow it to **Fayette St**, turning left. At **Calvert St** you will see the **Battle Monument**, commemorating all who died in the British attack on the city in 1814. A block further on is the ornate Second Empire-style **City Hall** with some of the country's best examples of architectural ironwork. A right turn on to **Commerce St** brings you back to the Visitors' Center at **Inner Harbor**.

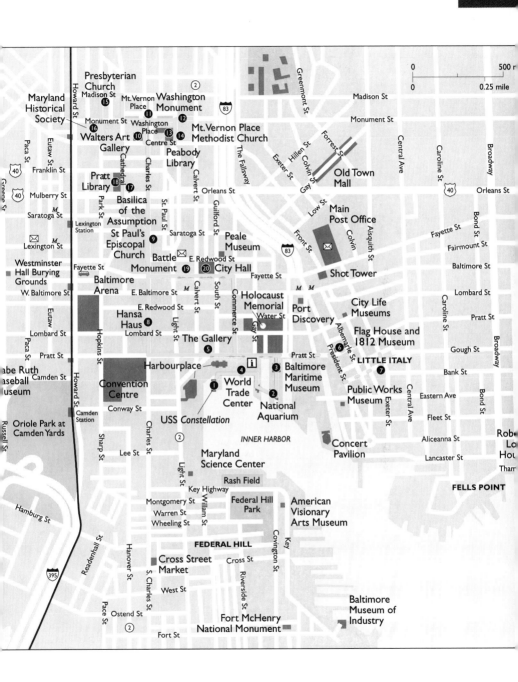

0 500 r
0 0.25 mile

Presbyterian Church
Maryland Historical Society
Madison St
Mt. Vernon Place
15
Washington Monument
2
Madison St
Monument St
12
Monument St
Washington Place
13 14
Mt. Vernon Place Methodist Church
Walters Art Gallery
16
10
Centre St
Peabody Library
Franklin St
Pratt Library
18
17
Orleans St
Old Town Mall
Mulberry St
Basilica of the Assumption
Orleans St
Saratoga St
Lexington Station
Saratoga St
Peale Museum
Main Post Office
Lexington St
St Paul's Episcopal Church
9
Battle Monument
19
E. Redwood St
20
City Hall
Shot Tower
Westminster Hall Burying Grounds
Fayette St
Fayette St
W. Baltimore St
Baltimore Arena
E. Baltimore St
City Life Museums
E. Redwood St
Holocaust Memorial
Pratt St
Lombard St
Hansa Haus
8
Lombard St
Port Discovery
Flag House and 1812 Museum
Gough St
Pratt St
The Gallery
5
Pratt St
LITTLE ITALY
7
Harbourplace
4
i
3
Baltimore Maritime Museum
Bank St
abe Ruth aseball useum
Camden St
Convention Centre
World Trade Center
1
Public Works Museum
Eastern Ave
Conway St
2
National Aquarium
Fleet St
USS Constellation
Oriole Park at Camden Yards
Camden Station
INNER HARBOR
Concert Pavilion
Aliceanna St
Lee St
Maryland Science Center
Lancaster St
Rash Field
FELLS POINT
Key Highway
Montgomery St
Federal Hill Park
American Visionary Arts Museum
Warren St
Wheeling St
FEDERAL HILL
Cross Street Market
Cross St
West St
Baltimore Museum of Industry
Ostend St
2
Fort McHenry National Monument
Fort St

Annapolis

Ratings

History	●●●●●
Gastronomy	●●●●
Shopping and crafts	●●●●
Beaches	●●●
Entertainment	●●●
Art and museums	●●
Nature and wildlife	●●
Children	●

Ships and boats are at the very heart of Annapolis. The town began as a province of Lord Baltimore's colony, to which he invited Puritans disenchanted with the religious restrictions of Virginia. This promise of freedom of worship soon attracted Catholics from Britain, who became influential as the town grew to become an important harbour and political centre. Most of the downtown historic district dates from the Colonial era.

Almost completely surrounded by water, Annapolis was a logical location for the US Naval Academy, whose presence in the town centre makes it very much a part of local life. When the midshipmen march to football games at Memorial Stadium, all Annapolis stops to watch them. Leisure life revolves around sailing, and in all but the foulest weather you'll see boats in the water.

Arriving and departing

ⓘ Annapolis Visitors Bureau 26 West St, just off Church Circle; tel: (410) 280-0445; open daily 0900–1700. An information kiosk is at City Dock.

US-301/50 runs east to west along northern Annapolis, connecting it to Washington, DC, and to the Eastern Shore via the Bay Bridge. Both Rte 2, which approaches Annapolis from Southern Maryland, and I-97 link it to the Baltimore Beltway.

Parking

Car parks are well signposted, off Main St and next to the Visitor Center, near Church Circle. When shopping, ask for discount parking validation. Metered parking has a well-enforced 2-hour limit. The Navy-Marine Corps Stadium, north of town, offers all-day parking and shuttle buses downtown, but check when the last bus returns.

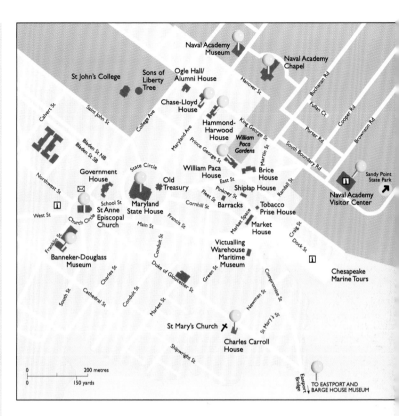

Getting around

Life in Annapolis centres around City Dock, from which Main St
climbs the hill to the Maryland Capitol. Its narrow winding Colonial
streets make Annapolis a charming place to walk. Driving is difficult,
with snarled traffic and limited parking. Most attractions are close to
downtown, best reached on foot. Other parts of Annapolis, such as
restaurants along Spa and Back Creeks, are connected by water taxi,
but are not a long walk from the central dock area.

Tours
Annapolis Walkabout $$ (223 S Cherry Grove Ave.; tel: (410) 263-8253;
open Apr–Oct Sat–Sun) is led by an architectural historian.
Beginagain $$$ (tel: (410) 626-1422; open daily) is a small sailing boat
with 3-hour tours from City Dock.
Chesapeake Marine Tours $$–$$$ (Slip 20, City Dock; tel: (410) 268-
7600; open Apr–Sept daily) cruise the harbour, river and into

Chesapeake Bay, and also make day excursions to St Michaels, on the Eastern Shore.

Schooner Woodwind $$$ *(tel: (410) 263-7837; open May–Sept)* has 2-hour sailing cruises from the Marriott Hotel, next to City Dock. The Wed evening sail includes watching sailing-boat races.

Discover Annapolis Tours $$ *(tel: (410) 626-6000)* has daily 1-hour minibus tours Apr–Nov from the Visitor Center on West St.

Historic Annapolis Foundation $ *(77 Main St; tel: (410) 268-5576, open Mon–Sat 1000–1700, Sun 1200–1700)* rents recorded self-guided tours, one highlighting African-American history.

Three Centuries Tours of Annapolis $$ *(48 Maryland Ave.; tel: (410) 263-5401; open Apr–Oct daily, Nov–Mar Sat)* conduct 2-hour walking tours of the historic district, leaving from the Visitor Center.

Sights

Banneker-Douglass Museum *84 Franklin St; tel: (410) 974-2893; open Tue–Fri 1000–1500, Sat 1200–1600.*

Banneker-Douglass Museum✦

In the former Mount Moriah African Methodist Episcopal Church, there are changing exhibits of photographs and collections relating to Maryland's Black heritage and the art of Africa and African-Americans.

Barge House Museum *Bay Shore Dr. at the end of Second St, Eastport; tel: (410) 268-1802; open Sat 1100–1600 or by appointment.*

Barge House Museum✦

Maritime collections and material give an interesting insight into the cultural history of the neighbourhood, once home to boat-builders and watermen.

Charles Carroll House $ *107 Duke of Gloucester St; tel: (410) 269-1737; open Fri, Sun and holidays 1200–1600, Sat 1000–1400.*

Charles Carroll House✦✦

The birthplace and home of Declaration of Independence signer Charles Carroll of Carrollton, a wealthy and influential man who helped found America's first railroad. The house, in restoration, sits above 18th-century terraced gardens and has frequent interactive programmes with costumed interpreters.

Chase-Lloyd House $ *22 Maryland Ave.; tel: (410) 263-2723; open Mon–Sat 1400–1600.*

Chase-Lloyd House✦✦

Begun in 1769 and completed by William Buckland on an unlimited budget, within its outstanding interior is possibly the finest cantilevered stairway built in the colony; ornate carvings and silver fixtures decorate the dining room.

Hammond-Harwood House $$ *19 Maryland Ave.; tel: (410) 269-1714; hourly tours Mon–Sat 1000–1530, Sun 1200–1530.*

Hammond-Harwood House✦✦✦

The last work of architect William Buckland, the house was built in 1774 at the height of Annapolis's Golden Age. In almost entirely original condition, it is among the most beautiful examples of late colonial architecture in America. The highlight is the dining room, with a rococo carved overmantel, finely detailed mouldings and carved window shutters. The quoined window above the stairway is

Maryland State House *State Circle; tel: (410) 974-3400; open daily 0900–1700; free 30-minute tours daily 1100 and 1500.*

The Naval Academy Chapel *Near Gate 3, Maryland Ave.; open Mon–Sat 0900–1600, Sun 1300–1600.*

inspired by the church of St Martin-in-the-Fields in London. The house has several Peale portraits and outstanding furniture by Charles Shaw, one of colonial America's finest cabinetmakers.

Maryland State House⁕

America's oldest State House in continuous use, and the only one to have served as the US Capitol. In this building the congress met in 1783 and 1784, George Washington resigned his command of the Continental Army and the Treaty of Paris was ratified, officially ending the American Revolution. The 1788 dome is the largest wooden dome in the United States.

The Naval Academy Chapel⁕⁕

The imposing dome forms a backdrop for Annapolis's historic district, and contains impressive stained-glass windows, several by Louis Comfort Tiffany. The baptismal font in St Andrew's Chapel is made of wood from the USS *Constitution*. Underneath the Rotunda lies the Crypt of John Paul Jones, the Revolutionary War hero.

Below
Tiffany window, Naval Academy Chapel

The signers

In Maryland much is made of those who signed the Declaration of Independence, pledging 'our lives, our fortunes and our sacred honor'. The four Annapolis men who signed for Maryland joined counterparts from other colonies to lead a cause which would cost many their lives and even more their fortunes. Charles Carroll of Carrollton, important in both Annapolis and Baltimore, was the only Catholic and one of the few lucky ones. He outlived all the others and continued to be one of the wealthiest and most influential men of his time.

The Naval Academy Museum
Near Gate 3, Maryland Ave.;
open Mon–Sat 0900–1700,
Sun 1100–1700.

The Naval Academy Visitor Center Gate 1,
King George St; tel: (410)
263-6933; open daily
Mar–Dec 0900–1700,
Jan–Feb 0900–1600.

William Paca House and Gardens $$ 186
Prince George St; tel: (410)
263-5553; open Mon–Sat
1000–1600, Sun
1200–1600; Jan–Feb
Sat–Sun only. Garden until
1700 Apr–Oct.

St Anne Episcopal Church Church Circle;
open daily 0800–1800.

Sandy Point State Park
East College Parkway,
signposted from US-301/50
west of Bay Bridge; tel: (410)
974-2149.

The Naval Academy Museum✦

Though small, the museum is filled with artefacts of naval history and academy traditions, such as the desk from the battleship *Missouri* on which Fleet Admiral Chester Nimitz signed the Japanese surrender in Tokyo Bay in 1945. One room contains ship models made contemporaneously with the original ships, dating back as far as 1650. A most unusual collection of intricate ship models was carved from bone by French sailors interned in British prison ships between 1756 and 1815.

The Naval Academy Visitor Center✦✦

The academy trains over 4000 cadets as Navy or Marine Corps officers and is filled with history and tradition. Guided tours ($$) begin here, where there are also exhibits and a film on the academy. Self-guided tours of the grounds are free.

William Paca House and Gardens✦✦✦

The restored home of a signer of the Declaration of Independence and Governor of Maryland is combined here with the city's premier historic garden. Thirteen period furnished rooms include an outstanding collection of antique American silver and decorative arts.

The beautiful gardens drop gently in terraces, and feature a boxwood parterre with topiary centrepieces and potted standards, five tall cone-shaped holly trees, a medicinal herb garden and a domed summer house. A visitors' centre has displays on historical garden themes. The re-creation of the original garden has been based on the site's archaeology and on a contemporary painting.

St Anne Episcopal Church✦✦

In Colonial days this was the royal governor's parish; King William presented the silver communion service in 1695, which is still in use. Three parishioners signed the Declaration of Independence. See the Tiffany stained-glass window, the needlepoint kneelers and the colony's last royal governor's grave in the churchyard.

Sandy Point State Park✦✦

A day-use beach park, with changing facilities, food vendors, trails, boats for hire, picnic areas and excellent windsurfing off the long beach. The waterfront is prime birding territory during spring and fall migrations.

Accommodation and food

Annapolis Accommodations (*66 Maryland Ave.; tel: (410) 280-0900 or (800) 715-1000*) represents hotels, motels and bed and breakfast homes, and can describe properties to help you find the right one.

The Blue Heron $$ (*172 Green St; tel: (410) 263-9171 or (888) 999-1839*) is a three-storey 1839 brick residence on a quiet street, a block from City Docks and Main St. Each guest room has a working fireplace and private bath.

The Charles Inn $$–$$$ (*74 Charles St; tel: (410) 268-1451*) close to Church Circle, is a nicely restored Civil War-era home with off-street parking. The three rooms have featherbeds and private baths with antique deep tubs or whirlpools. A full breakfast is elegantly served.

Country Inn and Suites (*2600 Housley Rd; tel: (410) 571-6700 or (800) 456-4000, www.countryinns.com*) has spacious suites in a location convenient to Rte 2, USA-301/50 and I-97, just east of the city, with bus shuttles to and from downtown Annapolis.

Flag House Inn $$ (*26 Randall St; tel: (410) 280-2721 or (800) 437-4825*), a historic district house, between City Dock and the academy, which has off-street parking and serves English breakfasts. Its brochure includes an excellent illustrated map of attractions, shops and restaurants.

Gibson's Lodgings $$ (*110 Prince George St; tel: (410) 268-5555*) is close to City Dock, in historic district houses, with parking. The beautifully decorated rooms have period antiques.

Harborview Boat and Breakfast $$ (*tel: (800) 877-9330, www.harborviewbnb.com*) offers staterooms in several classic yachts, including breakfast and an evening cruise.

Historic Inns of Annapolis $$ (*16 Church Circle; tel: (410) 263-2641*) includes four 18th- and 19th-century buildings close to the Capitol Building, with combined check-in at the Governor Calvert House, 58 State Circle. Rooms vary from slightly dowdy to newly renovated and period furnished, as in Robert Johnson House.

Loews Annapolis Hotel $$ (*126 West St; tel: (410) 263-7777*), a modern hotel within walking distance of the Naval Academy and City Dock, has a pool, tennis courts, health club and business centre.

Schooner *Woodwind* $$$ (*tel: (410) 263-8619, www.schooner-woodwind.com; available weekends only*) has four double-berth air-conditioned staterooms and includes a sunset cruise.

Most Annapolis restaurants are in the dock area, along Main St or in nearby Eastport, which is a short walk along the waterfront from the docks. Several more line West St, at the top of the hill past the Capitol.

Above
Annapolis Post Office

Opposite
The Naval Academy

All the restaurants listed below are open daily unless otherwise noted.

Aromi d'Italia Café $ (*8 Dock St, behind the information kiosk; tel: (410) 263-1300*) specialises in Italian ice cream, sandwiches, salads and pizza, with a few daily full meal specials.

Buddy's Crabs and Ribs $$ (*100 Main St; tel: (410) 626-1100*) is known for these two Maryland specialties, but serves a full seafood menu. Crispy sesame crackers and tangy pickles are on every table. The Blue Ridge beer is a good local choice. All-you-can-eat lunch buffets on weekdays. Sun breakfast buffet includes hearty seafood dishes.

**Carrol's Creek Restaurant $$** (*410 Severn Ave., Eastport; tel: (410) 263-8102*) commands a fine harbour view. Fresh seafood is prepared in elegant and innovative styles, with a new way each day for rockfish (bass), and a four-course Bay Dinner ($$$) including several of their specialties such as Maryland crab soup.

Griffin's $$ (*Market Space; tel: (410) 268-2576*) has sandwiches, pasta dishes and Caribbean jerked chicken breast in either the pub or adjacent dining room.

The Market House (*City Dock*) is a traditional market, small, but with a bakery, deli, raw bar, pizza, sandwiches and ice cream as well as ingredients for picnics.

Below
Annapolis Historic District

Phillips $$ (*City Dock; tel: (410) 990-9888*) is one of several in this small local chain, dependable for seafood. Crabcake platters and dishes of crabcakes with grilled fish are a good way to sample local fare.

Ram's Head Tavern $$ (*33 West St; tel: (410) 268-4545*) is also the Fordham Brewing Co, the town's only micro-brewery. Options for seating include the original cosy pub, a tiny tearoom or patio tables in fair weather. A cosmopolitan menu includes shepherd's pie, crabcakes, London Broil, Jambalaya, shellfish pie and, naturally, fine ales.

Treaty of Paris Restaurant $$ (*16 Church Circle; tel: (410) 263-2641*) offers continental favourites, such as Beef Wellington, as well as updated American dishes, served in an 18th-century setting. Three meals are served daily.

Annapolis Farmers' Market *Riva Rd at Truman Pkwy, accessible from Exit 22 off US-301/50; open Sat 0700–1200.*

Pennsylvania Dutch Farmers' Market *Annapolis Harbor Center, Solomons Island Rd; open Thur 1000–1800, Fri 0900–1800, Sat 0900–1500. Country foods, baked goods, vegetables, cheese and cured meats.*

Maryland Hall for the Creative Arts *801 Chase St; tel: (410) 263-5544; www.mdhallarts.org.*

Annapolis Opera, Inc *Tel: (410) 267-8135; www.mdhallarts.org.*

Annapolis Symphony Orchestra *Tel: (410) 269-1132; Oct–May.*

Ballet Theater of Annapolis *Tel: (410) 263-8289.*

The Annapolis Chorale *Tel: (410) 263-1906; Sept–May.*

Annapolis Summer Garden Theater *143 Compromise St; tel: (410) 268-9212; late May–Aug, Thur–Sun.*

Colonial Players *108 East St; tel: (410) 268-7373.*

Annapolis Sailing School *601 Sixth St; tel: (800) 638-9192. Adults and children are taught how to handle a sailing boat. To try without committing yourself to formal lessons, go any morning at 1000 for 'Try-Sail'.*

Shopping

Main St and nearby streets are lined with boutiques and shops, several featuring fine crafts and nautical items. Short Maryland Ave., between State Circle and the Academy Gate 3, has more, especially antique shops. Most are open Mon–Sat 1000–1500, Sun 1200–1700, often with longer summer evening hours.

Save the Bay Shop (*188 Main St*) carries books, crafts and gifts supporting the Chesapeake Bay Foundation's environmental work. **Historic Annapolis Foundation Museum Store** (*77 Main St*) offers quality crafts and historic reproductions, many with a maritime theme. At **Annapolis Pottery** (*40 State Circle*) demonstrations show stoneware pottery being made. **The League of Maryland Craftsmen** (*54 Maryland Ave.*) sells pottery, glass, wood, fibre arts and baskets. Shortly beyond Academy Gate 3, at the end of Maryland Ave., is the **Naval Institute Bookstore** (*open Mon–Sat 0900–1700, Sun 1100–1700*) in the ground floor of the museum, with books on every aspect of the sea and the US Navy, nautical gifts and Naval Academy insignia items.

Annapolis Antique Gallery (*2009 West St*) is where 40 antique dealers show their best furniture, china, decoys and collectibles.

Entertainment

Annapolis offers a rich and varied programme of performing arts events. Major performances are held at **Maryland Hall for the Creative Arts**, including grand operas, operetta and Broadway musicals presented by **Annapolis Opera**, classical concerts by the **Annapolis Symphony Orchestra** and classical and modern dance by the professional **Ballet Theater of Annapolis**. Popular and classical works can also be heard here, performed by **The Annapolis Chorale**, a 150-voice full chorus.

The **Annapolis Summer Garden Theater** presents Broadway musicals in an outdoor setting and the **Colonial Players** have five theatre-in-the-round productions a year.

Suggested walk

Distance: 2–3 miles, 3–4 with both detours.

Time: A leisurely stroll looking at the sights will take about 2 hours; but to explore the attractions thoroughly allow for a whole day.

Route: Begin at **City Docks** ❶, the historic heart of Annapolis, where you may see the *Stanley Norman*, a skipjack belonging to Save the Bay Federation, or possibly the sailing ship *Pride of Baltimore*, with its raked masts. Several harbour and river excursions begin at City Docks.

Maps

The free *Destinations* guide to Annapolis includes a good map, keyed to descriptions of 40 numbered sites, each coded to show its historic period. The list shows significant private buildings as well as those open for tours. The smaller but also excellent map inside the **Flag House Inn** brochure includes restaurants and other points of interest.

After touring the docks, head to the right-hand corner of Market Square, behind the market building, next to Maria's Restaurant. At the corner of Pinkney St is the **Tobacco Prise House ❷**, a warehouse from the early 1800s, and next door the **Shiplap House ❸**, built about 1715, and one of the oldest in the city. Follow Pinkney St to East St, where a right and a quick left will bring you to the **WILLIAM PACA HOUSE AND GARDENS ❹**, on Prince George St.

Detour: Take a few moments to wander through the narrow old streets that ascend the hill, including Cornhill and Fleet Sts, and to admire the restored residences and their doorways.

Continue on Prince George St to Maryland Ave., turning right to pass the 1774 **HAMMOND-HARWOOD HOUSE ❺**, around the corner, an excellent example of late Colonial architecture.

Across the street is the 1769 **CHASE-LLOYD HOUSE ❻**, known for its fine interior. Maryland Ave. leads on to Gate 3 of the US Naval Academy. Through the gate on your right is the grand dome of the **NAVAL ACADEMY CHAPEL ❼**, and the entrance to the **Crypt of John Paul Jones ❽**. Beyond, on the left is the **NAVAL ACADEMY MUSEUM ❾**. Return to the gate and turn right, walking one block to College St, following it to the left past the campus of **St John's College ❿**, where buildings date from as early as 1722. On the campus is the giant old **Sons of Liberty Tree ⓫**, a meeting place for patriots plotting the American Revolution.

A right on North St brings you to State Circle and **MARYLAND STATE HOUSE ⓬**. In its grounds are a small brick treasury building from 1737 and a cannon that arrived with the first settlers aboard the *Dove*, in 1634. Continue around State Circle to School St, on the corner of which is **Government House ⓭**, official residence of Maryland's Governor.

School St leads directly into Church Circle, with **ST ANNE EPISCOPAL CHURCH ⓮** in its centre. Directly opposite School St is West St, with several restaurants and the **Annapolis Visitors Bureau ⓯**.

Head downhill from Church Circle on Duke of Gloucester St to **CHARLES CARROLL HOUSE ⓰** at No 107 and its terraced gardens. Next to the house, **St Mary's Church ⓱**, a Victorian Gothic building with ribbed vaulting and a carved altar screen, is usually open during daylight. The cornerstone was laid in 1858 by Saint John Neuman. From the end of Duke of Gloucester St, a left on to Compromise St leads back along the waterfront to your starting point at City Dock.

Detour: Those with energy to spare can turn right on Compromise St, crossing the bridge over Spa Creek to explore the old watermen's and boat-building neighbourhood of Eastport.

Also worth exploring

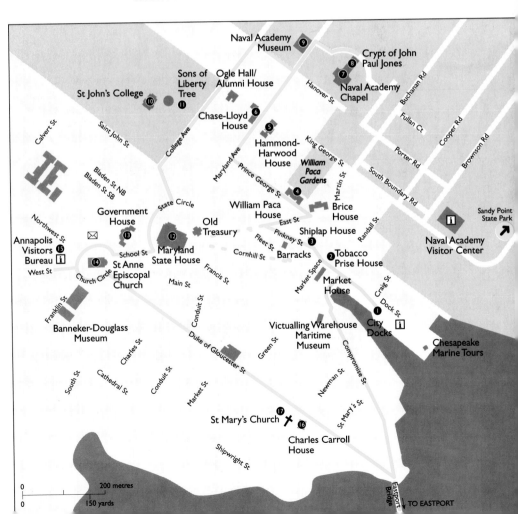 **London Town House and Garden**
$$ *London Town Rd, off Rte 253, Edgewater; tel: (410) 222-1919; open Mon–Sat 1000–1600, Sun 1200–1600. To reach Edgewater, follow Rte 2 south from the city.*

London Town House and Garden overlooks South River at the major ferry to Annapolis, where George Washington always crossed. Ships loaded tobacco from area plantations in a town of 300 people. But by 1800 London Town had almost disappeared. Today you can watch archaeologists dig up the long-vanished streets and uncover artefacts beneath **Rumney's Tavern**.

Only the large brick **William Brown House** remains, restored and furnished to 18th-century condition. The authentic household linens made by volunteers include handwoven linen nappies and embroidered bed hangings. Gardens surround the visitors' centre, above a dell filled with azaleas in the spring. The rare 1720 log-built tobacco house was relocated here.

Eastern Shore

Ratings

Nature and wildlife	●●●●●
Beaches	●●●●
Children	●●●
Gastronomy	●●●
Shopping and crafts	●●●
Art and museums	●●
Entertainment	●●
Historical sights	●●

Maryland's Eastern Shore joins with the state of Delaware and a tiny piece of Virginia to form the Delmarva Peninsula, based on the names of the three states. The landscape is flat or, at the most, gently rolling. Wide tidal rivers and estuaries cut it deeply, and the shore is further broken by islands and long fingers of water-surrounded land.

Facing the Atlantic Ocean to the east, a long strip of barrier island extends along all three states. Its smooth beaches, dunes and marshes provide a habitat for shore birds and for the famous wild horses, often called Chincoteague ponies. Historic small towns dot the peninsula, many of them fishing villages whence watermen once sailed in search of the Chesapeake's rich store of shellfish.

CAMBRIDGE✦✦

ℹ Dorchester County Visitors Center
Sailwinds Park; tel: (410) 228-1000 or (800) 522-8687;
www.tourdorchester.org.

Ⓟ Loblolly Lodge
South of Church Creek; tel: (410) 397-3033.
Canoes can be hired for paddling and birding in Blackwater Refuge.

The High Street's elegant Federal, Queen Anne, Second Empire and High Victorian homes give Cambridge an air of grace and make strolling a pleasure. The **Richardson Museum**✦✦ (*401 High St; tel: (410) 221-1871; open Apr–Oct, Wed, Sat–Sun 1300–1600*) records a rich maritime heritage, with a replicated boat shop and watermen's tools. Learn about skipjacks and bugeyes, and how they evolved from simple crabbing boats.

The **Dorchester County Historical Society**✦✦ (*LaGrange Ave.; tel: (410) 228-7953; tours year round Thur–Sat 1000–1600*) complex includes the 1760 Meredith House, furnished in fine antiques, with doll and toy collections. The adjoining Neild Museum preserves rural and agricultural tools, maritime trades and Native American artefacts.

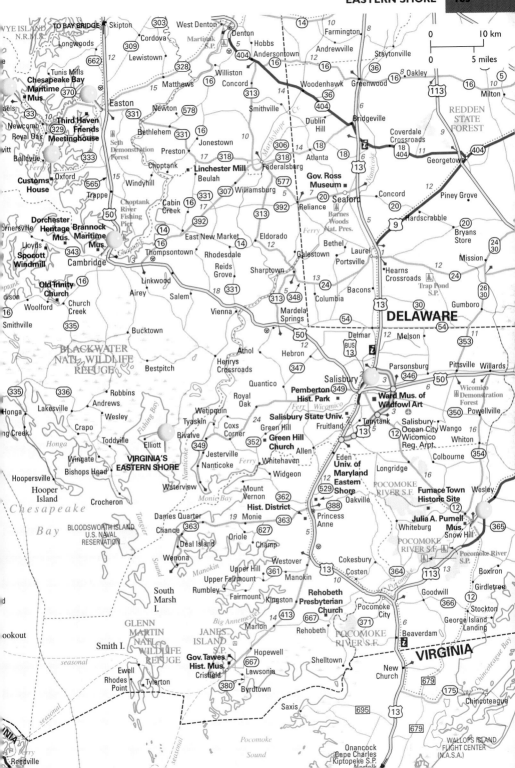

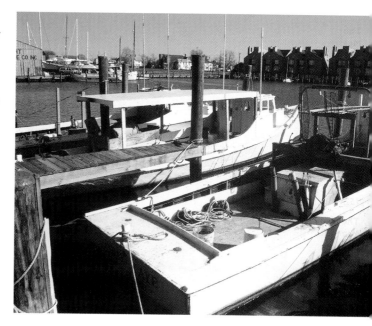

Blackwater National Wildlife Refuge $ *Rte 335, Church Creek; tel: (410) 228-2677; Visitors' Center open Mon–Fri 0800–1600, Sat–Sun 0900–1700.*

Cambridge Arts Center *High St; tel: (410) 228-7782; Mon–Sat 1000–1400. On sale are the works of local artists and craftsmen.*

Brooks Barrel Company *5228 Buckthorne Rd. Watch them work or buy barrels and buckets in the factory store.*

Antique Aircraft Fly-in *Dorchester Heritage Museum, off Rte 343; tel: (410) 228-1899. In late May antique and classic planes are put through their paces.*

The free *Historic Walking Tour of Cambridge* is an illustrated booklet explaining not only the history, but the architecture of the old waterfront neighbourhoods.

Lady Katie $$$ *Cambridge Creek; tel: (410) 228-6400. The only working skipjack out of Cambridge takes passengers on 2-hour cruises to see how oysters are harvested.*

Cambridge Lady $$ *Court and Gay Sts; tel: (410) 221-0776, www.shorenet.net/ cambridgelady; May–Oct Sat–Sun, June–Aug Fri. A classic motor yacht runs narrated cruises*

The Goldsborough Stable contains early vehicles and blacksmith, wheelwright and harnessmakers' tools.

Blackwater National Wildlife Refuge** is a vast tideland where you can drive, walk or canoe amid profuse bird life. Bald Eagles are common and between Oct and Mar Tundra Swans, Snow Geese and 20 duck species winter here. Trails lead to a marsh boardwalk and overlook platform.

Accommodation and food in Cambridge

Commodore's Cottages $ (*215 Glenburn Ave.; tel: (410) 228-6938 or (800) 228-6938*) has attractive guest cottages sleeping 4–6, set in lovely gardens.

Loblolly Landings and Lodge $ (*2142 Liners Rd, Church Creek; tel: (410) 397-3033*) combines B&B with hunting and fishing lodge and log cabins. Rooms are newly decorated and breakfast is memorable.

Tideland Park $ (*Taylors Island; tel: (410) 397-3473 or (800) 673-9052*) has waterfront log cabins and boat or bicycle rentals.

McGuigan's Pub $ (*411 Muse St; tel: (410) 228-7110*) serves Scottish and traditional pub foods.

Portside Seafood Restaurant $–$$ (*201 Trenton St; tel: (410) 228-9007; open Tue–Sun lunch and dinner*) serves local seafood overlooking the water.

EASTON AND OXFORD**

ⓘ Talbot County Visitors Center
Tred Avon Plaza, US-50; tel: (410) 822-4606 or (888) 229-7829; www.talbotchamber.org.

ⓠ Self-guided walking tour maps are at the **Historical Society.**

Oxford–Bellevue Ferry
$ *Tel: (410) 745-9023; every 20 minutes June–Aug Mon–Fri 0700–2100, Sat–Sun 0900–2100; Sept–Nov Mar–May Mon–Fri 0700–sunset, Sat–Sun 0900–sunset.*

ⓘ Historical Society of Talbot County
25 S Washington St; tel: (410) 822-0773; tours Apr–Nov Tue–Sat 1000–1600, 1000–1500, shorter in winter; gardens open Mon–Sat 1000–1600.

Third Haven Friends Meeting House *405 South Washington St; tel: (410) 822-0293.*

ⓐ Antique shops are on North Harrison St opposite the Tidewater Inn, on South Harrison, Washington and along US-50.

ⓦ Little Boat Rentals *846 Port St; tel: (410) 819-0881 or (800) 221-1523. Hire canoes here.*

The Oxford Mews *105 S Morris St, Oxford; tel: (410) 820-8222. Hire bicycles here.*

ⓐ Avalon Theater *40 East Dover St; tel: (410) 822-0345.*

The old Quaker settlement of Easton made its mark as a 19th-century steamboat port, a period recalled by the **Historical Society of Talbot County**** at three homes surrounding Federal-style gardens. The fine brick Federal James Neall House, the 1795 Joseph's Cottage and Ending of Controversie, a reconstruction of a 17th-century house, are all furnished. **Third Haven Friends Meeting House*** is probably the oldest active religious building in the USA.

Nearby Oxford was a thriving trading port long before the Revolution, and its quiet streets are lined with old homes. A ferry established in 1683 crosses the Tred Avon River to Bellevue.

Accommodation and food in Easton and Oxford

Tidewater Inn $$** (*101 East Dover St; tel: (410) 822-1300 or (800) 237-8775, www.tidewaterinn.com*) is Eastern Shore gentry to the core, catering for wildfowl hunters with details such as an 0430 autumn breakfast. The dining room (**$$) deserves its excellent reputation, and is the place to sample crab cakes. Buffet brunch Sat–Sun.

Ashby 1663 Bed and Breakfast $$$ (*27448 Ashby Dr.; tel: (410) 822-4235 or (800) 458-3622, fax: (410) 822-9288, www.ashby1663.com*) pampers guests (as they should for the price) in suites with whirlpool tubs, fireplaces and often private decks or patios. A swimming pool, lighted tennis courts, watercraft and formal gardens provide diversion.

The Robert Morris Inn $$** (*Morris St, Oxford; tel: (410) 226-5111, fax: (410) 226-5744*) is a local landmark, with rooms in the historic inn and newer waterside building. The restaurant (**$$) features local seafood in gracious surroundings: dinner daily, lunch Apr–Nov.

Le Zinc $–$$ (*101 Mill St, Oxford; tel: (410) 226-5776*) has the atmosphere of a continental café and a stylish New American menu: dinner Tue–Sat, pasta specials Wed–Thur.

Oxford Market and Deli (*203 South Morris St, Oxford*) has sandwiches, freshly baked breads, cheeses and meats for picnics, and also hand-dipped ice cream.

SALISBURY❖❖

ℹ️ **Wicomico County Visitors Center**
8480 Ocean Hwy (US-13); tel: (410) 548-4914 or (800) 332-8687; open daily summer 0800–1800, winter 0830–1700.

🏛️ **Salisbury Zoo** South Park Dr.; tel: (410) 548-3188; open daily summer 0800–1930, winter 0800–1630.

Ward Museum of Wildfowl Art $$ 909 S Schumaker Dr.; tel: (410) 742-4988; open Mon–Sat 1000–1700, Sun 1200–1700.

Pemberton Historic Park Rte 349 West; tel: (410) 548-4870.

🛍️ **The Local Artisan** 212 Downtown Plaza. On sale are the crafts of 30 potters, woodcarvers, jewellers and glass artists.

Salisbury Pewter Ocean Hwy (US-13); tel: (410) 546-1188; open Mon–Fri 0900–1700, Sat 1000–1700. Pewter is spun using Colonial techniques, which you can watch in the workshop. Prices may be half retail.

🎾 All **tennis courts**, many lighted at night, are free, often without reservations.

🌼 **Salisbury Festival**, in the first week of May, sees the town filled with a colourful display of blooming dogwood and azaleas.

Above
Salisbury Historic District

Walking and cycling paths follow the river through the free **Salisbury Zoo**❖❖, an outstanding community nature centre that introduces 90 species of native and exotic wildlife. Raised boardwalks and natural habitat enclosures make it easy to watch buffalo, spider monkeys, prairie dogs, sloths, otters, black jaguar and spectacled bears. The **Ward Museum of Wildfowl Art**❖❖ features historic decoy displays and collections of award-winning art.

Newtown Historic District is a living catalogue of Victorian, Queen Anne, Second Empire, Eastlake, Colonial Revival and cottage architecture.

Pemberton Historic Park❖❖ combines history with nature at an early plantation set in several ecosystems that provide the habitat for nearly 160 bird species. Programmes examine Colonial and Native American life.

Accommodation and food in Salisbury

Waterloo Country Inn $$ (*28822 Mount Vernon Rd, Princess Anne; tel: (410) 651-0883, fax: (410) 651-0883*) combines elegance with sublime comfort on the bank of a tidal creek where guests are welcome to use the inn's canoes.

Whitehaven B&B $ (*23844 River St, White Haven; tel: (410) 873-3294*) stresses comfort in its bright airy rooms. Owners will take guests by boat to a nearby yacht club for dinner.

David's at Waterloo $$ (*Waterloo Country Inn, see above*) matches the lodgings' world-class quality with a changing menu of creative dishes: evenings Thur–Sat.

English's Family Restaurant $ (*South Salisbury Blvd (US-13)*) is a diner specialising in traditional Eastern Shore dishes, such as sweet-potato biscuits.

Watermen's Cove $–$$ (*925 Snow Hill Rd; tel: (410) 546-1400*) stands out for its treatment of seafood, prepared in a variety of tasty ways: open daily for lunch and dinner.

ST MICHAELS✦✦✦

ⓘ St Mary's Square Museum *St Mary's Sq.; tel: (410) 745-9561; open May–Oct Sat–Sun 1000–1600.*

ⓘ Chesapeake Bay Maritime Museum *$$ Tel: (410) 745-2916; www.cbmm.org; open daily summer 0900–1800, spring and fall 0900–1700, winter 0900–1600.*

Artiste Locale *112 North Talbot St. A show of local crafts, including pottery, baskets, prints and metal arts.*

Canton Row Antiques *216C Talbot St. Several dealers specialising in quality pieces.*

Captain Dan Vaughn *Mission Rd, Tilghman Island; tel: (410) 886-2083. See decoys carved by Captain Vaughn at his shop.*

Island Kayak *Mission Rd, Tilghman Island; tel: (410) 886-2083. Rent a kayak or take a guided trip to watch herons and egrets.*

Town Dock Marina *305 Mulberry St; tel: (410) 745-2400. Hire a single-speed bicycle by the hour ($) or day ($$$).*

Maritime Arts Festival *Tel: (410) 745-2916. Chesapeake Bay Maritime Museum features music, decoys and seafood in mid-May.*

Tilghman Island Day *www.tilghmanisland.com. Exhibits, skipjack races, music and food in mid-Oct.*

Chesapeake Bay Maritime Museum✦✦✦ shows the breadth of the bay's influence on Eastern Shore life, history and culture through historic boats, exhibits on decoys, fishing, Native Americans, ship building, steamboating and watermen's skills. At its heart is the 1879 Hooper Straight Lighthouse with its restored keeper's cottage.

Tilghman Island has the last working fleet of skipjacks engaged in oyster dredging. Look for these sailing craft at Dogwood Harbor, after you cross the drawbridge.

St Michaels boasts of being 'the town that fooled the British' for tricking British ships during the War of 1812. Lanterns atop ship masts and in treetops above an otherwise darkened town caused the British to aim too high and most of the cannon fire flew over the rooftops.

Accommodation and food in St Michaels

Black Walnut Point Inn $$ (*Tilghman Island; tel: (410) 886-2452, fax: (410) 886-2053, www.tilghmanisland.com/blackwalnut*) fills its own private point, surrounded by the bay. A waterside cottage has a kitchen.

Victoriana Inn $ (*205 Cherry St; tel: (410) 745-3368*) has three rooms with shared baths, one private, close to the Maritime Museum.

Harrison's $$ (*Rte 33, Tilghman Island; tel: (410) 886-2123*) is both fishing centre and restaurant, serving seafood fresh from its own fleet's catch in a casual atmosphere.

SNOW HILL**

① Worcester County Tourism *105 Pearl St; tel: (410) 623-3617 or (800) 852-0335.*

⑪ Furnace Town Historic Site $ *Old Furnace Rd; tel: (410) 632-2032; open Apr–Oct daily 1100–1700.*

Pocomoke River State Park *US-113; tel: (410) 632-2566.*

🌐 Captain Bruce Wooten *6661 Snow Hill Rd; tel: (410) 632-1431.* Takes anglers on 8-hour fishing trips with as much instruction as needed.

Pocomoke River Canoe Company *312 North Washington St; tel: (410) 632-3971; open daily Apr–Nov.* The company rents kayaks and canoes, provides shuttles and runs guided trips.

Snow Hill sits astride the meandering Pocomoke River, which flows through a beautiful wilderness of cypress swamps. Bird life is abundant, and cypresses form a watery scene of tall trunks and knobbly half-submerged knees. Explore by canoe or on boardwalks in the Nassawango Creek Cypress Swamp Preserve, reached through **Furnace Town Historic Site***. Worth seeing for its giant brick iron furnace, this museum village thrived around the furnace in the early 1800s.

Pocomoke River State Park* has several sections along the river, with cypress swamps and forests and at Shad Landing swimming, fishing, camping, hiking and boat rentals.

Right
Pocomoke River State Park

Accommodation and food in Snow Hill

River House Inn $$ (*201 East Market St; tel: (410) 632-2722, fax: (410) 632-2866*) overlooks the river, with its own canoe landing and nicely decorated rooms furnished in antiques. Bicycles are free for guests' use.

Opposite
NASA Visitor Center

Snow Hill Inn $–$$ (*East Market St; tel: (410) 632-2102*) combines Chesapeake traditions with fine dining in dishes such as beef fillets topped with Maryland crab.

VIRGINIA'S EASTERN SHORE✧✧

ℹ New Church Welcome Center
US-13, New Church; tel: (757) 787-2460.

Chincoteague Chamber of Commerce 6733 Maddox Blvd; tel: (757) 336-6161.

📍 Every place in this narrow peninsula is close to its main artery, US-13.

🎫 Chincoteague National Wildlife Refuge $ Visitors Center open 0900–1600, longer in summer.

NASA Visitor Center Wallops Island, Rte 175; tel: (804) 824-1344; open Thur–Mon 1000–1600.

Kerr Place $ Onancock; tel: (757) 787-8012; open Mar–Dec Tue–Sat 1000–1600.

🛍 Hopkins & Bro. Store 2 Market St, Onancock; tel: (757) 787-3100. Operating since 1842, this is among the East Coast's oldest stores, selling gifts and foods.

🚤 Capt'n Bob's Marina Chincoteague; tel: (757) 336-6654. Get boat rentals and pontoon boats here.

Hopkins & Bro. Store See above. Hire bicycles here.

🐎 Assateague Pony Penning July last Wed–Thur. The wild horses swim the channel to Chincoteague.

Rural character pervades Virginia's Delmarva, where tourism is largely confined to Chincoteague and to motorists short-cutting south via the Chesapeake Bay Bridge-Tunnel.

Assateague Island extends from Maryland, and **Chincoteague National Wildlife Refuge✧✧✧**, which occupies much of it, is named after the smaller neighbouring Chincoteague Island just west, with resort facilities. The refuge on the fragile barrier island is a prime bird-watching area famous for wild horses, although these are easier to spot on Maryland's end of the island. A 1.2-mile (2km) trail leads to the 1867 Assateague Lighthouse.

NASA Visitor Center✧ follows the history of flight and rockets. See a piece of the moon, satellite photos of a hurricane and launch rockets. **Kerr Place✧** is a mansion dating back to 1799, with finely detailed plasterwork and woodwork, furnished and decorated to its period.

Accommodation and food in Virginia's Eastern Shore

1848 Island Manor House B&B $–$$ (4160 Main St, Chincoteague; tel: (757) 336-5436 or (800) 852-1505, fax: (757) 336-1333, www.chincoteague.com/b-b/imh) offers six antique-furnished rooms with shared and private baths.

Garden and the Sea Inn $–$$** (4188 Nelson Rd, New Church; tel: (757) 824-0672 or (800) 824-0672, fax: (757) 824-5605), built in 1802, is furnished with fine antiques and oriental rugs, some rooms with jacuzzis. The dining room (**$$) is among the Delmarva's best, serving Chincoteague oysters in peppercorn sauce and filling trout with Crab Imperial.

Miss Molly's Inn $–$$ (4141 Main St, Chincoteague; tel: (757) 336-6686 or (800) 221-5620, fax: (757) 336-0600, www.chincoteague.com/b-b/molly), built in 1886, serves fresh scones and trifle for tea.

Don's Seafood Restaurant $ (4113 Main St, Chincoteague; tel: (757) 336-5715) serves three casual meals daily, with chicken, shrimp and other Chesapeake specialties.

Eastern Shore Steamboat Co. Restaurant (2 Market St, Onancock; tel: (757) 787-3100) overlooks the harbour. A specialty is oysters stuffed with crabmeat.

Suggested tour

🎧 **St Michael's:
Dockside Express $**
*Tel: (410) 886-2643; open
mid-Apr–mid-Nov. Leads
general and themed
historic walking tours.*

Express Princess $$$ *Tel:
(410) 886-2643.
Reservations are suggested
for these morning 90-
minute nature cruises,
sunset and moonlight
cruises.*

Patriot $$ *Maritime
Museum Dock; tel: (410)
745-3100; cruises Apr–Oct
daily 1100, 1230, 1430 and
1600. A large tour boat
explores the Miles River.*

Rebecca T Ruark $$$
*Dogwood Harbor, Tilghman
Island; tel: (410) 886-2176.
Built in 1886, this ship
makes 2-hour sailing tours.*

ℹ️ **Crisfield Visitors
Center** *Somers Cove
Marina; tel: (410) 968-
2501; open May–Oct
Mon–Fri 0900–1630,
Sat–Sun 1000–1500.*

🎧 **Smith Island
Cruises** *Somers Cove
Marina; tel: (410) 425-
2771; June–Oct daily 1230.*

Tangier Island Cruises
*City Dock; tel: (410) 968-
2338; open mid-May–mid-
Oct daily 1230.*

Total distance: 202 miles.

Time: 5 hours driving time. Allow 2–3 days, longer with canoe or boat
trips. Those with limited time should concentrate on Furnace Town
and the Maritime Museum at St Michaels, if possible adding a skipjack
sailing tour.

Links: From Norfolk the Chesapeake Bay Bridge-Tunnel leads north to
the Eastern Shore. Snow Hill and Salisbury are close to Ocean City and
the Delaware Coast, and US-50 leads directly from Easton to Annapolis
or to US-301 and the Northern Chesapeake itinerary.

Route: From the Chesapeake Bay Bridge-Tunnel, follow US-13 past
Kiptopeke State Park, **Cape Charles** and **Onancock** to Rte 175,
turning right to **Chincoteague**.

Backtrack to US-13, turning right on to US-113 near **Pocomoke City**
and continuing to **SNOW HILL** ❶. Follow Rte 12 to **SALISBURY** ❷.

Head west on US-50 to **CAMBRIDGE** ❸, continuing over the
Choptank River to **EASTON** ❹. Follow Rte 333 to **OXFORD** ❺,
crossing the **Oxford–Bellevue Ferry** and turning left on Rte 33 to **ST
MICHAELS** ❻. Return to US-50, heading north to the Bay Bridge.

Also worth exploring

Already a sailing port in the late 17th century, **Crisfield** prospered on
fishing and by 1910 had the nation's largest sailing fleet. **Janes Island
State Park** *(tel: (410) 968-1565)*, accessible by shuttle or rented boats,
has canoe and walking trails through marshes and pine forests. The
campsite and marina are on the mainland. Ferries leave Crisfield for
Smith and **Tangier Islands**.

Right
Bison in Salisbury Zoo

TO BAY BRIDGE • Skipton
303 West Denton
Longwoods
309 Cordova
662 Lewistown
Denton
Hobbs
Andersontown
404
328
Williston
Concord
Matthews
16
313
Smithville
Newton 578
331
Chesapeake Bay Maritime Mus. 370
Easton 331
Third Haven Friends Meetinghouse 329
Bethlehem 331 16
Newcomb
Royal Oak
333
Jonestown
Preston
318
Choptank
Linchester Mill
Beulah
Customs House 5 Oxford
565 Windyhill
Trappe
50 331
Cabin Creek
East New Market
392
16 14
313
16 14
Thompsontown
Rhodesdale
Reids Grove
Eldorado
Dorchester Heritage Mus.
Brannock Maritime Mus. 3
Cornersville
Lloyds
Spocott Windmill
343 Cambridge
Old Trinity Church 16
Madison
Woolford
Church Creek
335
Airey
Salem
331
Linkwood
Vienna
313 348
Mardela Springs
Columbia
Bucktown
Athol
Hebron
347
Henrys Crossroads
Bestpitch
Quantico
Royal Oak
Salisbury 349
Pemberton Hist. Park 2
Ward Mus. of Wildfowl Art
335 336
Robbins
Andrews
Wesley
Lakesville
Crapo
Toddville
Wetipquin
Tyaskin
Bivalve
Coxs Corner
Green Hill
Salisbury State Univ.
Green Hill Church
352
349
Jesterville
Nanticoke
Allen
Whitehaven
Widgeon
Fruitland
Tonytank
13
12
Salisbury-Ocean City Wicomico Reg. Arpt.
Wango
Whiton
354
Colbourne
Honga
Wingate
Bishops Head
VIRGINIA'S EASTERN SHORE
Waterview
Mount Vernon
362
Hist. District
Monie
363
Eden
Univ. of Maryland Eastern Shore
Longridge
529
Oakville
Princess Anne
388
Fumace Town Historic Site
Wesley
12
Julia A. Purnell Mus. 1
Whiteburg
Snow Hill
365
Hoopersville
Crocheron
Dames Quarter
Chance
Deal Island
Oriole
Champ
627
363
Wenona
Upper Hill
Westover
Manokin
361
13
Cokesbury
Costen
364
113
Boxiron
Girdletree
Goodwill
12
366
Stockton
Rumbley
Upper Fairmount
Fairmount
Kingston
Marion
413
Rehobeth
Rehobeth Presbyterian Church
667
Pocomoke City
371
Beaverdam
VIRGINIA
South Marsh I.
Smith I.
Lookout
Ewell
Rhodes Point
Tylerton
Gov. Tawes Hist. Mus.
Crisfield
Lawsonia
Byrdtown
380
Hopewell
667
Shelltown
New Church
679
Saxis
695
13
679
Onancock
Cape Charles
Kiptopeke S.P.
WALLOPS ISLAND FLIGHT CENTER (N.A.S.A.)
Chincoteague
175
Reedville

Third Haven
14 Farmington
Andrewville
36 Staytonville
16 Woodenhawk
Greenwood
Oakley
16
113
5
Milton
404
Dublin Hill
Bridgeville
Coverdale Crossroads
18 404
Georgetown
404
Atlanta
18
13
Gov. Ross Museum
577
Federalsburg
Williamsburg
307
Reliance
Seaford 20
Concord
20
Piney Grove
Hardscrabble
9
Bryans Store
24 30
Mission
26 30
Gumboro
Bethel
Galestown
Laurel
Portsville
Hearns Crossroads
Bacons
24
Trap Pond S.P.
Sharptown
DELAWARE
Delmar
BUS 13
Melson
353
Parsonsburg
346
Pittsville
Willards
50
Powellville
350
0 10 km
0 5 miles
5

Rockville to Frederick

Ratings

Historical sights	●●●●
Shopping and crafts	●●●●
Gastronomy	●●●
Art and museums	●●
Children	●●
Entertainment	●●
Nature and wildlife	●●
Beaches	●

History is the hallmark of this area north of Washington, DC. The C&O Canal begins here (and began building here in 1828), bypassing one of the region's premier natural features, the torrential Great Falls of the Potomac. Today the canal is the focus of a linear National Park that protects its 184-mile length.

The region was a corridor through which both armies coursed in the Civil War, as General Lee sought to demoralise the Union and surround its capital. Frederick was an important crossroads and storage centre for Union supplies, and a crucial battle at Monocacy saved Washington from invasion. More peaceful today, Frederick's history is evident in its streets of beautiful old homes.

CATOCTIN MOUNTAIN✤✤

ⓘ Tourism Council of Frederick County
19 E Church St, Frederick;
tel: (301) 663-8687 or
(800) 999-3613;
www.co.frederick.md.us;
open daily 0930–1630.

Catoctin Mountain Park Visitors Center
Rte 77, Thurmont; tel: (301) 663-9330.

Catoctin Mountain Park is set in wild mountainous landscape, where 'moonshine' whiskey was made secretly during the prohibition era. The restored remains of Blue Blazes Whiskey Still, destroyed by 'revenuers' in the 1930s, is reached by a short trail. Hog Rock Nature Trail is under a mile long, with interpretive nature signs.

Cunningham Falls State Park✤✤ lies directly south, named after the 70ft Cunningham Falls, which cascade over a series of rock ledges. The 1.5-mile trail to the falls has several uphill sections. A large lake offers swimming and canoes for hire and the park runs outdoor and nature programmes as well as having picnic areas and playgrounds.

Catoctin Wildlife Preserve and Zoo✤✤ is designed for family outings, with a blend of pettable and exotic creatures, including

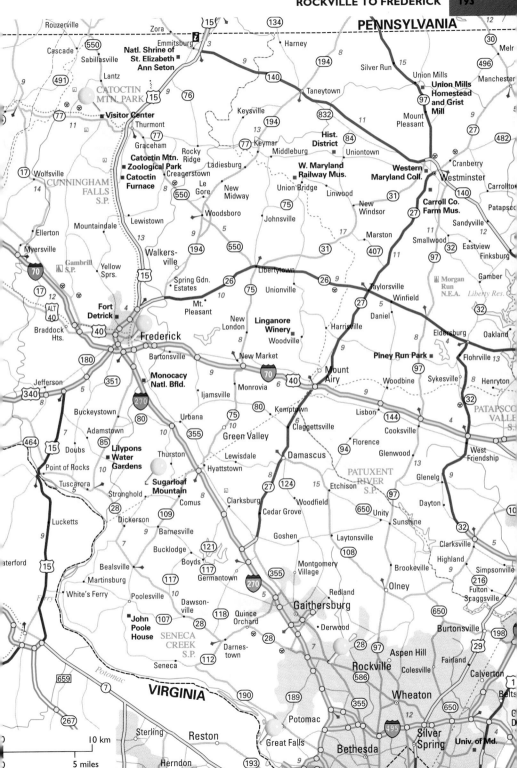

Rouzerville
Zora
Cascade
Sabillasville
Lantz
CATOCTIN MTN. PARK
Visitor Center
Thurmont
Graceham
Rocky Ridge
Catoctin Mtn. Zoological Park
Catoctin Furnace
Le Gore
Creagerstown
Ladiesburg
New Midway
Woodsboro
Johnsville
Wolfsville
CUNNINGHAM FALLS S.P.
Myersville
Gambrill S.P.
Yellow Sprs.
Mountaindale
Lewistown
Walkersville
Spring Gdn. Estates
Mt. Pleasant
Fort Detrick
Braddock Hts.
Jefferson
Frederick
Bartonsville
Monocacy Natl. Bfld.
Buckeystown
Adamstown
Urbana
Lilypons Water Gardens
Thurston
Point of Rocks
Doubs
Tuscarora
Sugarloaf Mountain
Comus
Stronghold
Dickerson
Barnesville
Bucklodge
Bealsville
Martinsburg
White's Ferry
Poolesville
Dawsonville
John Poole House
SENECA CREEK S.P.
Seneca

Emmitsburg
Natl. Shrine of St. Elizabeth Ann Seton
Harney
Silver Run
Union Mills
Union Mills Homestead and Grist Mill
Melr
Manchester
Taneytown
Keysville
Keymar
Middleburg
Uniontown
Mount Pleasant
Hist. District
W. Maryland Railway Mus.
Western Maryland Coll.
Westminster
Cranberry
Carrollto
Union Bridge
Linwood
New Windsor
Carroll Co. Farm Mus.
Sandyville
Smallwood
Eastview
Finksburg
Marston
Libertytown
Unionville
Taylorsville
Winfield
Gamber
Morgan Run N.E.A.
Liberty Res.
Daniel
New London
Linganore Winery
Woodville
Harrisville
Eldersburg
Oakland
New Market
Mount Airy
Piney Run Park
Woodbine
Sykesville
Henryton
Monrovia
Ijamsville
Lisbon
Cooksville
West Friendship
PATAPSCO VALLE S.
Kemptown
Claggettsville
Florence
Glenwood
Green Valley
Lewisdale
Damascus
Etchison
PATUXENT RIVER S.P.
Glenelg
Dayton
Hyattstown
Clarksburg
Woodfield
Cedar Grove
Unity
Sunshine
Goshen
Laytonsville
Clarksville
Highland
Simpsonville
Fulton
Scaggsville
Montgomery Village
Brookeville
Olney
Germantown
Boyds
Gaithersburg
Redland
Burtonsville
Quince Orchard
Derwood
Aspen Hill
Fairland
Calverton
Darnestown
Rockville
Colesville
Belts
Potomac
Wheaton
Univ. of Md.
Sterling
Reston
Great Falls
Bethesda
Silver Spring
Herndon

VIRGINIA

10 km

5 miles

Cunningham Falls State Park $ *Rte 77 and Rte 15, Thurmont; tel: (301) 271-7574.*

Catoctin Wildlife Preserve and Zoo $$ *13019 Catoctin Furnace Rd (Rte 806), Thurmont; tel: (301) 271-3180; www.CWPZoo.com, open May–Sept daily 0900–1800, April and Oct 1000–1700, Nov–Mar weekends.*

Catoctin Iron Furnace *Catoctin Furnace Rd (Rte 806), Thurmont; tel: (301) 271-7574; www.dnr.state.md.us.*

Catoctin Mountain Orchard *Rte 15, Thurmont; open June–Oct daily 0900–1700.* You can buy berries, cherries, apricots, peaches, apples and grapes in season.

Catoctin Colorfest In the second weekend in Oct at Thurmont Community Park the work of over 350 craftspeople is on show and for sale.

golden tigers, black jaguars, monkeys, bears, alligators and a giant tortoise. The emphasis is on learning about the animals and interacting when possible.

Catoctin Iron Furnace**, almost across the road, was built in 1776 to make cannonballs for the Revolution, providing 100 tonnes of shells used at Yorktown alone. The ruins of the ironmaster's house have been consolidated. Three of Maryland's five covered bridges cluster nearby – the closest to US-15 is Roddy Road Covered Bridge.

Accommodation and food in Catoctin

Bowling Brook Country Inn $$ (*6000 Middleburg Rd, Middleburg; tel: (410) 876-2893 or 857-4445*) is a quiet country B&B whose rooms are beautifully appointed, some with jacuzzis.

Cozy Country Inn $–$$ (*103 Frederick Rd (Rte 806), Thurmont; tel: (301) 271-4301, www.cozyvillage.com*) is often used by journalists and government officials accompanying US presidents to nearby Camp David. Rooms are themed on past presidents and Winston Churchill, a guest in the 1940s. The popular restaurant, hardly cozy, serves traditional dishes and an all-you-can-eat buffet ($) on Sun.

Mountain Gate Family Restaurant $ (*133 Frederick Rd (just off US-15), Thurmont; tel: (301) 271-4373*) serves unbelievably cheap turkey, ham, roast beef and roast pork dinners, sandwiches and breakfasts.

Mountain Gate Convenience Store $ (*130 Frederick Rd (just off US-15), Thurmont*) has takeaway lunches and dinners at even lower prices.

Above
Catoctin Zoo

FREDERICK✧✧✧

ℹ **Tourism Council of Frederick County**
19 E Church St; tel: (301) 663-8687 or (800) 999-3613; www.co.frederick.md.us; open daily 0930–1630. Tourist information centre (TIC).

🚶 **Guided Walking Tours** $ Apr–Dec Sat–Sun 1330. These start from the TIC, which also publishes an excellent walking tour map, leading past the most historically important buildings, with historic photos and descriptions.

Frederick Carriage Company $$$ TIC or tel: (301) 694-7433. Horse-drawn carriages tour the old city.

🏛 **National Museum of Civil War Medicine** $ 48 E Patrick St; tel: (301) 695-1864; www.CivilWarMed.org; open Mon–Sat 1000–1700, Sun 1100–1700.

Rose Hill Manor $$ 1611 N Market St; tel: (301) 694-1646; open Apr–Oct Mon–Sat 1000–1600, Sun 1300–1600, Nov weekends.

Schifferstadt Architectural Museum $ 1110 Rosemont Ave.; tel: (301) 663-3885; open mid-Apr–mid-Dec Tue–Sat 1000–1600.

Monocacy National Battlefield Rte 355, southeast of Frederick; tel: (301) 662-3515; open Apr–Oct daily 0800–1630, Nov–Mar Wed–Sun 0800–1630.

Frederick's streets are lined with well-kept commercial blocks and residences from the Civil War era and earlier. The city's role in that war is portrayed uniquely at the **National Museum of Civil War Medicine**✧✧, whose innovative displays show period medical practices. Re-enactors stage live action on W Patrick St, where a Civil War skirmish took place.

Barbara Fritchie House recalls its 90-year-old owner, who challenged Confederate troops to tear down her Union flag. They didn't. Collections of The Historical Society of Frederick County are shown in an 1820s home, and include fine furniture, paintings and decorative arts. The Community Bridge, a *trompe-l'oeil* mural incorporating hundreds of images from the community, spans a canalised river, with a promenade and entertainment space.

Rose Hill Manor✧✧ is a classic 18th-century plantation with a Farm Museum exhibiting early agriculture, and a Children's Museum with hands-on programmes teaching about life in the manor house and plantation. The 1756 **Schifferstadt Architectural Museum**✧✧, an example of a German colonial home, has thick stone walls, a built-in iron stove, wishbone chimneys and other unusual features.

Monocacy National Battlefield✧✧ is the site of the 1864 Civil War battle that, although it was 'lost', stopped the Confederate march on Washington, DC, and saved the capital. The Visitor Center has an orientation programme and self-guided tour maps.

Accommodation and food in Frederick

McCleary's Flat $–$$ (121 E Patrick St; tel: (301) 620-2433 or (800) 774-7926, www.fwp.net/mcclearysflat) combines a perfect downtown location, lush décor and warm genial hosts, all in a lovingly restored Second Empire-style mansion of 1876. Thoughtful touches abound and off-street parking is close.

Tyler Spite Inn $$–$$$ (112 W Church St; tel: (301) 831-4455) dates from 1810, a fine antique-furnished mansion in a beautiful historic downtown neighbourhood. More rooms in the adjacent mansion are just as comfortable, with fireplaces and featherbeds.

Frederick Brewing Company $–$$ (124 N Market St; tel: (301) 631-0089) includes pub fare and more upmarket dishes, such as Louisiana *boudin* with jumbo shrimp. The atmosphere is bright, busy, noisy and youngish.

The Province Restaurant $$ (129 N Market St; tel: (301) 663-1441; Tue–Thur prix-fixe *dinners, daily lunch, closed Mon*) has a bistro style and imaginative American and international dishes such as veal Amontillado with almonds. Desserts are brilliant.

ROCKVILLE AND GREAT FALLS✧✧

❶ Conference and Visitors Bureau of Montgomery County 12900 Middlebrook Rd, Ste 1400, Germantown MD 20874; tel: (800) 925-0880; www.cvbmontco.com.

❷ Rockville is an amorphous commercial and residential area just north of the Beltway, bisected by I-270, which leads north to Frederick. To reach Great Falls from Rockville, take Exit 5 to Rte 189, Great Falls Rd.

❸ Weiner Judaic Museum 6125 Montrose Rd, just west of Rockville Pike (Rte 355); tel: (301) 881-0100; open Sun–Thur 0900–2230, Fri 0900–1700, except Jewish holidays.

Canal Clipper Tel: (301) 299-3613; mid-Apr–Oct. A replica canal boat adapted for passengers is drawn by mules along the C&O Canal from Great Falls Tavern, rising through the canal lock.

Great Falls Tavern Visitor Center 11710 MacArthur Blvd, off Great Falls Road (Rte 189); open year-round daily 0900–1700.

Swain's Lock Swain's Lock Rd, off River Rd (Rte 190), Potomac; tel: (301) 299-3613; canoe lessons ($) Thur 1900.

Above
Great Falls lock hands

The jazz-era literary stars F Scott and Zelda Fitzgerald are buried at St Mary's Church Cemetery (*Viers Mill Road (Rte 586) and Rte 355*). Collections of the **Weiner Judaic Museum**✧ focus on Judaic history, from archaeological artefacts to contemporary culture and art.

The **C&O Canal National Historic Park**✧✧ follows the Potomac River northwest from Washington. George Washington envisioned this canal to bypass the river's un-navigable parts and open the western frontier. One of the major obstacles was the thundering Great Falls of the Potomac, as impressive today as in Washington's time, plunging over jagged rocks into a gorge where bald eagles circle. **Great Falls Tavern Visitor Center**✧✧✧ explains the canal and its locks. For the best view of the falls, follow the path to Olmstead Bridges.

Swain's Lock✧ (Lock 21), about 2 miles from Great Falls Tavern, is an original lockmaster's house, now a small recreational area with picnic tables, bicycle and canoe rentals. The canal has water in it for several miles here, perfect for quiet paddling, and the tow path is a favourite of walkers and cyclists.

Accommodation and food in Rockville and Great Falls

Cabin John Regional Park $ (*7400 Tuckerman Ln., Rockville MD, tel: (301) 299-4555*) has camp pitches and a full range of recreational facilities for campers.

Woodfin Suites Hotel $$ (*1380 Piccard Dr., at I-270 Exit 8; tel: (301) 590-9880*) has tasteful suites and studios, some with kitchens, in a motel-style building.

Old Anglers Inn $$$ (*10801 MacArthur Blvd, near Great Falls, Potomac; tel: (301) 365-2425*) serves well-prepared upmarket cuisine in a historic setting long favoured by sportsmen, including President Theodore Roosevelt.

SUGARLOAF MOUNTAIN✦✦

To explore this region's C&O Canal locks, gate houses and aqueducts from the well-kept and wide towpath trail, rent a bicycle from **Swain's Lock** (*Swain's Lock Rd, off River Rd (Rte 190), Potomac; tel: (301) 299-3613*).

Lilypons Water Gardens *6800 Lilypons Rd, off Rte 85, Buckeystown; open Oct–Feb Mon–Sat 0930–1630, Mar–Sept Mon–Sat 0930–1730, Sun 1100–1730.*

Sugarloaf Mountain has scenic picnic areas with tables near the parking area on top and in wooded groves surrounding its rocky outcrops.

President Franklin Roosevelt tried to buy Sugarloaf Mountain as a presidential retreat, but its owner wouldn't sell. Trail maps for the surprisingly steep ascent are in a box at the entrance or you can drive to the top to explore its rocky summit and admire the views from its look-outs. The building stone for nearby Monocacy Aqueduct was quarried here, and although this bridge which carried the canal over the river is now in poor condition, the quartzite blocks are as good as the day they were cut. The seven-arched aqueduct, built 1828–33 and an icon of American transportation history, is under restoration.

Lilypons Water Gardens✦ are among America's leading growers of water lilies and aquatic plants. Small show gardens demonstrate the use of water plants in the landscape and large pools form the nurseries for a collection of flowers in shades of yellow, pink and red. It is a favourite haunt of blue herons.

Food in Sugarloaf Mountain

Meadowlark Inn $$ (*19611 Fisher Ave., Poolesville; tel: (301) 428-8900; closed Mon*) is a country restaurant serving homemade breads and traditional foods.

Right
Lilypons Water Gardens

Suggested tour

The ferry *Jubal A Early* crosses the Potomac River daily 0500–2300.

Carroll County Tourism *210 E Main St; tel: (301) 848-1388; www.carr.org/tourism; open Mon–Sat 0900–1700, Sun 1000–1400.*

Frederick has over 20 **antique shops** along *E Patrick St, Carroll St and corner of 2nd E Sts.*

New Market *I-70 east of Frederick.* Over two dozen antique shops to browse through.

Shab Row Farmers' Market *Frederick; open June–Oct, Thu 1500–1800.*

Westminster Inn *$–$$ 5 S Center St; tel: (410) 876-2893.* Antique-furnished guest rooms each have a jacuzzi. The dining room serves a stylish and creative menu using fresh local ingredients.

Union Mills Homestead *$ 3311 Littlestown Pike (Rte 97); tel: (410) 848-2288; open Jun–Aug Tue–Fri 1000–1600, Sat–Sun 1200–1600.*

Basilica of The National Shrine of St Elizabeth Ann Seton *333 S Seton Ave., Emmitsburg; tel: (301) 447-6606.*

White's *24801 White's Ferry Rd, Dickerson; tel: (301) 349-5200.* Hire canoes or rowing boats here.

Total distance: 80 miles, 104 with detours.

Time: Allow 2 days with or without detours, 3 if you explore Frederick in depth or add Westminster to the itinerary. Those with limited time should stop to see Great Falls and the C&O Canal, then concentrate on Frederick.

Links: From Washington, DC, Rte 355 leads to Rockville, or from the Beltway, take I-270. US-340 connects Frederick to Harpers Ferry and I-70 connects it to Hagerstown.

Route: Leave **ROCKVILLE ❶** on Rte 189, Great Falls Rd, which crosses I-270 at Exit 5, and follow it to MacArthur Blvd, following signs to **GREAT FALLS ❷**. Take Rte 189 back to Rte 190, River Rd, turning left, with a diversion left on Swain's Lock Rd. Continue past **Seneca Creek State Park** to the attractive old town of **Poolesville**.

Detour: From Poolesville, follow an un-numbered road signposted **White's Ferry**, to the last ferry across the Potomac. Confederate troops controlled this crossing point during the Civil War.

Follow Rte 109 to **Bealsville**, then Rte 28 to **Dickerson**, following Sugarloaf Rd, right immediately after the railway underpass, to **SUGARLOAF MOUNTAIN ❸**. Return to Dickerson and turn right on Rte 28, making a short diversion left to **Monocacy Aqueduct**. North of Dickerson, go right on Rte 85, and right again on Lilypons Rd to the gardens, returning to Rte 85, which leads north to **FREDERICK ❹**.

From Frederick, follow US-15 north past **Cunningham Falls Park** and **CATOCTIN MOUNTAIN ❺**, to **Thurmont**. For variety, return to Frederick by following Rte 77 east to **Keymar** and heading south on Rte 194.

Detour: From Thurmont, continue north on US-15 to **Emmitsburg**, visiting the **Mother Seton Shrine**, honouring the first American Roman Catholic saint.

Also worth exploring

Westminster, east of Frederick via Rtes 26 and 31, is a charming town filled with historic buildings, which you can explore on a guided or self-guided walking tour from the tourist information centre. **Uniontown**, west of Westminster, is lined by buildings that span the entire 19th century. To the north, in Union Mills, **Union Mills Homestead** assembles over 200 years of history in a 1797 home, grist mill and saw mill.

Western Maryland and borderlands

Ratings

Art and museums	●●●●○
Historical sights	●●●●○
Children	●●●○○
Entertainment	●●●○○
Gastronomy	●●●○○
Nature and wildlife	●●●○○
Shopping and crafts	●●●○○
Beaches	●●○○○

To Americans, the names of Antietam and Harpers Ferry are synonymous with the Civil War, and that era's history still pervades the region. Western sites reflect earlier history: the French and Indian Wars stronghold of Fort Frederick and George Washington's first command at Cumberland. While here, Washington envisioned the C&O Canal, which borders the Potomac River, its entire length marked by a National Park and multi-use towpath trail.

Rolling mountain roads further west are less explored, except by fishermen, hikers and whitewater enthusiasts, to whom the area's vast public parklands are well known. Beautiful in any season, this landscape is most glorious in autumn, when maples paint the hillsides red and orange.

CUMBERLAND❖❖

ⓘ Allegany County Visitor and Convention Bureau *13 Canal St; tel: (301) 777-5138 or (800) 508-4748; www.mdmountainside.com.*

Rocky Gap Information Center *Exit 50, I-68, Rocky Gap; open daily 0830–1800.*

Washington St is lined by fine old homes built in Cumberland's glory days, a living catalogue of American Victorian architectural styles from turreted brick and patterned slate to 'painted ladies'. A prime example is the 1867 **History House❖❖**, a tour of which is filled with stories of life in that opulent era.

Fort Cumberland, George Washington's first command, sat at Washington St's crest, and at Prospect Sq. is a plan of the fort, its outer walls marked by paving stones. Emanuel Church sits directly over the site of this French and Indian war fort and is a very early Gothic-Revival church, redesigned by Louis Comfort Tiffany. Sole remnant of Fort Cumberland is the tiny log **George Washington's Headquarters**, from 1755, now on Greene St below.

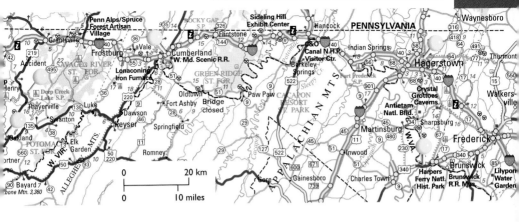

A *Self-Guided Walk into History*, free at History House, leads along Washington St and through the historic centre. *Fort Cumberland Walking Tour*, free from the Visitor Center, lists 28 stops with descriptions. Corresponding audio tours are available.

Western Maryland Scenic Railroad $$$
Cumberland Station; tel: (301) 759-4400 or (800) 872-4650; www.wmsr.com; May–Dec 1100 or 1130, reservations recommended. Scenic steam and diesel rail excursions travel to Frostburg.

History House $
Washington St; open June–Oct Tue–Sun 1100–1600, Nov–May Tue–Sat 1100–1600.

Rocky Gap State Park
16701 Lakeview Rd, exit 50 I-68; tel: (301) 784-8400 or (800) 724-0828; fax: (301) 784-8408; www. rockygapresort.com.

Rocky Gap State Park✦✦ is highly developed, featuring a luxury hotel, Jack Nicklaus golf course and polished facilities, along with more rustic camp pitches, hiking trails, fishing, swimming, boats for hire and scheduled activities (*see page 202*).

Right
George Washington's Headquarters

The Gallery
8 Greene St. Art and fine crafts are on display.

Historic Cumberland Antique Mall 55–57 Baltimore St. Many dealers occupy this five-storey shop.

The Inn at Walnut Bottom 120 Greene St; tel: (301) 777-0003. You can hire bicycles for use in the area and the inn arranges bikes and shuttles for towpath trips.

Allegany Expeditions 10310 Columbus Ave.; tel: (301) 722-5170. You can hire kayaks, canoes, and camping gear or take guided Potomac canoe trips.

Cumberland Theater $$$ 101 N Johnson St; tel: (301) 759-4990; mid-June–Oct. The theatre produces professional plays and musicals.

Railfest Tel: (301) 759-4400 or (800) 872-4650; www.wmsr.com; mid-Oct. There are special train excursions (by reservation) to Oakland and railroading events.

Accommodation and food in Cumberland

The Inn at Walnut Bottom $–$$ (120 Greene St; tel: (301) 777-0003) has the flavour of a European inn, with nicely decorated rooms and a large pleasant common area. Most rooms have private baths, all have TV and telephone. The owners will arrange bike towpath trips with shuttle.

**Rocky Gap Lodge and Golf Resort $$** (16701 Lakeview Rd, Flintstone; tel: (301) 784-8400 or (800) 724-0828, fax: (301) 784-8408, www.rockygapresort.com) sits above a long lake, surrounded by hills. Rooms are spacious, the dining room excellent, and a full range of activities and sports is offered. Camp pitches ($) are across the lake in a wooded setting.

The Bourbon St Café $ (82 Broadway; tel: (301) 722-1116) blends Cajun flavours with Maryland ingredients, a happy marriage indeed. It serves lunch and dinner Mon–Sat.

Uncle Tucker's $ (I-68 exit 46; tel: (301) 777-7232) serves generously embellished pizza and baby back ribs, with entertainment on the deck during summer weekends.

When Pigs Fly $ (18 Valley St; tel: (301) 722-7447) serves updated home-style dishes with an emphasis on pork ribs, in a bright casual setting. The sausage chilli is delicious.

Above
Washington St, Cumberland

Opposite
Swallow Falls

DEEP CREEK ✦✦

ⓘ Garrett County Chamber of Commerce *Rte 219, McHenry; tel: (301) 245-4400; www.deepcreeklake.org.* Publishes an excellent magazine-style guide with a detailed map. TIC.

Visitors Center *Tel: (301) 387-4386; open Sun–Thur 0900–1700, Fri–Sat 0900–1800.*

ⓘ Expect summer traffic on narrow US-219 around the lake to be at a standstill at weekends.

Deep Creek Lake Shuttle $ *Garrett Transit; tel: (301) 334-9431; operates Sun–Thur 1000–2200, Fri–Sat 1000–0100.* Twenty sites around the lake are linked in a 1-hour circuit that includes campsites, markets, hotels and the State Park.

The Evening Star $$ *Deep Creek Outfitters, 1899 Deep Creek Dr.; tel: (301) 387-6977; Mon–Fri 1600, Sat–Sun 1400.* Take a cruise round Deep Creek Lake on an enclosed catamaran – reservations important.

ⓘ Deep Creek Lake State Park $ *898 State Pk Rd; tel: (301) 387-5563; fax: (301) 387-4462.*

ⓘ High Mountain Sports *US-219; tel: (301) 387-4199.* Equipment for hire and lessons in mountain biking, water skiing and other water sports. Specialises in teaching beginners.

Deep Creek Lake is the nucleus of a surprisingly sophisticated resort region, with Wisp Golf Club, world-class fly-fishing streams and miles of hiking trails in state parks and forests. One of these leads to the beautiful **Swallow Falls** and a rocky, scenic river canyon. **Deep Creek Lake State Park** ✦ adjoins the artificial lake with a sandy beach, marina, fishing pier, bike paths and a playground. The Discovery Center offers hands-on activities and programmes, including field trips. An aquarium there shows native fish and historical exhibits describe mining and lumbering.

Accommodation and food in Deep Creek

Streams and Dreams $$ *(8214 Oakland-Sang Rd, Hoyes Landing; tel: (301) 387-6881, www.streams-and-dreams.net)* is a B&B that specialises in fishing. Offers fly-fishing trips; guests can fish in the private pond.

Carmel Cove $$ *(Glendale Rd; tel: (301) 387-0067)* sits above a cove where the inn keeps canoes for guests. Individually decorated rooms have queen-size beds and phones, and some have whirlpool tubs, fireplaces or decks. Breakfasts are bountiful.

Point View Inn $ *(Rte 219; tel: (301) 387-5555)* combines motel-style rooms with a good restaurant, overlooking the lake and serving three meals daily.

Deep Creek State Park $ *(898 State Pk Rd; tel: (301) 387-5563, fax: (301) 387-4462)* has 112 pitches, 25 with caravan hookups.

Canoe on the Run Café $ *(Rte 219 next to tourist information centre; tel: (301) 387-5933)* serves soups, sandwiches and salads at lunch and dinner, plus a few breakfast favourites.

Arrowhead Deli $ *(Rte 219 opposite tourist information centre; open 24 hours)* has inexpensive hot and cold foods for picnics, trail lunches or a whole dinner.

HAGERSTOWN**

i **Hagerstown Convention and Visitors Center** *16 Public Sq.; tel: (301) 791-3246; www.marylandmemories.org.*

↔ Hagerstown is near the crossroads of I-70 and I-81. US-40 passes through its centre.

P A large garage ($), free weekends, is off E Washington St in the town centre.

⌖ Neatly arranged in a grid, Hagerstown streets have quadrant designations to help you locate addresses.

The tourist information centre has several free *Hagerstown Downtown Walking Tour* maps, including one featuring 25 Civil War sites and another of 18 churches.

🏛 **Washington County Museum of Fine Arts** $ *City Park, Key St; tel: (301) 739-5727; www.washcomuseum.org; open Tue–Sun.*

Hager House $ *City Park, Key St; tel: (301) 739-8393; open Apr–Nov Tue–Sat 1000–1600, Sun 1400–1700.*

Miller House $ *135 W Washington St; tel: (301) 797-8782; open Apr–Dec Wed–Saturday 1300–1600.*

The **Washington County Museum of Fine Arts***** far exceeds the collections of many big city art museums. See works by Titian, Tintoretto and Veronese, a Lalique gallery, Tiffany and Steuben art glass, Whistler graphics, Rodin and Daumier bronzes, Peale portraits, American silver, folk art and fine furniture. Within sight is the period-furnished stone **Hager House***, built 1739–40 by the city's founder, a German immigrant; an adjacent small museum shows hundreds of artefacts from excavations. Also in City Park is the 1912 Engine 202 Steam Locomotive and Caboose, the last of its type, joined by eight cabooses.

A tour of **Miller House**** explores not only its many rooms of collections, but its own fascinating architectural and social history, beginning in 1818 as a potter's home and shop. The elegantly furnished parlour, Civil War collections, pottery, toys, 19th-century European dolls and over 200 clocks are notable.

Accommodation and food in Hagerstown

Indian Springs Campground $ (*10809 Big Pool Rd (Rte 56), Big Pool; tel: (301) 842-3336*) has tent pitches and caravan sites.

Sundays Bed and Breakfast $ (*39 Broadway; tel: (301) 797-4331 or (800) 221-4828*) has 14 nicely decorated rooms in an 1890 Queen Anne-style mansion, serving full breakfast and afternoon tea.

Winnie Price's Wilgrove Manor $–$$ (*635 Oak Hill Ave.; tel: (301) 733-6328*) is another grand mansion surrounded by a columned porch, where continental breakfast is served in good weather.

The Plum $ (*6 Rochester Pl., off West Washington St; tel: (301) 791-1717; open 0730–1430*) makes generous sandwiches to order, which you can eat in the quilt-decorated café or take away.

Rococo $$ (*20 W Washington St; tel: (301) 790-3331; lunch and dinner Mon–Sat*) creates sophisticated New American dishes and presents them elegantly. Veal specials are outstanding.

Schmankerl Stube Bavarian Restaurant $$ (*58 Sth Potomac St; tel: (301) 797-3354; open lunch Tue–Fri, dinner Tue–Sun*) serves *haupt*-German cuisine, with a few nods to lighter American tastes. In the summer there's a beer garden.

Above
Doll collection, Miller House

Maryland Theater
*21 S Potomac St; tel:
(301) 790-2000.*

**Western Maryland
Blues Fest** *Tel: (301) 739-
8577 ext 116; www.blues-
fest.com.* The first weekend
in June fills the city with
some of the best current
Blues artists.

Maryland Symphony
*Tel: (301) 791-3132; 4 July,
1930.* A concert at the
Antietam National
Battlefield on
Independence Day,
followed by fireworks.
Bring a picnic.

Right
Miller House

HARPERS FERRY❖❖❖

ℹ West Virginia Welcome Center US-340 at Washington St; tel: (304) 535-2627 or (800) 848-8687.

🅿 Follow signs to the National Historic Park car park, from which buses shuttle to the restored area. There is no parking in the historic district.

🏛 Harpers Ferry National Historic Park $ Visitors Center, Shenandoah St; tel: (304) 535-6223; open daily 0800–1700.

Antietam National Battlefield $ Rte 65, Sharpsburg; tel: (301) 432-5124. A 2-hour tour in your own car, led by a ranger, is free with park entrance.

🌐 Blue Ridge Outfitters Tel: (304) 725-3444; www.brocraft.com. Either hire bicycles and equipment, or take a guided trip along the C&O Canal.

The Shenandoah and Potomac rivers meld under tall cliffs, and the town of Harpers Ferry grew along the least steep of the junction's plunging hillsides. Also through this break in the Appalachian Mountains passes a historic route west, the train line and the C&O Canal, reached by a footbridge from the historic district.

Harpers Ferry National Historic Park❖❖❖ includes restored buildings housing static displays occasionally enlivened by costumed interpreters. John Brown's Fort is the relocated brick armoury where Brown's band made their stand and were captured. Beyond is a river overlook with signs relating local Civil War history, quite literally a tug of war as the town passed between Union and Confederate control.

Other stops include the Civil War Museum, John Brown Museum, industry displays, a dry goods store and a building showing historic construction techniques. Most compelling is the small **Black Voices Museum**, which chronicles slaves and freed Blacks in *ante-bellum* Harpers Ferry. Harper House, the oldest in town and furnished with Civil War-era antiques, is reached by steps from High St. The message at Harpers Ferry is a puzzling one, seeming to make a hero of John Brown for waging civil insurrection.

North of Harpers Ferry is **Antietam National Battlefield❖❖**, scene of the bloodiest single-day battle of the Civil War. A vivid film shown at the Visitors Center describes it, giving meaning to Sunken Road and Burnside Bridge, where Union troops finally forced the southern withdrawal. The loss at Antietam stopped Lee's northward advance and dissuaded the British from supporting the Confederacy.

Above
Harpers Ferry National Historic Park

Accommodation and food in Harpers Ferry

Hilltop House $–$$ (*400 E Ridge St; tel: (304) 535-2132 or (800) 338-8319*), a large traditional country inn, overlooks the rivers from a high bluff. The menu is equally traditional, serving three meals daily and specialising in fried chicken.

Hostelling International Harpers Ferry $–$$ (*19123 Sandy Hook Rd, Knoxville; tel: (301) 834-7652, fax: (301) 834-7652, www.members.aol.com/FerryLodge/Hostel; open mid-Mar–mid-Nov*), reached from Rte 340 in Maryland via Keep Tryst Rd, has bunks and private rooms.

Jacob Rohrbach Inn $–$$ (*138 W Main St, Sharpsburg; tel: (877) 839-4242 or (301) 432-5079*) is a comfortable 1832 home with engaging innkeepers. Antiques and reproductions furnish guest rooms and a summer kitchen now houses a hot tub.

The Anvil $–$$ (*1270 Washington St; tel: (304) 535-2582*) features seafood, chicken, steak and veal in a rustic setting – lunch and dinner daily.

Cliffside Inn $ (*Rte 340; tel: (304) 535-6302 or (800) 782-9437*) serves three home-style meals daily with weekend buffet.

Right
Kennedy Farm, near Harpers Ferry

OAKLAND**

Garrett County Visitors Center
US-219, McHenry; open Sun–Thur 0900–1700, Fri–Sat 1800.

Greater Oakland Business Association
Tel: (301) 533-4470; www.oaklandmd.com.

The free *Walking Guide* to Downtown points out interesting sights in Oakland – or Mayor Asa McCain will guide you on a personal free walking tour if available!

Garrett County Historical Museum
107 S Second St; tel: (301) 334-3226; open June–Sept Mon–Sat 1100–1600, or by appointment.

Grace's Craft Room 372 Joni-Miller Rd (off Mason Rd); tel: (301) 334-1010; Mon–Sat 0800–2000. This is the place to buy Amish quilts, woven rugs and other fabric arts.

The Oakland Farmers' Market Near the old railway station; open Wed–Sat 1000–1300. Browse around for farm produce and baked goods.

Sugar and Spice Bakery US-219 S; open Mon–Sat 0700–1730. Try the homemade cheese along with breads and delicious apple dumplings.

Welcoming the many prestigious guests who came to Oakland's resorts by train was the elegant 1884 B&O Railroad Depot, now under restoration. So many dignitaries visited that St Matthew's Church, across the street, was called 'The Church of Presidents'. The nearby **Garrett County Historical Museum**◆ is like a county attic, filled with bits and pieces of local history that include Archaic period Native American artefacts, folk art, coal-mine tools and Civil War items.

A number of Amish farms are south of Oakland on US-218, some with bakery or dairy shops. You will know when you are near Amish settlements when you encounter cautionary road signs for buggies and see them parked in dooryards.

Accommodation and food in Oakland

Deer Park Inn $$** (*65 Hotel Rd, Deer Park; tel: (301) 334-2308*) occupies one of the Victorian 'cottages' of the long-gone Grand Deer Park Hotel. The elegant dining room (**$$) serves innovative New American cuisine by reservation.

Oak and Apple B&B (*208 N Second St; tel: (301) 334-9265, www.oakandapple.com*) is a comfortable home with four guest rooms, two of which share a bath. Continental breakfast includes homemade breads and fresh fruit.

Cornish Manor Restaurant $$ (*Memorial Drive; tel: (301) 334-6499, fax 334-7848*) also ranks high in the fine dining class, with a continental (but never stodgy) menu. Eclectic décor and friendly hosts add to the evening.

Right
Oakland railway station

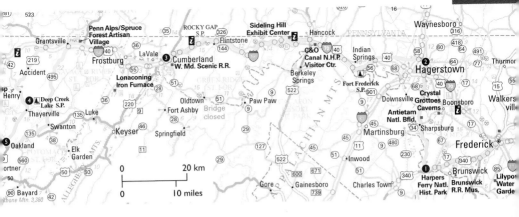

Suggested tour

Sideling Hill Information
Center *I-68, Harvey; open daily 0830–1800.*

Fort Frederick State Park $ *Rte 56, Big Spring; tel: (301) 842-2155.* Here you can find a picnic area, tent pitches and access to the C&O Canal towpath.

C&O Canal Hancock Visitors Center *326 E Main St; tel: (301) 678-5463; open daily June–Aug, Fri–Tue spring and fall.*

Thrasher Carriage Museum *19 Depot St; tel: (301) 689-3380; www. cumberland.com/thrasher; open May–Sept Tue–Sun 1100–1500, Oct daily, Nov–Dec Sat–Sun.*

Total distance: 294 miles.

Time: 8 hours' driving time. Allow 4 days minimum, 5 if you plan to enjoy any of the sports or activities.

Links: The tour begins in Frederick, a point on the North of Washington itinerary or easily reached from the capital by I-270. I-70 connects Frederick to Baltimore.

Route: Leave **FREDERICK** on US-340 to **HARPERS FERRY ❶**, following the un-numbered Scenic Route (designated by yellow flower signs) to Sharpsburg, where Rte 65 takes you past **Antietam Battlefield** to HAGERSTOWN ❷. Leave town on US-40 past historic stone Wilson Bridge to **Indian Springs**, following Rte 56 left to **Fort Frederick**, a rare stone Vauban-type defence built by the British during the French and Indian Wars. Backtrack to I-70/US-40 and continue west to **Hancock**, where the **C&O Canal Visitor Center** shows an excellent 1917 film with rare old footage.

From Hancock, US-40 and I-68 sometimes join, passing through **Sideling Cut**, an 800ft notch carved through the mountain, exposing a 20-million-year slice of geological history. Displays in **Sideling Hill Exhibit Center** explain this. Continue past **Rocky Gap State Park** to CUMBERLAND ❸. Leave via US-40, passing tiny **Toll Gate House** in LaVale and stopping in **Frostburg** to visit the outstanding **Thrasher Carriage Museum**, filled with restored horse-drawn vehicles.

Continue on US-40, crossing the **Eastern Continental Divide** at Meadow Mountain east of **Grantsville**. West of Grantsville, turn south (left) on US-219, along a scenic ridge to **Accident**, stopping to see the **Drane House**, a 1797 log farmhouse. Pass **DEEP CREEK LAKE ❹** before arriving in OAKLAND ❺. From **Oakland**, follow Rte 135 east to Rte 495, following it north (left) to Grantsville and I-68, which returns you to Hancock and I-70, back to Frederick.

Southern Maryland

Ratings

Art and museums	●●●●
Beaches	●●●●
Nature and wildlife	●●●●
Children	●●●
Entertainment	●●●
Historical sights	●●●
Gastronomy	●
Shopping and crafts	●

Separated from neighbouring land by the Chesapeake Bay on the east and the broad Potomac River on the south and west, Southern Maryland's wide peninsula is itself cut by several wide tidal rivers. The traveller in this relatively low and flat land is never far from water. This is the oldest part of the state, where its first settlers came in 1634 on two small ships, the *Ark* and the *Dove*, to establish a colony under Lord Baltimore.

Although the area has much of the charm and attraction of the Eastern Shore, it has never drawn many tourists, so you will find its beaches and parks uncrowded and the people you meet there will most likely be Marylanders. Those who enjoy fishing, fossil hunting or history will like this area especially, for it offers all three in abundance.

CHESAPEAKE BEACH✦

Breezy Point Beach $ *Breezy Point Rd, off Rte 261; tel: (410) 535-0259; open June–Aug 0600–2100.*

Chesapeake Beach Railway Museum $ *Main St; tel: (410) 257-3892; open May–Sept daily 1300–1600, Apr, Oct Sat–Sun 1300–1600.*

Beaches are what made Chesapeake Beach a popular resort in the 19th century, and they still bring people to the area. North Beach, just north of Chesapeake Beach, has a small public beach with a half-mile boardwalk. Bay Front Park, known locally as Brownie's Beach, is just south of Chesapeake City. You may find fossils there. **Breezy Point Beach✦✦** is a half-mile stretch of sand lapped by the Chesapeake, with picnic areas, a bathhouse, playground and a fishing and crabbing pier.

Chesapeake Beach Railway Museum✦ occupies the former station of the Chesapeake Beach Railroad, once the favoured way to arrive at this seaside resort. Old photographs and artefacts show the resort in its heyday. A 1914 Model-T Ford Depot Hack and half an 1889 railway

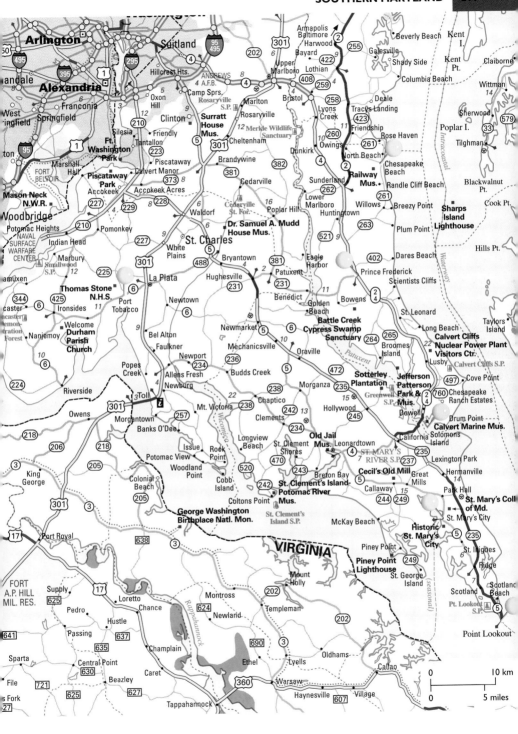

Arlington
Suitland
Andale
Alexandria
Franconia
West
ingfield Springfield
ton
Mason Neck
N.W.R.
Woodbridge
Potomac Heights
Indian Head
amuxen
Marbury
caster
emon-
ration
Forest Nanjemoy
King
George
FORT
A.P. HILL
MIL. RES.

Hillcrest Hts.
Oxon Hill
Camp Sprs.
Silesia
Ft. Washington Park
Piscataway Park
Accokeek
Accokeek Acres

ANDREWS
A.F.B.
Rosaryville S.P.
Clinton
Friendly
Tantallon
Piscataway
Calvert Manor
Waldorf
Pomonkey
White Plains
La Plata
Port Tobacco
Ironsides

Surratt House Mus.
Marlton
Cheltenham
Brandywine
Cedarville
Cedarville St. For.
Dr. Samuel A. Mudd House Mus.
St. Charles
Bryantown
Hughesville
Newtown
Bel Alton
Faulkner
Newport
Allens Fresh
Newburg
Budds Creek

Upper Marlboro
Bristol
Lyons Creek
Owings
Dunkirk
Sunderland
Lower Marlboro
Huntingtown
Eagle Harbor
Patuxent
Benedict
Bowens
Golden Beach
Newmarket
Mechanicsville
Oraville
Morganza
Chaptico
Clements

Annapolis
Baltimore
Harwood
Bayard
Lothian
Deale
Tracys Landing
Friendship
Rose Haven
North Beach
Chesapeake Beach
Railway Mus.
Randle Cliff Beach
Breezy Point
Plum Point
Dares Beach
Prince Frederick
Scientists Cliffs

Beverly Beach Kent I.
Galesville
Shady Side Kent Pt.
Columbia Beach
Wittman
Sherwood
Poplar I.
Tilghman

Blackwalnut Pt.
Sharps Island Lighthouse
Hills Pt.

St. Leonard
Battle Creek Cypress Swamp Sanctuary
Broomes Island
Long Beach
Sotterley Plantation
Jefferson Patterson Park & Mus.
California
Solomons Island
Calvert Marine Mus.
Hollywood
Old Jail Mus.
Leonardtown
ST. MARY'S RIVER S.P.
Cecil's Old Mill
Lexington Park
Hermanville
Great Mills
Callaway
Park Hall
St. Mary's Coll. of Md.
St. Mary's City
Historic St. Mary's City
St. Inigoes
Ridge
Scotland
Scotland Beach
Pt. Lookout S.P.
Point Lookout

Calvert Cliffs Nuclear Power Plant Visitors Ctr.
Lusby Calvert Cliffs S.P.
Taylors Island
Cove Point
Chesapeake Ranch Estates
Drum Point

Thomas Stone N.H.S.
Welcome
Durham Parish Church
Popes Creek
Riverside
Owens
Morgantown
Banks O'Dee
Issue
Potomac View
Woodland Point
Colonial Beach
George Washington Birthplace Natl. Mon.
Port Royal
Supply
Pedro
Hustle
Passing
Sparta
File
s Fork

Longview Beach
St. Clement Shores
Breton Bay
St. Clement's Island Potomac River Mus.
Coltons Point
St. Clement's Island S.P.
McKay Beach
Piney Point
Piney Point Lighthouse
St. George Island
Mount Holly
Loretto
Chance
Montross
Newland
Champlain
Central Point
Beazley
Caret
Tappahannock
Haynesville
Warsaw
Village
Oldhams
Lyells
Ethel
Templeman

VIRGINIA

Intracoastal Waterway
Patuxent
Wicomico
Rappahannock
St. Mary's River S.P. (seasonal)

Smallwood S.P.
Marshall Hall
FORT BELVOIR

Cook Pt.

0 ___ 10 km
0 ___ 5 miles

495 395 295 1
202 301 255 422
408 259 258 423 260 261
4 2 262 263
521 402 472 264 265 497 760 235 245 237 243 470 520 242 244 249
381 382
488 231 238
234 236
257 206 218 205
344 425 224
625 17 624 637 635 630 627 641 721 625
227 228 229 223 210
344 6
202 3 360 607

At North Beach:
**Chesapeake
Antique Center** *4133
7th St.* Stocks collectibles
and Victoriana.

**Nice and Fleazy
Antique Center** *7th and
Bay Ave.* Sells fine silver,
nautical items, jewellery.

Bay Avenue Antiques
9132B Bay Ave. Fine glass
and crystal, porcelain,
decoys.

**Chesapeake Beach
Fishing Charters**
Tel: (301) 855-4665.
Fifteen boats are
represented, including
Mary Lou II *(tel: (301)
855-0784). Half-day, full-day
and evening trips, June–Sept.*

carriage complete the collection. The fishing capital of the bay,
Chesapeake Beach is close enough to prime fishing grounds for a 6-
hour trip to be productive.

Right
Railway museum,
Chesapeake Beach

Accommodation and food in Chesapeake Beach

Tidewater Treasures B&B $$ *(7315 Bayside Road; tel: (410) 257-0785)*
is a modern home overlooking Bay Front Park and its beach, each
room with a view of the bay.

Breezy Point Campground $ *(Breezy Point Rd, off Rte 261; tel: (410)
535-0259 or (410) 535-1600 out of season for reservations – call in mid-
Jan for July–Aug weekends; open June–Oct)* has caravan sites on the water,
with or without electric hookup, with a playground, 300ft fishing and
crabbing pier and a half-mile beach.

Rod and Reel Restaurant $$ *(Rte 261 and Mears Ave.; tel: (410) 257-
2735 or (301) 855-8351)* serves traditional seafood, many dishes
broiled instead of fried.

POINT LOOKOUT*

Point Lookout State Park *Rte 5, Scotland; tel: (301) 872-5688.*

Scheible's Fishing Center *48342 Wynne Rd, Ridge; tel: (301) 872-5185, or (800) 895-6132; www. webgraphic.com/scheibles.* Scheible's is a major outfitter for fishing in the Potomac and Chesapeake, with 15 charter boats and an 80-passenger headboat.

Blue and Gray Days *Fort Lincoln, Point Lookout State Park; tel: (301) 872-5688.* Civil War activities are re-enacted in late June.

Below
Point Lookout Civil War camp

Point Lookout State Park* is at the tip of the peninsula where the Potomac meets Chesapeake Bay. Along with good canoeing (rentals available) and swimming, there is fishing from the shore and from a pier extending 250m into Chesapeake Bay. Fort Lincoln served as a prisoner-of-war camp for Confederate soldiers during the Civil War, and monuments honour the 3 364 buried there. The earth embankments of the old fort are open to the public, and some of the buildings have been reconstructed. The park's Visitors Center has displays on the Civil War camp, as well as nature exhibits, including live reptiles and amphibians. At the very tip of the point, Point Lookout Lighthouse is replete with ghost stories.

Accommodation and food in Point Lookout

Point Lookout State Park (*Rte 5, Scotland; tel: (301) 872-5688*) has a large camp-pitch, one area of it on the water. Inland sites may have annoying biting insects.

Scheible's Crab Pot Restaurant $–$$ (*48342 Wynne Road, Ridge; tel: (301) 872-5185*) serves seafood, plus Maryland fried chicken. Look for bargains weeknights and by ordering 'basket' style meals.

PORT TOBACCO❖

ℹ Charles County Tourism Division
8190 Port Tobacco Rd; tel: (301) 934-9305 ext 195 or (800) 766-3386 ext 146.

🏛 Port Tobacco Courthouse and Museum $ *Chapel Point Rd, off Rte 6; tel: (301) 934-4313; open Wed–Sun 1200–1600.*

Thomas Stone House $ *6655 Rose Hill Rd, between Rtes 225 and 6; tel: (301) 934-6027; open June–Aug daily 0900–1700, rest of the year Thur–Mon.*

St Ignatius Church *Chapel Point Rd; Mass Sat 0900, 1700, Sun 0730, 0900, 1100, 1800, weekdays 0800 and 1200.*

🎣 Reel Bass Adventures *10100 Old Franklin Ave., Seabrook; tel: (301) 839-2858. Charter fishing trips are tailored to individual skills and interests, all led by expert fishermen. They provide top-notch equipment and lures.*

🌊 Blessing of the Fleet *First Sat in Aug 1530. This is part of the Potomac River Festival.*

Port Tobacco, founded in 1634, was a thriving seaport, but all that is left of it now is a pretty cluster of 18th-century homes and a reconstruction of the brick **Courthouse❖**, now a museum. A museum gift shop has local crafts and books. **Thomas Stone House❖❖** is a gracious five-part Georgian plantation built about 1770 by Thomas Stone, a signer of the Declaration of Independence and Articles of Confederation. The beautifully panelled East Room is the highlight.

Overlooking Chapel Point, **St Ignatius Church❖** dates from 1798, on the site of the first Catholic services, which were then illegal. It is the oldest continuously active Roman Catholic parish in the USA, with a relic of the True Cross brought by its founder. Beside St Thomas Manor, a Jesuit residence built 100 years later, the small Cook's House has an open bulkhead leading to a tunnel out to the hillside. Originally used to smuggle priests, it later hid slaves on the Underground Railroad. The sunset view from the church, the stones of its churchyard silhouetted against the orange sky, is outstanding.

Accommodation and food in Port Tobacco

La Plata Inn $ (*400 Sth Hwy 301, La Plata; tel: (301) 934-4900 or (800) 528-1234*) is a modern and comfortable hotel on the major route through the region.

Smallwood State Park $ (*Rte 224, Marbury; tel: (301) 743-7613, reservations (800) 784-5380*) has 16 camp pitches overlooking the water, with a marina, boat rental and fishing.

Captain Billy's $–$$ (*Pope's Creek Rd, off Rte 301; tel: (301) 932-4323*) is renowned for its big trays of hardshell crabs 'in the rough'. Don't be shy, they will show you how to attack these delicacies with a mallet and extract every last morsel. Crabcakes, fried oysters, scallops and fried chicken are on the menu if you don't relish this quintessential Maryland feast.

**Casey Jones Restaurant $$** (*417 E Charles St, La Plata; tel: (301) 932-6226*) has fine (very fine indeed) dining and a separate pub ($) serving unique pizzas. In the restaurant expect the likes of grilled duck with *foie gras*.

Above
St Ignatius Church

PRINCE FREDERICK❖❖

Calvert County Tourism *175 Main St; tel: (410) 535-4583 or (800) 331-9771.*

Battle Creek Cypress Swamp Sanctuary *Gray's Rd, off Rte 506; tel: (410) 535-5327; open Apr–Sept Tue–Sat 1000–1700, Sun 1300–1700, Oct–Mar until 1630.*

Calvert Cliffs State Park $ *Rte 765, off Rte 2/4, Lusby; tel: (301) 872-5688; open daylight hours.*

Jefferson Patterson Park *10515 Mackall Rd (Rte 256), St Leonard; tel: (410) 586-8500; open year-round; Visitors Center mid-Apr–mid-Oct Wed–Sun 1000–1700.*

Chesapeake Antique Flea Market and Specialty Shops *Calvert Beach Rd, St Leonard; tel: (410) 586-3725; open Wed–Sun 1000–1700, auctions Wed and Fri. Seventy dealers ply their wares here.*

Calvert County's Farmers' Market *Rte 2/4 South; tel: (410) 535-4583; Sat 0900–1600, Sun 1300–1800, Wed 1500–1900. While you shop your children can explore the children's playground.*

Penn Auto *5 Church St; tel: (301) 855-1781 or (410) 535-2222. Penn Auto hire out bicycles.*

Battle Creek Cypress Swamp Sanctuary❖❖ is a fascinating, if somewhat spooky world of tall cypress trees whose knobbly knees poke up through the water. The Nature Center shows the life cycles of the trees and the swamp, which a boardwalk takes you through with dry feet. At **Calvert Cliffs State Park**❖❖❖, few can resist the lure of a beach strewn with fossils from the Miocene Epoch, teeth of sharks that swam there millions of years ago. The beach is accessed by a woodland trail.

Evidence of human history dates back 12,000 years at **Jefferson Patterson Park**❖❖. Trails and exhibits show how people used the land, and the Discovery Room provides binoculars, field guides, and Indian and Colonial tools and games you can use outside. Other excellent hands-on activities teach about early life and archaeologists' work. Exhibits illustrate the conservation of artefacts, underwater archaeology, the Battle of Leonard's Creek and local ecology. A replica Native American campsite with a reed house is on the Woodland Trail. At the Agricultural Center old tools are displayed and often demonstrated.

Accommodation and food in Prince Frederick

Serenity Acres B&B $–$$ *(4270 Hardesty Rd, Huntingtown; tel: (410) 535-3744, www.bbonline.com/md/serenity)* combines the warmth of a private home with the privacy of an inn. Nicely decorated rooms overlook beautiful gardens and a swimming pool.

Old Field Inn $$ *(485 Main St; tel: (410) 535-1054 or (301) 855-1054)* serves interesting updates on continental and Chesapeake classics. Veal Wellington, for example, is stuffed with blended cheeses and pignoli nuts before wrapping in puff pastry to roast.

Right
Jefferson Patterson Park, Native American dwelling

SOLOMONS ISLAND❖❖❖

ℹ️ **Tourist Information**
Solomons Island Rd; tel: (410) 326-6027; open daily 0900–1700, later in summer.

Solomons Water Taxi Tel: (410) 535-7022; daily in summer. There are stops at 24 locations, including inns, restaurants and the Calvert Marine Museum.

William B Tennyson Calvert Marine Museum; tel: (410) 326-2042; runs May–Oct Wed–Sun 1400, July–Aug weekends 1230, 1400, 1600. One-hour cruises feature the bay's natural and human history.

Calvert Marine Museum and Drum Point Lighthouse $$ Solomons Island Rd; tel: (410) 326-2042; open 1000–1700 daily.

J C Lore and Sons Oyster House Solomons Island Rd; open June–Aug daily 1000–1630, May and Sept weekends.

Annemarie Garden Dowell Rd, off Rte 2/4; tel: (410) 326-4640; open daily 1000–1600.

Sea Dive and Bicycle Rte 2/4, S&W Shopping Center, Solomons Island; tel: (410) 326-4386.

Bunky's Charter Boat Rentals $$$ Solomons Island Rd; tel: (410) 326-3241. The headboat Marchelle leaves 0700 and 1300 daily, as well as charters.

Almost completely surrounded by water, Solomons is popular for fishing, boating and the outstanding **Calvert Marine Museum**❖❖❖, whose well-designed exhibits illuminate the natural and human history of the Chesapeake, covering everything from the Miocene Sea to the Triangle Trade and the War of 1812. Undersea exploration vehicles, the Navy in World War II, watermen and oyster packing are all explored and fossil collections help recognise those found on the beaches. An aquarium and a pair of river otters named Bubble and Squeak are highlights for children.

Drum Point Lighthouse stands outside on tall stilts, and you can climb inside to see the keepers' quarters and light. In the water and sheds below are vintage craft, including the *William B Tennyson*. **J C Lore and Sons Oyster House**❖ is a working 1888 cannery with all of its original equipment. A video tells the story of the island, fishermen and packers.

Annemarie Garden❖❖ combines gardens with public art space, a series of outdoor rooms, each by a prominent artist or sculptor. One is a small dance stage, another a series of wooden ramps leading to treetop level in the lovely wooded grounds.

Accommodation and food in Solomons Island

Solomons Victorian Inn $–$$ (*125 Charles St; tel: (410) 326-4811, www.chesapeake.net/solomonsvictorianinn*) eight rooms and a suite have private baths; those in the new Carriage House have private entrances. A full breakfast is served in a glass-enclosed porch overlooking the harbour and gardens.

CD Café $–$$ (*14350 Solomons Island Rd; tel: (410) 326-3877*) offers espresso and pastries or creative dinners using fresh local ingredients. It may be crowded at dinnertime.

St Mary's City❖❖❖

ℹ St Mary's County Tourism *Washington St, Leonardtown; tel: (410) 326-6027.*

🏛 Historic St Mary's City **$$** *Rte 5; tel: (301) 862-0990; www.webraphic.com/hsmc; open May–Nov Wed–Sun 1000–1700.*

Patuxent River Naval Air Museum *Rte 235, Patuxent River; tel: (301) 863-7418; open Wed–Sun 1200–1700.*

⛵ St Mary's County Crab Festival *Leonardtown; tel: (301) 475-8403; mid-June.* As well as the obvious, this includes an antique car show and craft sale.

Tidewater Archaeology Dig *Historic St Mary's City; tel: (301) 862-0990; late July.* Visitors can join in archaeological excavations.

Grand Militia Muster *Historic St Mary's City; tel: (301) 862-0990; 2nd weekend Oct.* The largest 17th-century military re-enactment in the country.

If you look for the 'city' in tiny St Mary's City, you are not alone: archaeologists and historians have been digging it up for years, trying to reconstruct what was once Maryland's thriving first settlement. Costumed interpreters at **Historic St Mary's City**❖❖❖ re-create the setting, even speaking in early 1600s language.

Buildings are being reconstructed on their original sites in four main areas connected by roads and wide walking paths. Begin at the Visitors Center for background displays and film, then visit the nearby cluster of reconstructed bark and thatch longhouses. A farmhouse shows homely arts and period farm skills.

Around the reconstruction of the imposing brick 1676 State House are the Ordinary, an early lodging, and the merchant ship *Dove*, replicating the one that brought the original settlers from England. The house skeletons along the roads mark the sites of buildings identified by archaeologists, to be reconstructed by costumed interpreters.

Patuxent River Naval Air Museum❖ will fascinate anyone interested in the space programme or flight, with collections of aircraft and air-related hardware and exhibits. Learn how a jet engine works, what test pilots do, how gear and equipment are tested. Ask to see the films, especially the one on the Blue Angels, the US Navy's Red Arrow counterpart.

Accommodation and food in St Mary's City

See Solomons Island for all tourist services.

Opposite
Archaeologist at work in Calvert Marine Museum

Right
Historic St Mary's City

Suggested tour

Cecil's Old Mill
Indian Bridge Rd, Great Mills; tel: (301) 994-1510; open mid-Mar–Oct Thur–Sun 1000–1700, daily Nov–Dec.

Potomac River Museum *Coltons Point; tel: (301) 769-2222; open Apr–Sept Mon–Fri 0900–1700, Sat–Sun 1200–1700, Oct–Mar Wed–Sunday 1200–1600.*

Below
St Mary's City

Total distance: 182 miles.

Time: Driving time 5–6 hours. Allow 3 days. Those with limited time should see Historic St Mary's City, Calvert Cliffs and the Calvert Marine Museum.

Links: From Annapolis, follow Rte 2 south. From Fredericksburg, Virginia, US-301 crosses the Potomac and joins the route south of Port Tobacco. From Washington, Rte 5 (Beltway Exit 7) connects Washington to the end of the suggested route.

Route: Travel south from **Annapolis** on Rte 2, diverting left on Rte 260 to **CHESAPEAKE BEACH ❶** and following Rte 261 south past **Breezy Point Beach** to Rte 263. Rejoin Rte 2, now 2/4, and continue south to **PRINCE FREDERICK ❷**. Continue south past **Calvert Cliffs State Park** and turn off to **SOLOMONS ISLAND ❸** just before the bridge over the Patuxent River. Cross the bridge and turn left on to Rte 235.

Follow Rte 235 south past the **Patuxent River Naval Air Museum** to its junction with Rte 5, following Rte 5 left (south) to its end at **POINT LOOKOUT ❹**. Retrace your route to the intersection, continuing north on Rte 5 to **ST MARY'S CITY ❺**. Continue on Rte 5, which heads west, through Great Mills, worth a stop for historic **Cecil's Old Mill**, an artisan's shop selling and demonstrating Maryland-made crafts.

Rte 5 continues through **Leonardtown**, with a museum in an old jail. Shortly past Leonardtown, bear left on to Rte 234 through the town of **Clements**.

Continue west on Rte 234 until it ends at US-301, turning right. In about 4 miles, turn left on to Chapel Point Rd, passing **St Ignatius Church** and continuing to **PORT TOBACCO ❻**. Turn left on Rte 6, and almost immediately right on to Rose Hill Rd to visit the **Thomas Stone House**. Continue to Rte 225, turning right to **La Plata** and left on US-301, which will return you to Annapolis or take you to Rte 5, north to the Beltway or into Washington, DC.

Farthing's Ordinary

North Chesapeake Bay

Ratings

Entertainment	●●●●
Historical sights	●●●●
Beaches	●●●
Children	●●●
Gastronomy	●●●
Nature and wildlife	●●●
Art and museums	●●
Shopping and crafts	●●

The land at the head of the Chesapeake lies between wide rivers that feed the bay, and the entire shore is deeply cut by tidal estuaries: the Wye, the Chester, the Sassafras, the Elk and the Northeast. Kent and Wye islands form stepping stones that narrow the bay enough for a bridge to span it. Few cities, none of any size, intrude on the rural land and seascapes of the Eastern Shore's northern reaches.

Apart from the destruction of Havre de Grace and Georgetown in the War of 1812, this corner of the bay has enjoyed a relatively quiet history. Today its towns look much as they have for the last century, with gracious old homes, the harbours on their tidal rivers now filled with pleasure boats instead of the skipjacks that once formed the core of the economy.

CHESAPEAKE CITY✦✦

P Chesapeake City is famed for police who ticket non-residents at any excuse, even while unloading luggage. Use only your lodging, restaurant or the museum car parks.

The Chesapeake and Delaware Canal saves ships bound for Baltimore about 300 miles and the local amusement is watching barges go by. Learn more about this interesting waterway at the well-designed **C&D Canal Museum**✦, where an animated model shows how locks work. The town's historic buildings centre around Bohemia Ave.

C&D Canal Museum *Beside the canal; open Mon–Sat 0800–1615, Sun Apr–Sept 1000–1800.*

Accommodation and food in Chesapeake City

The Blue Max $–$$ (*300 South Bohemia Ave.; tel: (410) 885-2781*) has large attractive rooms and a lovely guest parlour, as well as a long front veranda for relaxing.

Bayard House Restaurant $$$ (*11 Bohemia Ave.; tel: (410) 885-5040*)

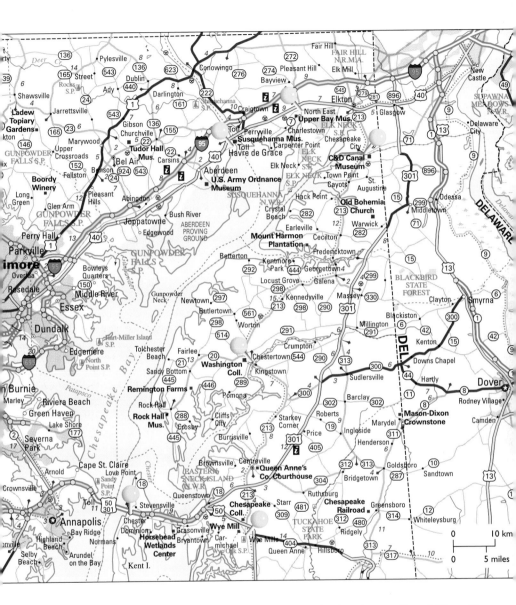

Boutiques, craft shops and antique emporia fill historic buildings along Bohemia Ave.

does wonderful things with local seafood, such as stuffing chillies with crab and shrimp.

Chesapeake Inn Restaurant $$ (*605 Second St; tel: (410) 885-2040*) skilfully blends Italian culinary traditions with local seafood. In summer lighter dishes of soft-crab or crabcake sandwiches, pasta and creative pizzas are served on the deck.

CHESTERTOWN✦✦✦

ⓘ Kent County Tourism *100 N Cross St; tel: (410) 778-0416.*

ⓖ Historic Walking Tours $ *High St; tel: (410) 778-2829; Mar–Nov Sun 1100.* Tours of Chestertown begin at the park.

ⓗ Geddes-Piper House $ *101 Church Alley; tel: (410) 778-3499; open May–Oct Sat–Sun 1300–1600.*

On the last weekend of May, Chestertown commemorates its own 'Tea Party' in 1774, similar to Boston's, when crates of tea were dumped into Chester River, with costumed re-enactments, crafts and a parade.

Prim rows of homes from the Colonial and later eras form Chestertown's historic district, highlighted by the restored 1780s **Geddes-Piper House**✦, furnished with fine period pieces. Widehall is an elaborate 1770 town home next to the town landing, where Chestertown's Tea Party took place. Queen Street is lined by tradesmen's and merchants' homes from the 18th and early 19th centuries.

Accommodation and food in Chestertown

The Parker House $–$$ (*108 Spring Ave.; tel: (410) 778-9041, fax: (410) 778-7318, www.chestertown.com/parker*) is close to the historic centre, with large rooms and Victorian beds. No credit cards.

White Swan Tavern $–$$ (*231 High St; tel: (410) 778-2300, fax: (410) 778-4543*) dates from 1733, with beautifully restored rooms and suites furnished in period antiques. The original kitchen has a walk-in fireplace. Afternoon tea is included, also served to the public (*Thur–Tue 1500–1700*), reservation suggested.

Blue Heron Café $$ (*Cannon St; tel: (410) 778-0188*) features regional ingredients in creative New American dishes, for lunch and dinner Tue–Sun.

Play It Again Sam $ (*108 South Cross St; tel: (410) 778-2688; open Mon–Sat 0700–1530, Sun 0900–1600*) serves bountiful croissant sandwiches, pie, cake, gourmet coffees and ice cream.

HAVRE DE GRACE**

ⓘ Chamber of Commerce 220
North Washington St; tel: (410) 939-3303 or (800) 851-7756; www.hdgtourism.com. An excellent Self-Guided Tour and street map from the Chamber of Commerce describes the fine architecture in its historical context.

ⓐ A Tours *Tel: (410) 939-1133; Tue–Sun. Explore the Underground Railroad and Civil War-era sites by appointment.*

Skipjack *Martha Lewis* *Congress Ave.; tel: (302) 777-5488 or (800) 406-0766; tours every 2 hours Sat–Sun 1200–1800. A rare working oyster boat offers sailing tours focusing on the environment, oysters, birds and marine life.*

ⓘ Concord Point Lighthouse *Concord and Lafayette Sts; open Apr–Oct Sat–Sun 1300–1700.*

Decoy Museum $ *215 Giles St; tel: (410) 939-3739; www.decoymuseum.com; open daily 1100–1600.*

Susquehanna Lockhouse Museum $ *Erie St; tel: (410) 939-5780; open May–Oct Sat–Sun 1300–1700.*

US Army Ordnance Museum *Aberdeen Proving Ground, Rte 22; tel: (410) 278-3602; www.ordmusfound.org; open daily 1000–1645.*

British travellers are far more welcome today than they were in 1813, when they torched the town. Only the Flemish-bond brick Episcopal Church and a few homes remained, but the result was the town rebuilt in the elegant Victorian mansions that you see today, especially on Union Street.

Granite **Concord Point Lighthouse** was built in 1827 and the stone house opposite was the keeper's house. A boardwalk promenade through a bird-filled tidal marsh connects to the **Decoy Museum**, where displays show the history of decoy-making and their artists. Tydings Park, at the end of the promenade, has picnic tables and a playground.

At the opposite side of town, the **Susquehanna Lockhouse Museum** was home and office to the lock-keeper. A reconstructed pivot bridge is at the site.

In neighbouring Aberdeen, the **US Army Ordnance Museum** explores the history of firearms with collections of rare breech-loaders, Sharps and other early arms. Outside, the 'Mile of Tanks' fills fields row on row.

Accommodation and food in Havre de Grace

Currier House Bed and Breakfast $–$$ *(800 South Market St; tel: (410) 939-7886 or (800) 827-2889, www.currier-bb.com)* is one of the few homes to survive the War of 1812, in a quiet neighbourhood with a view of the lighthouse.

Vandiver Inn $–$$ *(301 South Union Ave.; tel: (410) 939-5200 or (800) 245-1655, www.vandiverinn.com)* occupies a grand and elegantly decorated 1886 mansion, listed on the National Historic Register.

The Crazy Swede $$ *(400 N Union Ave.; tel: (410) 939-8020)* gives Chesapeake seafood dishes a new look, combining veal with shrimp and crabmeat and offering many non-seafood choices. One- and two-bedroom suites include breakfast.

Price's Seafood $–$$ *(654 Water St; tel: (410) 939-2782)* is a really old-fashioned crab house, with no pretensions and lots of character.

Tidewater Grille $$ *(300 Franklin St; tel: (410) 939-3313)* overlooks the bay, serving lunch and dinner from a varied menu that includes fried or broiled crabcakes.

KENT ISLAND AND WYE MILLS❖❖

ℹ️ Queen Anne's County publishes an excellent free *Explore Our History and Heritage* packet covering the area from its aboriginal inhabitants. Available at most inns.

🏨 **Pintail Point Farm** $$$ *511 Pintail Point Ln., Queenstown; tel: (410) 827-7029.*

Horsehead Wetlands Center $ *600 Discovery Ln., Grasonville; tel: (410) 827-7029.*

Wye Grist Mill $ *Wye Mills; open mid-Mar–mid-Nov Mon–Fri 1000–1300, Sat–Sun 1000–1600, operating first and third Sat.*

🏕️ **Matapeake State Park** $ *Kent Island.* Picnic tables overlook a long fishing pier, especially scenic at sunset. Free picnic sites are at Wye Grist Mill and Wye Oak.

🛍️ **Prime Outlets** is a giant mall filled with cut-price shops, on US-50 near its split from US-301, near Wye River.

Pintail Point Farm❖, in a beautiful bayside setting, offers a 24-station sporting clays (clay pigeons) shooting course and both fresh and saltwater fly fishing, with an Orvis-endorsed instruction programme. An 18-hole Scottish links golf course is open to the public. **Horsehead Wetlands Center**❖ preserves bird habitats, where you can see natives and exotics wild and in aviaries. Trails lead through coastal forest to a marsh boardwalk and blinds.

Wye Grist Mill❖❖ still grinds grain as it has since the Revolution. A small museum has displays on local agriculture. Old Wye Church was built in 1721, with box pews, a graceful centre pulpit and a rare royal coat of arms. Most were destroyed during the Revolution.

Accommodation and food in Kent Island and Wye Mills

Kent Manor Inn $$ (*500 Kent Manor Dr., Kent Island; tel: (410) 643-5757 or (800) 820-4511*) occupies a beautifully restored plantation home on a tidewater farm, with its own docks and walking trails, and serves peerless crabcakes, and other delicacies at lunch and dinner daily.

The Queenstown Inn Bed and Breakfast $$ (*7109 Main St, Queenstown; tel: (410) 827-3396*) blends modern and antique furniture in comfortable large rooms. Breakfast features homemade breads.

Tuckahoe State Park $ (*Crouse Hill Rd, Queen Anne; tel: (410) 820-1668; open mid-Apr–mid-Oct*) has caravan sites and tent pitches, no reservations.

Harris Crab House $–$$ (*Kent Narrows, Grasonville; tel: (410) 824-9500; open daily from 1100*) is big, noisy and busy, so expect to wait in the evening for a brown-paper-covered table and a tray of crabs – messy, but delicious.

Hemingway's $$ (*US-50/301, Kent Island; tel: (410) 643-CRAB*) brings unusual flair to seafood favourites, with Spanish-style shrimp sautéed in olive oil and garlic or flounder stuffed with shrimp mousse. Open year-round, daily from 1100.

Above
Kent Manor Inn, Kent Island

NORTH EAST❖

ⓘ Cecil County Tourism *129 E Main St, Elkton; tel: (410) 996-5300.*

ⓘ Upper Bay Museum *219 Walnut St; tel: (410) 287-2675; open June–Aug Sat 1000–1500, Sun 1000–1600.*

Elk Neck State Park *Rte 272; tel: (410) 287-5333.*

⬤ Day Basket Factory *714 Main St; tel: (410) 287-6100.* Baskets are made entirely by hand, starting with white oak planks. Watch the process and buy these individually crafted signed baskets at the shop.

⬤ Elk Neck State Park $ has a beach on the Susquehanna which is shallow water for some distance, especially good for children.

⬤ A Decoy Show takes place at the Upper Bay Museum (*tel: (410) 287-2675*) on the third weekend in Oct.

The **Upper Bay Museum**❖❖ records the culture of the upper bay, along with collecting boats, watermen's tools, decoys and Native American stone weapons.

Elk Neck State Park❖❖ crowns the high point that separates Elk River from the Susquehanna at the head of the Chesapeake. Turkey Point Lighthouse guards the tip, its steady solar-powered beacon still active. The main C&D Canal channel is to the left, a good place to watch ships and barges. Walk the trail around the point, but shun the dangerously undercut cliffs.

Accommodation and food in North East

Crystal Inn $–$$ (*1 Center Dr. at I-95 exit 100; tel: (410) 287-7100 or (800) 631-3803, fax: (410) 287-7109*) is plain but comfortable, with a 24-hour restaurant, indoor pool and buffet breakfast included.

The Mill House Bed and Breakfast $–$$ (*102 Mill Lane; tel: (410) 287-3532*) is in the town centre, dating from the early 1700s.

Woody's Crab House $ (*29 Main St; tel: (410) 287-3541; open Mar–Dec*) is a casual waterside eatery with trays of hardshell crabs and fried fish.

Right
Elk Neck Lighthouse

Suggested tour

Skipjack Cove Marina Tel: (410) 275-2122. On the Sassafras River in Georgetown, you can hire a kayak or take a guided trip up the tidal creeks.

Mount Harmon Plantation $ Grove Neck Rd, Earleville; tel: (410) 275-8819; open for tours Tue, Thur 1000–1500, Sun 1300–1600.

Watermen's Museum Tel: (410) 778-669; open Sat–Sun 1000–1700. Enquire at adjacent Marina for key Mon–Fri.

Rock Hall Museum Town Hall, Main St; tel: (410) 778-1399; open Wed–Fri 1400–1630.

Kitty Knight House $ Rte 213, Georgetown; tel: (410) 648-5777 or (800) 404-8712, fax: (410) 648-5729. Overlooks the Sassafras River with a variety of rooms and some suites for families. The dining room ($$) is popular, serving dishes such as cashew-crusted chicken breast or tomato-basil crab crêpes.

Total distance: 160 miles, 208 with detours.

Time: 4 hours driving time – allow 2–3 days. Those with limited time should concentrate on Chestertown and Havre de Grace.

Links: Baltimore and Annapolis are part of the route. At the eastern end of the Bay Bridge, follow US-50 south to Easton to begin the Eastern Shore itinerary, or connect to the Ocean City–Dover itinerary in Chestertown via Rte 291, which becomes Delaware Rte 6, meeting US-13 north of Dover.

Route: From **Baltimore** follow Rte 2 to US-50/301 East, crossing the Bay Bridge to **KENT ISLAND ❶** and **WYE MILLS ❷**. Head north on Rte 313 to **CHESTERTOWN ❸** and continue to follow it north, crossing the Sassafras River at Georgetown.

Detour: In Cecilton, turn left on to Rte 282 to **Mount Harmon Plantation**, at the end of a long lane, its terraced boxwood parterre gardens framed by wisteria vines. The Georgian manor house dates from 1730 and is furnished with American and British antiques.

Continue on Rte 213 to **CHESAPEAKE CITY ❹** and north to **Elkton**, where a left turn on to Rte 7 leads to **NORTH EAST ❺**.

Detour: Rte 213 continues north to Fair Hill, and the large **Fair Hill Natural Resource Management Area**, known for its thoroughbred racing centre and excellent fishing in Big Elk Creek. The 1860 Tawes Drive Covered Bridge is in the northern section.

From North East, Rte 272 leads south into **Elk Neck State Park**. Backtrack to Rte 7, going west to **HAVRE DE GRACE ❻**. US-40 continues south past Aberdeen and back to Baltimore.

Also worth exploring

Rock Hall, west of Chestertown on Rte 20, celebrates its roots at the **Watermen's Museum**, where exhibits show tools used by the crabbing, fishing and oyster fleets that worked from its harbour. The **Rock Hall Museum** continues in the same theme, with models and displays on shipping, plus Native American artefacts. Beyond, Eastern Neck Wildlife Refuge is a good place to spot migrating birds or the many others that nest there.

Right
Chestertown

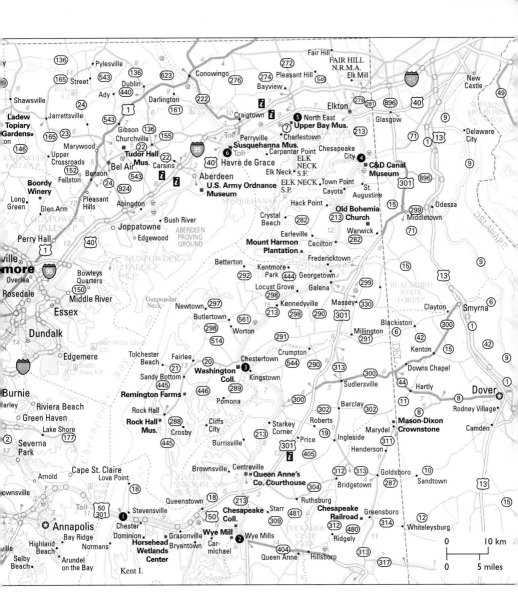

Ocean City and Delaware Shore

Ratings

Beaches	●●●●●
Children	●●●●●
Nature and wildlife	●●●●●
Entertainment	●●●○○
Gastronomy	●●●○○
Historical sights	●●●○○
Shopping and crafts	●●●○○
Art and museums	●○○○○

Beaches are what the area does best, and travellers can choose between two sharply contrasting styles. The major resorts of Ocean City and Rehoboth Beach are filled with activity, entertainment and people, while the state and national parks of Assateague, Fenwick Island and Cape Henlopen offer miles of beach with quiet stretches even in mid-summer.

A long narrow barrier island lies offshore from Cape Henlopen to Assateague, a national park known best for its wild horses. During a hurricane in 1933, the ocean cut an inlet between Ocean City and Assateague, but this is the only break. Between the barrier island and mainland are wide salt ponds that provide bird habitats and opportunities for water sports.

ASSATEAGUE AND BERLIN✦✦✦

ℹ️ **Delaware Tourism** 99 Kings Hwy, Dover 19903; tel: (302) 739-4271 or (800) 441-8846.

Assateague Island National Seashore Visitors Center Rte 611, Berlin; tel: (401) 641-1441; open daily 0900–1700.

Inside the federally managed Assateague National Seashore is Assateague Island State Park, both with tourist services, such as campgrounds and canoe/bicycle rentals. At the Visitors Center are exhibits, several excellent films and a touch tank where you can play with sea creatures. Adjacent is a picnic area. To see the wild horses, which roam freely, drive slowly along the park roads. On hot summer days, look for them on the beach.

Three short nature trails explore park ecosystems, including dunes, forest and marsh, a habitat rich in song and wading shore birds. Three miles of bike paths explore other areas. Several historic sites are marked by signs, one explaining the remains of a shipwreck.

Often used as a movie set, Berlin has an attractive downtown of

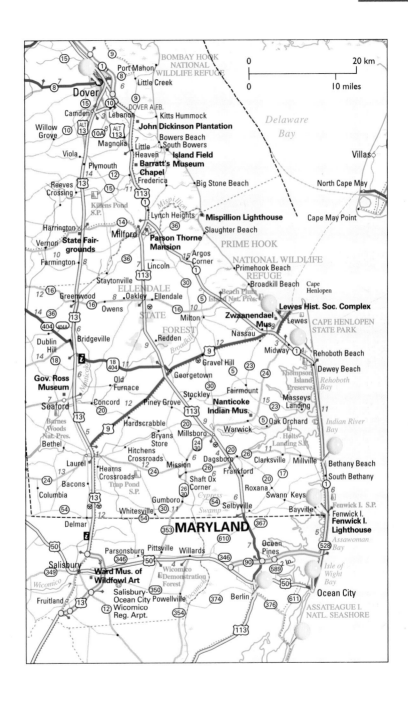

P The only car parks on Assateague are at the Visitors Center, from which you can walk or cycle into the park, or at the beaches. There are few roads on the island.

Taylor House Museum $ *Main and Baker Sts; tel: (410) 641-1019; open June–Sept, Wed, Fri–Sat 1300–1600.*

In the Berlin–Ocean City area more than a dozen golf courses are open to the public.

Assateague National Seashore *Tel: (401) 641-2120.* Crabbing and bay explorations in canoes furnished by the park need to be reserved beforehand. Canoes may be hired at the Bayside picnic area, past the campsite.

Rainy Day *Race Track Rd, Berlin; tel: (410) 641-5029; open daily 0700–1600.* Canoes can also be hired here.

On Assateague, bicycle hires are at the end of Bayside Dr., near the picnic area.

The **Globe Theater** in Berlin has a crafts gallery on the second floor, with baskets, pottery, woodenware, quilts, decoys and more. Downstairs is a bookstore and gourmet food shop.

historic buildings, including the art-deco Globe Theater, now a venue for crafts, a café, shops and classic films. The **Taylor House Museum**◆ is known for interior decorative features, with furnished rooms and local artefacts. A short nature trail with boardwalks enters the waterfowl nesting habitats at the Stephen Decatur Memorial Park.

Accommodation and food in Assateague and Berlin

On **Assateague Island $$** *(tel: (410) 641-2918 or (410) 641-1441)* camp pitches face both the bay and ocean sides of the island, open, unshaded and insect-ridden, but close to beaches, fishing, canoeing, biking and walking trails.

The Atlantic Hotel $–$$ *(2 North Main St; tel: (410) 641-3589 or (800) 814-7672)* is a historic hotel with restored Victorian rooms furnished with matching suites of marble-topped and other Victorian pieces. The elegant dining room **($$$)** updates a continental menu. The informal **Drummer's Café ($$)** serves lunch and dinner daily, with a pianist and singing waiter Wed–Sat.

Merry Sherwood Plantation $$ *(US-13; tel: (410) 641-2112 or (800) 660-0358, fax: (410) 641-9528)* is an eye-catching plantation house surrounded by trees and gardens. The interior is sumptuous, decorated with fine antiques and works of art, and a full breakfast is served in the formal dining room.

Assateague Crab House $$ *(Rte 611 near the park entrance)* serves seasonal seafood dishes, including calamari, along with hard and soft-shelled crabs.

DOVER**

Delaware State Visitors Center
Duke of York and Federal Sts; tel: (302) 739-4266; open Mon–Sat 0830–1630, Sun 1330–1630.

Victorian Dover Historic District Tour *Tel: (302) 678-2040; daily by appointment.*

Meetinghouse Galleries *$ 316 S Governors Ave.; tel: (302) 739-4266.*

Delaware Agricultural Museum and Village *$ 866 N DuPont Hwy (US-13); tel: (302) 734-1618; open Tue–Sat 1000–1600, Sun 1300–1600.*

John Dickinson Plantation *$ Kitts Hummock Rd, off US-113; tel: (302) 739-3277; open Tue–Sat 1000–1530, Sun 1330–1630.*

Bombay Hook National Wildlife Refuge *$ Smyrna; tel: (302) 653-6872.*

Spence's Bazaar *Sth and New Sts; tel: (302) 734-3441; open Tue and Fri.* This flea market also has auctions and an Amish food market.

Public gardens bloom all over town, with the biggest display in the Plaza on Loockerman St. **Meetinghouse Galleries***, in a 1790 church, shows Delaware archaeology and small town life.

Delaware Agricultural Museum and Village** demonstrates farm life throughout the state's history, with exhibits and historic buildings. **John Dickinson Plantation**** is furnished with 18th-century antiques and reconstructed outbuildings show life on a plantation of the time.

Bombay Hook National Wildlife Refuge** preserves coastal habitat for birds migrating on the Atlantic Flyway. Roads and trails lead to observation towers.

Accommodation and food in Dover

Chain lodgings run the gamut from Budget Inn to Sheraton, with few other choices.

Tango's Bistro $–$$ *(Sheraton Hotel, 1570 N DuPont Hwy; tel: (302) 678-8500)* serves contemporary dishes with an emphasis on fresh produce and lighter cooking styles.

Right
Victorian house in Dover

FENWICK ISLAND AND BETHANY BEACH*

ℹ Bethany-Fenwick Area Chamber of Commerce *Rte 1, north of Fenwick Island; tel: (302) 539-2100 or (800) 962-7873.*

🎡 Fenwick Island State Park $ *Rte 1; tel: (302) 539-9060; open year-round 0800–sunset.*

Assawoman Wildlife Area $ *Bayville; tel: (302) 739-5297.*

Discoveries From the Sea Museum $ *708 Ocean Hwy, Fenwick Island; tel: (302) 539-9366; open daily June–Aug 0900–2100, Sept–Oct 1100–1600, Nov–Mar Sat–Sun 1100–1600.*

● Bethany Beach Boardwalk There are often art and craft shows in the summer.

Seaport Antique Village *Rte 54; tel: (302) 436-8962.* The merchandise is shown off in a museum-house setting of fully furnished rooms.

Far less crowded and commercialised than the big beach resorts to its north and south, this area features quiet dune-backed beaches enjoyed primarily by residents. Fenwick Island Lighthouse, built in 1859, is open alternate Weds. At the northern edge of **Fenwick Island State Park*** is a round World War II coastal defence observation tower with views as far as Cape May. The park has boat rentals, fishing, bathhouses and miles of beach. **Assawoman Wildlife Area***, on the bay enclosed by the barrier island, invites birds with its variety of habitats and people with an observation tower and nature trails for good viewing.

Coins, jewellery, pottery, weapons and gold bars recovered from local shipwrecks fill the **Discoveries From the Sea Museum****, collected by a local underwater archaeologist.

Accommodation and food in Fenwick Island and Bethany Beach

Harbor View Motel $–$$ (*Rte 1, Bethany Beach; tel: (302) 539-0500*) is close to the beach and all rooms have balconies.

Sedona $–$$ (*26 Pennsylvania Ave., Bethany Beach; tel: (302) 227-3888*) serves seafood, Angus beef and wild game with a southwestern flavour.

House of Welsh $–$$ (*1106 Ocean Hwy, Fenwick Island; tel: (302) 541-0728*) is a century-old Baltimore tradition, recently moved to the shore. The pub and dining room are known for steaks, seafood and daily pub specials.

Delvecchio's Bakery $ (*Rte 54, Fenwick Island; tel: (302) 436-9618*) bakes bread, pastries and doughnuts, serving them with tea or coffee at café tables.

OCEAN CITY**

ⓘ Ocean City Visitors Information
Center *Coastal Hwy (Rte 528) at 40th St; tel: (410) 289-8181; open Mon–Fri 0830–1700, Sat 0900–1700, Sun 0930–1700, later in summer.*

ⓟ Rte 528/Coastal Hwy widens to eight lanes in the northern part of the city, with numbered short streets branching off like centipede legs. You can't possibly get lost, although trying to drive in the summer is a nightmare. A public tram ($) circles the beach and business district.

Bike World *6 Caroline St and the boardwalk at 15th and 17th Sts; tel: (410) 289-2587; open 0600–1600.* You can hire bicycles here.

Discovery Nature Cruises $$$ *First St Pier; tel: (410) 289-2896; available May–Sept. Each day there are five naturalist-led 90-minute trips, landing on Assateague Island.*

Shantytown Nature Cruises $$$ *Fishing Center, Shantytown Rd; tel: (410) 213-0926. Go out looking for sea birds, dolphins, whales and sea turtles.*

ⓟ Ocean City Lifesaving Station Museum $ *Boardwalk at the Inlet; tel: (410) 289-4991; open June–Sept daily 1100–2000, May and Oct 1100–1600, winter weekends 1100–1600.*

Ocean City seems about to sink the narrow strip of sand it occupies, with the sheer weight of its high-rise hotels, which line the 10-mile white sand beach, crowded and lively in the summer. A 3-mile boardwalk stretches from the Inlet to 27th St, open to bicycles in the off season.

The 1902 carousel at Trimper's Rides has the original hand-carved and painted animals, although it is now run by electricity. **Ocean City Lifesaving Station Museum***, an 1891 Life-Saving Station, shows the old beach resort and describes lifesaving in the region, with photographs of storm damage.

Accommodation and food in Ocean City

Commander Hotel $–$$ *(1404 Baltimore Ave.; tel: (410) 289-6166 or (888) 289-6166)* offers modern beachfront suites with refrigerators, microwave ovens and in-room safes, all wheelchair accessible.

Inn on the Ocean $$ *(1001 Atlantic Ave.; tel: (410) 289-8894 or (877) 466-6662)* also overlooks the boardwalk, each luxurious room decorated in a different colour scheme and theme.

Harrison's Harbor Watch $$ *(on the Inlet; tel: (410) 219-5121)* is far from intimate, but a good reliable destination for traditional and some innovative seafood dishes.

Phillips by the Sea $$ *(Boardwalk at 13th St; tel: (410) 289-9121)* serves a predictable, but well-prepared dinner menu of fresh seafood.

Windows on the Bay $$ *(61st St Bayside; tel: (410) 723-3463)* adds more creative seafood treatments, such as shrimp marsala, and non-seafood dishes. Frequent off-season specials make this a favourite of locals.

REHOBOTH BEACH AND LEWES✧✧

ⓘ Rehoboth Chamber of Commerce *501 Rehoboth Ave.; tel: (302) 227-2233 or (800) 441-1329.*

ⓦ The Rehoboth Beach trolley connects beaches, hotels and restaurant areas.

Queen Anne's Railroad *730 Kings Hwy, Lewes; tel: (302) 644-1720 or (888) 456-8668; www.ridetherails. com.* You can combine a train excursion with a lunch or dinner trip in 1940s dining carriages.

Fisherman's Wharf Lewes *Tel: (302) 645-8862; July–Aug.* This is the centre for whale and dolphin watching cruises and daily sunset cruises.

ⓗ The Homestead $ *12 Dodds Lane, Henlopen Acres; tel: (302) 227-1105; open Mon–Sat 1000–1600, Sun 1300–1600.*

Lewes Historical Complex $ *110 Shipcarpenter St; tel: (302) 645-8073.* Several sites are included on a combined ticket.

Zwaanendael Museum $ *Kings Hwy and Savannah Rd; tel: (302) 645-9418; open Tue–Sat 1000–1630, Sun 1330–1630.*

Cape Henlopen State Park $ *US-9; tel: (302) 645-6852; open 0800–sunset; Nature Center 0900–1600 daily.*

Above
Lewes, historic house

On summer weekends, it seems as though the entire population of Washington, DC, has migrated to Rehoboth, which is sometimes called 'The Nation's Summer Capital'. The beach is superb, although not a place for quiet contemplation. **The Homestead**✧✧, built in 1743, is surrounded by formal boxwood gardens, a medicinal herb garden and one commemorating the coronation of Queen Elizabeth II in 1953.

Lewes is Delaware's oldest town, settled by the Dutch in 1631. It was bombarded during the War of 1812, and Cannonball House, hit in the attack, is part of the **Lewes Historical Complex**✧✧✧, along with Burton-Ingram House, Blacksmith Shop, Thompson Country Store and an early plank house. Also included is Lightship Overfalls Museum, a former seagoing beacon. **Zwaanendael Museum**✧ tells the story of HMS *DeBraak*, a British warship sunk near Lewes in 1798.

Cape Henlopen State Park✧✧ is among the east coast's finest birding sites, with forest, beach, marsh and saltwater lagoon habitats. Seaside Nature Center has an aquarium and information on current bird sitings and nature trails.

Accommodation and food in Rehoboth Beach and Lewes

The Beach House $$ (*15 Hickman St, Rehoboth; tel: (302) 227-7074 or (800) 283-4667*) provides guests with beach chairs, towels and coolers with ice to carry to the beach, just a few steps away.

The Inn at Canal Square $$ (*122 Market St, Lewes; tel: (302) 645-8499 or (800) 222-7902*) has waterfront rooms with balconies, breakfast included.

Elizabeth's $–$$ (*23 Baltimore Ave., Rehoboth; tel: (302) 226-2444*) raises pizza to an art form with toppings you won't find elsewhere and a smart setting.

Thyme Square $–$$ (*31 Robinson Dr., Rehoboth; tel: (302) 227-3100*) pleases all tastes with both traditional and innovative dishes featuring veal, lamb and local seafood.

Millpond Paddler
*Rte 26, Millville; tel:
(302) 539-2339.* Tours
several nearby bays and
ponds in sea kayaks.

Free concerts are
held on weekend
evenings in the summer, in
the bandstand on the
boardwalk at Rehoboth
Ave.

Right
Dutch-style architecture at the
Zwaanendael Museum

Suggested tour

Total distance: 88 miles, with detour 118 miles.

Time: 2–3 hours' driving time, depending on seasonal beach traffic.
Allow 1–2 days. Those with limited time should concentrate on
Assateague and the historic sites of Lewes.

Links: Berlin and Ocean City are close to Salisbury and Snow Hill,
both on the Eastern Shore itinerary, and from US-13 north of Dover,
Rte 6 (which becomes Rte 291 in Maryland) connects to Chestertown,
on the Northern Chesapeake itinerary.

Route: Leave **BERLIN** ❶ via Rte 376 to **ASSATEAGUE** ❷, continuing
to **OCEAN CITY** ❸ on Rte 611. Rte 528 leads to **FENWICK ISLAND**
❹, where it becomes Delaware Rte 1 from **BETHANY BEACH** ❺ to
REHOBOTH ❻.

Detour: From Bethany Beach, follow Rte 26 west to Millsboro, to visit
the **Nanticoke Indian Museum**.

Rte 1 continues north, past **LEWES** ❼ and Cape Henlopen, and on to
DOVER ❽.

Also worth exploring

From Lewes, you can take the 70-min **Cape May–Lewes Ferry** across
Delaware Bay to visit the Victorian seaside town in New Jersey. Leave
your car in Lewes and ride on the trolley or buses that meet arriving
boats. Along with its streets of well-manicured Victorian cottages, the
village offers shopping, carriage rides, sailing and a lighthouse.

Above
Fisher-Martin House, Lewes

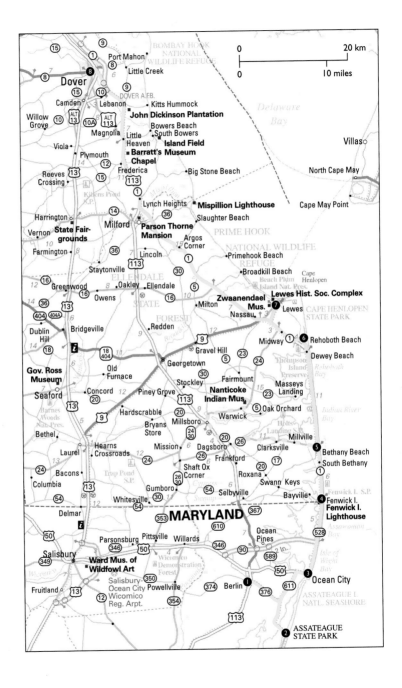

Wilmington

Ratings

Art and museums	●●●●
Historical sights	●●
Nature and wildlife	●●
Shopping and crafts	●●
Beaches	●
Children	●
Entertainment	●
Gastronomy	●

With Delaware's business-friendly tax policies and Wilmington's strategic location almost exactly 100 miles from Washington, DC, and New York, the city has evolved into a financial capital and the titular home of some of America's largest corporations, most notably E I Du Pont de Nemours. The du Pont family settled here in 1803 and flourished. Scions of the family built great mansions, constructed some of America's finest gardens and endowed the region's museums and other cultural attractions. Their estates constitute the most-visited attractions in and near Wilmington. Although Swedes founded Wilmington in 1638, the Dutch soon took over and were succeeded by the British by 1665. Quakers laid out the current city in 1731, and their legacy of social justice and business acumen remains Wilmington's guiding spirit. The main residential sections of the city have shifted towards the surrounding countryside, making Wilmington's downtown very quiet at night.

ⓘ Greater Wilmington Convention and Visitors Bureau *100 W 10th St; tel: (302) 652-4088; www.wilmcvb.org.*

Parking

Most major attractions outside the city centre have free parking lots. **Community Service Parking** (*jct Orange and 11th Sts*) is convenient for central Wilmington sightseeing.

Getting around

DART buses service downtown Wilmington and surrounding attractions frequently on weekdays and Saturdays, but streets are well signposted, making it simplest for visitors to drive their own vehicles.

Brandywine Christmas

The fascination with grand houses and gardens so typified by the various du Pont family properties finds its most lavish expression at Christmas, when the museums and museum houses of Wilmington and the surrounding Brandywine Valley go all out for the holidays. These annual extravaganzas include:

• Brandywine River Museum (see pages 246–8): o-gauge model railroad and Victorian dolls' houses.

• Hagley Museum: Victorian Christmas decorations and evening tours.

• Longwood Gardens (see pages 249–50): lavish poinsettia displays in conservatory; daily concerts.

• Winterthur: 22 period rooms show three centuries of holiday décor.

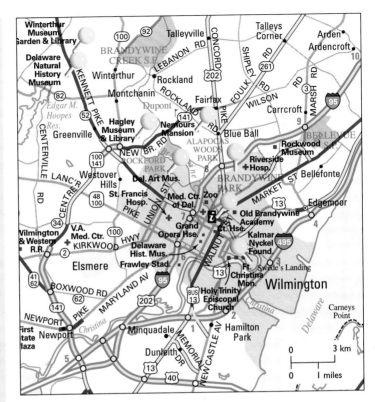

Brandywine Park $
Park Dr.; open dawn to dusk.

Brandywine Zoo $$
1001 N Park Dr.; tel: (302) 571-7788; open daily 1000–1600. Free Nov–Mar.

Sights

Brandywine Park⁺

Stretching along 1 mile of Brandywine Creek, the park is renowned for its classic bridges and is popular with cyclists, joggers and dog-walkers. It also serves as the centrepiece of the 1.8-mile Brandywine Nature Trail, which continues west to Rockford Park and east to the ornate concrete Market St bridge. Within the park are the dramatic Josephine Garden of roses and the **Brandywine Zoo⁺**, which houses many North American animals as well as Siberian tigers.

Delaware Art Museum⁺⁺

Rich in English Pre-Raphaelite art, paintings and illustrations by Howard Pyle and early works by American realist painters of the 'Ashcan School', the Delaware Art Museum's holdings are narrow but deep. The museum was created to house works by Wilmington native Pyle, who operated an influential school for illustrators. It soon expanded to embrace the 1900–20 'Golden Age of Illustration' by

Delaware Art Museum $$ *2301 Kentmere Pkwy; tel: (302) 571-9590; open Tue, Thur–Sat 0900–1600, Wed 0900–2100, Sun 1000–1600.*

Delaware Museum of Natural History $$ *5 miles NW of Wilmington on Rte 52; tel: (302) 658-9111; open Mon–Sat 0930–1630, Sun 1200–1700.*

Delaware History Museum and Old Town Hall $$ *505 Market St; tel: (302) 655-7161; open Mon–Fri 1200–1600, Sat 1000–1600.*

Hagley Museum and Library $$$ *Rte 141 (3.5 miles N of Wilmington); tel: (302) 658-2400; open mid-March–Dec daily 0930–1630, Jan–mid-March Sat–Sun 0930–1630.*

acquiring works by Pyle protégés N C Wyeth, Frank Schoonover and Maxfield Parrish, among others. Temporary exhibitions are often outstanding.

Delaware Museum of Natural History⁺

Serving scholars with its specimen collection and schoolchildren with its interpretive exhibits, the natural history museum spotlights Delaware's fauna and operates a clearing house for sightings of rare birds. Thematic environmental exhibits include representations of an African watering hole and the Great Barrier Reef.

Downtown Wilmington⁺

The high-rise office buildings empty daily at 1700, and downtown virtually closes. But by day it bustles on the pedestrianised stretch of Market St between Rodney Sq. and the Delaware History Museum. Rodney Sq., marked by an equestrian statue of Delaware's signer of the Declaration of Independence, is anchored by the Hotel du Pont. The du Pont industrial family constructed the hotel in 1913 and it remains a centre for civic activities, complete with lavish public rooms and an active theatrical stage. Symphonic concerts and ballet are presented at the nearby Grand Opera House, an 1871 marvel of cast-iron design.

The **Delaware History Museum⁺**, set in a renovated 1940s Woolworth's 'dime store', features interactive exhibits tracing the city's growth from its 1638 trading-post origins to its present role as a corporate capital. The adjacent Georgian-style **Old Town Hall⁺** was the site of abolitionist meetings, although the jail beneath often held 19th-century fugitive slaves. The northernmost city in a border state between the 'free' north and the 'slave' south, Wilmington was often the final stop on the Underground Railroad, the network used by slaves to escape to freedom.

Wilmington's most active anti-slavery neighbourhood was Quaker Hill, reached by walking up 4th or 5th Sts from Market St. Settled in 1738, it is the city's oldest residential neighbourhood, and boasts fine examples of 19th-century brick town house architecture on the verge of gentrification. Central to Quaker Hill is the Friends Meeting House. The New-Wark Meeting, formed in 1682, built this structure in 1816. In the graveyard rests Quaker abolitionist Thomas Garrett, who worked with Harriet Tubman and others to guide more than 2700 fugitive slaves to freedom.

Hagley Museum and Library⁺⁺

The Hagley Museum and Library chronicles the American origins of the du Pont family and their industrial legacy, the E I Du Pont de Nemours company, which grew from a single gunpowder mill in 1804 to the largest manufacturer of black powder in the USA to the modern petrochemical giant. Five generations of du Ponts lived in the Georgian-style home built by E I du Pont in 1803 to overlook his first

Nemours Mansion and Gardens $$$
1600 Rockland Rd; tel:
(302) 651-6912; open
May–Nov Tue–Sat, tours at
0900, 1100, 1300, 1500;
Sun at 1100, 1300, 1500.

powder mills on the Brandywine River. In addition to the house and formal gardens, the 235-acre property includes a preserved workers' community with costumed interpreters and a working 19th-century machine shop. A shuttle bus delivers visitors to each site, but a map also details nature trails and a riverside walk through blooming azaleas, dogwoods and rhododendrons in the spring.

Nemours Mansion and Gardens✧✧

The du Pont legacy takes a decidedly French twist at this Louis XVI-style château constructed by Alfred I du Pont in 1909–10 and surrounded by some of the finest French-style formal gardens in North America. The guided tour highlights the antique furniture, paintings and decorative arts on three levels of the house, while a bus tour through the gardens concludes at the garage to see the family's collection of antique cars.

Below
Delaware Art Museum

Swede's Landing⁕

In March 1638 Swedish settlers landed on the north bank of the Christina River, where they built Fort Christina. This first successful European settlement of the Delaware valley is poignantly reflected in Old Swede's Church (**Holy Trinity Church⁕**), built in 1698 and the oldest Protestant church in North America. Its graveyard has been in continuous use since 1638. The 1690 **Hendrickson House⁕**, built by Swedish settlers, was moved to Wilmington from Pennsylvania and is now a museum. West along the Christina River at the foot of 7th St is a shipyard that has been a fixture since the 1600s. A 136ft replica of the *Kalmar Nyckel*⁕⁕, one of the vessels that brought the first settlers, can be boarded when she is in port.

Winterthur Museum, Garden and Library $$$ Rte 52 (6 miles NW of Wilmington); tel: (302) 888-4600; open Mon–Sat 0900–1700, Sun 1200–1700. Garden tram operates Mar–Dec. Reservations required for some seasonal tours.

Winterthur⁕⁕⁕

Winterthur legend holds that one Sunday in the 1920s Henry Francis du Pont skipped church to look for antiques. He came home with a 1737 Pennsylvania walnut chest, and turned his attention and fortune to acquiring and displaying American decorative arts. Today Winterthur holds one of the country's leading collections of American furniture and decorative arts and even offers a PhD degree in American Studies in conjunction with the University of Delaware. The two museum buildings (one with 175 period rooms) and the 965-acre estate (including 60 acres of gardens) can be overwhelming. Scholars and connoisseurs spend days at Winterthur. Visitors with more casual interests should select the 'Introduction to Winterthur' ticket, which includes admission to the decorative arts galleries, a guided tour of selected period rooms and a tram ride through the gardens.

Above
Winterthur in spring

Right
Winterthur house

Events

Wilmington's house museums sponsor a vast number of seasonal special events that reach a frenzied peak at Christmas time.

Point to Point Races Tel: (800) 448-3883. First Sun in May, three and an eighth-mile steeplechase course in the grounds of the Winterthur estate.

St Anthony's Italian Festival Tel: (302) 421-3790. Week-long ethnic festival in June with cafés, music, rides.

Winterthur's Craft Festival Tel: (302) 888-4600. Labor Day weekend festival featuring crafts and demonstrations by more than 180 artists.

Brandywine Arts Festival Tel: (302) 656-0135. During Sept, 300 exhibitors set up along the Brandywine River in downtown Wilmington.

Delaware Antiques Show Tel: (302) 888-4600. Mid-Nov show at the Tatnall School, with the emphasis on cultivating connoisseurship.

Shopping

No sales tax on goods makes Delaware a shoppers' Mecca.

Shipyard Outlets (*900 S Madison St – on riverfront*) is the first outlet centre featuring stores previously accessible only by catalogue.

Winterthur Museum Store (*Rte 52 – 6 miles NW of Wilmington; tel: (302) 888-4600*) has extraordinary displays of decorative art objects for sale, displayed in co-ordinated rooms.

Accommodation and food

Wilmington has the usual complement of business hotel chains, including Sheraton, Marriott, Wyndham, Best Western, Days Inn, Doubletree, Hilton, Holiday Inn, Ramada. Some central city hotels offer substantial discounts on weekends.

Bed and Breakfast Delaware (*tel: (302) 479-9500*) co-ordinates reservations for area bed and breakfast operations.

Hotel DuPont $$$ (*11th and Market Sts; tel: (800) 441-9019 or (302) 594-3100*). The elegant *grande dame* of Rodney Sq. has 217 rooms with outstanding public spaces, sometimes small private ones.

The Market Street mall is lined with casual eateries for breakfast and lunch on weekdays. Trolley Square (*Delaware St between Rodney and Union Sts*) has the city's best concentration of contemporary restaurants serving evening meals.

Bistro 1717 $$ (*1717 Delaware St; tel: (302) 777-0454*). New American bistro, hard by the rail overpass.

Brandywine Brewing Company $$ (*3801 Kennett Pike, Greenville Ctr (jct Rtes 52 and 141); tel: (302) 655-8000*). This restaurant brews ten beers on the premises to accompany an American grill menu.

Brandywine Room $$$ (*Hotel DuPont, 11th and Market Sts; tel: (302) 594-3100; dinner Sun–Thur only*). The fanciest room with the highest prices and the most meticulously prepared American-continental cuisine in Wilmington.

Green Room $$ (*Hotel DuPont, 11th and Market Sts; tel: (302) 594-3100*). The more casual side of dining at the Hotel DuPont. Open daily for all meals, including the city's most popular Sunday brunch.

Tavola Toscana $$$ (*Rockford Shopping Center, 14th and DuPont Sts; tel: (302) 654-8001*). Elegant, updated northern Italian fare with crisp white linen table settings and prices to match.

Suggested tour

Playhouse Theater at Hotel DuPont
11th and Markets Sts; tel: (302) 656-4401. The classically designed 1250-seat theatre, known as 'Wilmington's Little Broadway', presents touring shows and productions of the Wilmington Ballet Company.

Grand Opera House
818 Market St; tel: (302) 658-7897. This main venue for musical events is home to the Delaware Symphony and Opera Delaware.

Above
Hagley Museum

Length: 1 mile walking, 12 miles driving; 14 miles with detour.

Duration: 2–3 days.

Route: The walking tour of **DOWNTOWN WILMINGTON** ❶ begins at Rodney Sq. and takes in the city's historic roots. After an appreciative look at the lavish lobby of the Hotel DuPont, continue west down Market St, which becomes a pedestrian way, past the Grand Opera House for a quarter of a mile to the **Delaware History Museum** and **Old Town Hall**.

Detour: Continue two blocks west on Market St and turn left on 4th St, walking down two blocks to Walnut St. Turn left and proceed three blocks to 7th St, turning right and continuing a quarter of a mile to **SWEDE'S LANDING** ❷.

From Market St, turn uphill (north) on 5th St and walk four blocks to Quaker Hill. Turn right on West St to walk through the neighbourhood to 10th St, turning right to return to Rodney Sq.

The driving portion of the tour passes through a bucolic landscape to visit some of the great mansions and gardens of the du Pont clan. Although it's possible to stop briefly at each in a 1-day drive, the

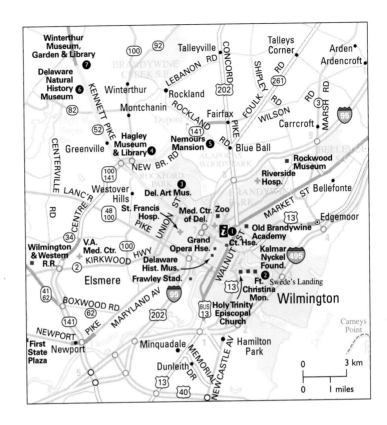

mansions deserve at least 3–4 hours each to see them properly.

From Downtown Wilmington follow Delaware Ave. 1.2 miles to Union St, turn right and follow signs for three blocks to **DELAWARE ART MUSEUM** ❸. From the parking lot, follow signs for half a mile to Rte 52 (Pennsylvania Ave./Kennett Pike) and turn right. Follow Rte 52 for 3 miles north to Rte 141; turn right and drive 0.3 miles to **HAGLEY MUSEUM** ❹. Continue east on Rte 141 to the junction with Rte 202 to visit **NEMOURS MANSION AND GARDENS** ❺. Backtrack to Rte 52, turn right (north) and continue 2 miles to **DELAWARE MUSEUM OF NATURAL HISTORY** ❻ or 2.3 miles to **WINTERTHUR** ❼. Return to Wilmington on Rte 52.

Also worth exploring

Brandywine Creek State Park $ *Off Rte 100, 5 miles N of Wilmington; tel: (302) 577-3534; open daily dawn–dusk.*

Brandywine Creek State Park was created from part of the Winterthur estate. Nineteen miles of walking trails snake through Tulip Tree Woods, a stand of tulip poplars nearly 200 years old. The park's fresh water marshes teem with bog turtles and wading birds.

Brandywine Valley

Ratings

Art and museums	●●●○○
Historical sights	●●●○○
Shopping	●●●○○
Wildlife	●●●○○
Gastronomy	●●○○○
Beaches	●○○○○
Children	●○○○○
Entertainment	●○○○○

Genteel country living is the theme of the Brandywine Valley communities north of Wilmington, Delaware, where it seems that every third shop sells either country home décor, garden accessories or antiques. The rolling green countryside and lush farmlands of this area straddling the Pennsylvania–Delaware border have fascinated landscape painters for two centuries, and the pastoral visions of American realist Andrew Wyeth are especially prized here. Most visitors never see the modest town centres of Brandywine Valley communities, as principal attractions lie on the Baltimore Pike, Rte 1. The Delaware River towns south of Wilmington complement the Brandywine Valley with a more pervasive sense of history, augmented by the preservation of an entire early Colonial town and an important Union fortress from the Civil War. Both areas boast superb bird watching, as they lie along the principal migratory flyway of North America's Atlantic coast.

CHADDS FORD, PENNSYLVANIA❖❖

Chester County Visitors Center
Longwood Gardens, Rte 1, Kennett Square, Penn; tel: (800) 228-9933; www.brandywinevalley.com.

Brandywine Battlefield Park
$–$$ Rte 1; tel: (610) 459-3342; open Tue–Sat 0900–1700, Sun 1200–1700.

The heart of 'Wyeth country' in the Brandywine Valley, Chadds Ford boasts three attractions that summarise the appeal of the region: history, art and agriculture. **Brandywine Battlefield Park❖** is the site of a critical American defeat in the Revolutionary War. At the Visitors Center, costumed interpreters explain how General William Howe outmanoeuvred George Washington's attempt to block the British advance on Philadelphia, leaving the colonials to spend the winter of 1777–8 at nearby Valley Forge (*see page 276*). Visitors can drive through the battlefield and tour the Quaker farmhouses that served as headquarters for Washington and the Marquis de Lafayette, who saw his first military action in America here.

Setting, collections and architecture make the **Brandywine River Museum❖❖** a quintessential regional experience. The building is an artfully modern adaptation of a Civil War-era grist mill. The museum holds the largest collection of work by American realist painters and

Brandywine River Museum $$ *Rte 1, just S of Rte 100; tel: (610) 388-2700; open daily 0930–1630.* Additional charge for shuttle bus and tour of N C Wyeth studio.

Chaddsford Winery $$ *638 Baltimore Pike (Rte 1, 5 miles S of Rte 202); tel: (610) 388-6221; open daily 1200–1700, closed Jan–1 Apr, Mon.*

Pennsbury-Chadds Ford Antique Mall *Rte 1; tel: (610) 388-1620; open Thur–Mon.* The displays of antique furniture, jewellery and other collectibles are unusually spacious.

The Village Peddler *161B Baltimore Pike (Rte 1); tel: (610) 388-2828.* Among the country and primitive antiques, the reproduction redware pottery is outstanding.

Annual Fall Harvest Market *Tel: (610) 388-2700; weekends from mid-Sept–mid-Oct.* More than 20 regional artisans exhibit their work in the courtyard of Brandywine River Museum.

Candlelight Christmas *Tel: (610) 459-3342; first Sat in Dec.* A self-driving tour of six historic properties decorated for Christmas season.

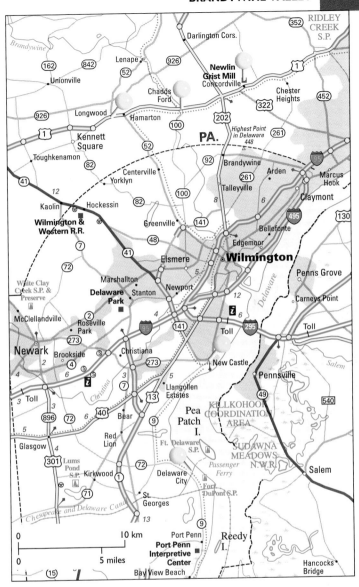

illustrators N C, Andrew and Jamie Wyeth. Also on display are works by regional 19th-century landscape painters and key American illustrators, including Howard Pyle, Maxfield Parrish and Rockwell Kent. Tours of the N C Wyeth studio are available Apr–Nov.

The **Chaddsford Winery** pioneered the production of serious table wines in Pennsylvania in the early 1980s. As the European varietal vines have matured, the wines compete well with California offerings. Tastings and winery tours are available daily.

Accommodation and food in Chadds Ford

A Bed and Breakfast Connection *Tel: (800) 448-3619.* Makes reservations for B&Bs in Brandywine Valley.

Brandywine River Hotel $$ (*Rte 1 and Rte 100; tel: (610) 388-1200*) presents an elegant interpretation of Colonial-Revival style, decorated extensively with prints and paintings in the regional realist tradition.

The Gables at Chadds Ford $$$ (*423 Baltimore Pike (Rte 1); tel: (610) 388-7700*) serves bright contemporary New American food in stylish surroundings.

Hank's Place $ (*Rtes 1 and 100; tel: (610) 388-7062; closes at 1900 Mon–Sat, at 1500 on Sun*) serves classic American grill food, starting with breakfast before dawn. Locally famous for homemade sausages.

Art runs in the family

Three generations of Wyeths have made the world intimately familiar with the rural landscape of the Brandywine Valley. Illustrator and painter N C Wyeth (1882–1945) studied with the famous illustrator of fantasy romances, Howard Pyle, and developed an expressive and atmospheric style much favoured for boys' adventure novels. He settled in Chadds Ford in 1906, and his commission to illustrate *Treasure Island* in 1911 launched a very successful career. (A re-issue of this edition and many other Wyeth books are available at the Brandywine Valley Museum shop.) N C Wyeth was the sole teacher of his son, Andrew Wyeth, who was born in 1917. Andrew paints primarily in watercolours and tempera, infusing a precise naturalism with a studied visionary light. The most famous Wyeth painter, he is a member of the French Académie des Beaux-Arts and Britain's Royal Academy. Andrew's son, Jamie, born in 1946, continues the realist painting tradition, often working in extreme close-up views, and illustrates children's books.

Right
The Brandywine River Museum

DELAWARE CITY, DELAWARE

Delafort ferry $$
Tel: (302) 832-7708.
Departs from Delaware
City Battery Park.

Fort DuPont $$ Off
Rte 9, S of Delaware
City; tel: (302) 834-7941;
open daily 0800–sunset.

**C&D Canal Wildlife
Area $** Off Rte 9, S of
Delaware City; tel: (302)
834-7941; open daily dawn
to dusk.

**Fort Delaware State
Park $** Pea Patch Island; tel:
(302) 834-7941; open late-
Apr–Sept Sat–Sun and
holidays, also mid-June–early
Sept Wed–Sun 1000–1800.

**Wiso's Seafood
and Tackle $** 107
5th St; tel: (302) 834-2279.
Ultra-casual spot near the
public marina has extensive
picnic grounds.

**MD Bait and
Tackle** 46 Clinton St;
tel: (302) 834-7473.
Everything one could need
to fish, including local
licences.

Delaware City has three chief attractions: sport fishing, bird watching and a Civil War living history museum. The C&D Canal joins the waters of the Chesapeake Bay to the Delaware River in marshy lowlands, creating ideal conditions for striped bass, white perch and channel catfish. Many fishermen simply drop their lines at Battery Park in the centre of town. More than 200 migrant and nesting species of birds have been documented in the marshlands on the edges of **Fort DuPont*** and in the adjacent **C&D Canal Wildlife Area***, where grasslands attract vireos and other songbirds.

A ferry makes the 10-minute crossing to **Fort Delaware State Park*** on Pea Patch Island, where interpreters re-create life during the Civil War, when the fort served as a Union prison. The ramparts provide close-up views of large sea-going vessels heading upriver. The park includes a picnic area with tables and grills, a hiking trail and a bird-watching observation tower. Nine species of herons, egrets and ibis nest on Pea Patch Island, making it the largest nesting ground for wading birds on the Atlantic coast north of Florida.

LONGWOOD GARDENS***

**Longwood Gardens
$$$** Rte 1, Kennett Sq.,
Penn; tel: (610) 388-1000;
open daily 0900–1700
(Apr–Oct until 1800),
conservatory opens 1000,
July–Aug and Dec Tue, Thur,
Sat extended evening hours.

Above
Longwood Gardens

Longwood Gardens is a vast 1050-acre complex of 20 outdoor gardens, woodlands and meadows and an additional 20 gardens under glass. In all, more than 11,000 varieties of plants grow at Longwood, attracting garden enthusiasts from around the globe. An English Quaker family named Peirce bought the Longwood property from William Penn in 1700 and had begun planting ornamental trees by 1798. Pierre S du Pont (of the Wilmington family) purchased Longwood in 1906 to save the trees from destruction, and constructed elaborate gardens and built the vast conservatory over the next three decades. Three spectacular fountains, each with hundreds of jets lit by coloured lights on summer nights, dot the property. Exhibits at the Peirce-du Pont House trace the evolution of the property.

Phillips Place *909 E Baltimore Pike (Rte 1);* tel: *(610) 388-6082.* The town of Kennett Square claims to be the mushroom capital of the eastern USA. Phillips Place offers fresh and dried mushrooms and houses a small 'museum' ($) of mushroom cultivation.

Gateway Stables Riding Center $$$ *Old Merrybell Ln., S Chester Cty;* tel: *(610) 444-1255.* Guided trail rides and horse hire for off-premise rides.

Accommodation and food in Longwood Gardens

Longwood Inn $ (*815 E Baltimore Pike (Rte 1, half a mile south of Longwood Gardens); tel: (610) 444-3515*) is a modest motor hotel with 28 large rooms.

Mendenhall Hotel and Conference Center $$ (*Rte 52 – 1 mile south of Rte 1, Mendenhall; tel: (610) 388-2100*) is a modern country hotel near Longwood Gardens.

Terrace Restaurant $$ (*Longwood Gardens; tel: (610) 388-6771; open Apr–Dec daily for lunch, also for dinner June–Sept Tue, Thur and Sat 1700–1930*) does speciality salads and gourmet American fare.

Right
Longwood Gardens

NEW CASTLE, DELAWARE✦✦✦

ℹ Historic New Castle Visitors Bureau *W door of Old Courthouse, 211 Delaware St; tel: (800) 758-1550 or (302) 325-7888.*

🏛 New Castle Court House $ *211 Delaware St; tel: (302) 323-4453; open Tue–Sat 1000–1530, Sun 1330–1630.*

Dutch House $$ *32 E Third St; tel: (302) 322-2794; open Apr–Dec Tue–Sat 1100–1600, Sun 1300–1600.*

Amstel House $$ *4th and Delaware Sts; tel: (302) 322-2794; open Apr–Dec Tue–Sat 1100–1600, Sun 1300–1600.*

Read House $$ *42 The Strand; tel: (302) 322-8411; open Mar–Dec Tue–Sat 1000–1600, Sun 1200–1600.*

⛓ Separation Day *Tel: (302) 322-9802; first Sat in June.* A celebration of Delaware's separation from England, with a parade, crafts show and fireworks.

Concerts in Battery Park *Tel: (302) 325-7888; late-June–mid-Aug Wed evenings.* A regular series of free concerts at Battery Park.

Local lore claims that the New Castle town fathers rebuffed early 19th-century preservationists, forcing them to settle for the Virginia site that became Colonial Williamsburg. Old New Castle's handsome 18th- and 19th-century buildings are filled with 21st-century life. No museum village, New Castle bustles with boutiques, antique dealers, cafés and restaurants.

Located 6 miles south of Wilmington on the Delaware River, New Castle had great strategic importance during the struggles of European nations to colonise the region. The **New Castle Court House✦** flies the flags of Sweden, the Netherlands, Great Britain and the USA, a reminder of the world powers who have laid claim to the site since 1609. New Castle was the capital of Delaware until 1777 and the interior shows a British courtroom of the colonial era. Vintage portraits of William Penn and other early settlers hang in a ground-level hallway and changing historical exhibits are mounted upstairs.

Old New Castle begins at the waterfront with The Strand, a broad street with brick sidewalks, and progresses three blocks up from the river. This compact district contains more than 60 well-preserved historic buildings. Three homes open to the public illustrate the town's history. The **Dutch House✦** is a home typical of the early colonists around 1700. The Georgian **Amstel House✦** of about 1738, built when New Castle was the seat of colonial government, served as the governor's home. The **Read House✦✦**, a 22-room mansion built in 1801, represents the height of Federal grandeur and the wealth of New Castle's merchant class. The 2.5-acre formal garden, added in 1847, is the oldest surviving garden in the region.

Accommodation and food in New Castle

Armitage Inn $$ (*2 The Strand; tel: (302) 328-6618*) is an elegant 1732 house adjacent to Battery Park and the riverfront with four rooms and one suite.

Terry House Bed and Breakfast $ (*130 Delaware St; tel: (302) 322-2505*) has three queen-bedded rooms in a Federal-Revival town house with capacious rooms.

Jessop's Tavern $$ (*114 Delaware St; tel: (302) 322-6111; closed on Sun*), a renovated 1724 colonial tavern, serves contemporary updates on traditional fare, including wild mushroom potpie and fried oyster sandwiches.

O'Donald's Ice Cream and Sandwich Shop $ (*308 Delaware St; tel: (302) 322-4272*), with its pressed tin ceilings and Victorian arched windows, makes a dandified setting for casual sandwiches and huge scoops of ice cream.

NEWLIN GRIST MILL✧

**Newlin Grist Mill and Park $–$$** *219 S Cheyney Rd (jct Rte 1, S Cheyney Rd); tel: (610) 459-2359. Park open daily 0800–dusk, grist mill 0900–dusk. Trout fishing Mar–Oct weekends 0900–1600 ($).*

Newlin Grist Mill✧ is a low-key yet charming historic site. The water-powered grist mill built in 1704 is the oldest active mill in the USA, still grinding cornmeal for sale at the Visitors Center. Other buildings on the Concordville, Pennsylvania, property include the 1739 miller's house and a blacksmith shop. Three miles of walking paths follow the mill race and its feeder stream and pass trees that predate European settlement. A small trout pond offers fishing.

Suggested tour

Concordville has a Ramada Inn and Best Western.

Length: 40 miles, 45 miles with detour.

Duration: 3 driving hours, 2 days with stops.

Buckley's Tavern *$$ 5812 Kennett Pike, Centreville (Rte 52); tel: (302) 656-9776. Casual tavern fare and upmarket American-continental dining room.*

Route: From Wilmington, Delaware, follow Rte 52 (Kennett Pike) north for 6 miles to **Centreville**, Delaware. The community of venerable country homes dates from 1750 and 17 of its structures are on the National Historic Register. More than 30 small speciality shops, mostly devoted to home décor and antiques, line Rte 52.

Continue 1.5 miles north to Rte 1, turning south for 2.5 miles to **LONGWOOD GARDENS ❶**. Drive north on Rte 1 for 5 miles to **CHADDS FORD ❷** and a stop at the Chaddsford Winery and the excellent antiques mall next door. Continue 1.5 miles north on Rte 1 to the **Brandywine River Museum**. Another 1 mile north is the **Brandywine Battlefield Park**. Continue an additional 1.5 miles north to the junction with Rte 202.

Below
Newlin Grist Mill

Detour: Continue north on Rte 1 for 2.5 miles to **NEWLIN GRIST MILL ❸** for a leisurely woodland walk along the mill stream.

Turn south on Rte 202 for 5.5 miles to I-95. Follow I-95 2 miles south to exit 6, I-295. Follow I-295 north 1 mile towards Delaware Memorial Bridge, taking the Rte 9 exit. Rte 9 meanders southward 2 miles through marshlands to **NEW CASTLE ❹**. The road hugs the often-industrial marshy bank of the Delaware River for another 10 miles to **DELAWARE CITY ❺**.

Also worth exploring

West Chester, Pennsylvania, is only 7 miles north of Longwood Gardens on

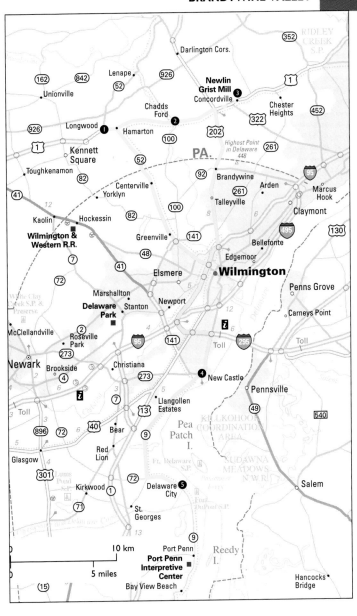

QVC Studio Tour
$$ *Off Wilson Rd; tel:*
(800) 600-9900; tours daily
1000–1600.

Rtes 100 and 52 or 7 miles north of Rte 1 on Rte 202. The drive winds through rustic countryside with calendar-picture vistas. The extensive downtown shopping district teems with bistros and coffee bars. Yet most visitors come to see the studios of **QVC**, the cable-shopping network that bills itself as the 'world's largest electronic retailer'. Call for reservations to be part of the live studio audience.

Philadelphia

Ratings

Historical sights	●●●●●
Art	●●●●
Entertainment	●●●●
Gastronomy	●●●●
Children	●●●
Shopping	●●●
Beaches	●
Nature	●

Founded in 1682 by Quaker William Penn as the 'City of Brotherly Love', Philadelphia was the second largest English-speaking city in the world at the outbreak of the American Revolution and served as the insurgent colonies' first seat of 'national' government. The Declaration of Independence and the US Constitution were written here, and the city remained the capital of the new USA until 1800. Often overshadowed today by New York and Washington, Philadelphia has much to offer in addition to its venerable historic sites. It boasts lively performing and visual arts scenes, bustling market-places and even its own eponymous fast food, the 'Philadelphia cheesesteak'. Laid out on a grid on the flat lands between the Delaware and Schuylkill rivers, Philadelphia is a walker's delight. Most attractions lie close to each other, and other interesting quadrants of the city can be reached quickly by public transport.

ⓘ Philadelphia Convention and Visitors Bureau Information Center 1525 John F Kennedy Blvd; tel: (215) 636-1666 or (877) 334-2238; www.pcvb.org.

✈ Philadelphia International Airport Tel: (215) 937-6800.

Amtrak Tel: (800) USA–RAIL; www.amtrak.com.

Greyhound 1001 Filbert St; tel: (800) 231-2222.

Arriving and departing

More than 20 US and international airlines service Philadelphia International Airport. The taxi fare from the airport to the central city is about $20. The convenient train service is about $5. Amtrak stops in Philadelphia as part of its Northeast Corridor and Metroliner service between Boston, Massachusetts, and Washington, DC. Trains arrive at 30th Street Station, close to central city hotels and the convention centre. Greyhound provides bus services from all parts of the USA.

Drivers approaching Philadelphia from the south on I-95 or from the west on the Pennsylvania Tpk should look for exits marked 'Central Phila./I-676' and follow signs to '15th St/Central City'.

Parking

Limited metered on-street parking is available and most larger hotels have parking lots. Private lots are well distributed throughout the city.

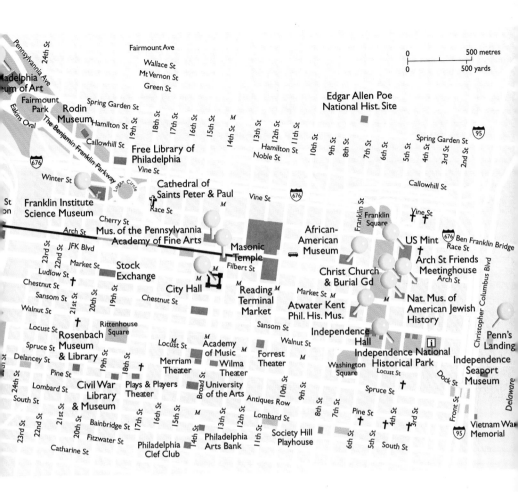

Getting around

Phlash minibuses
$$ Tel: (215) 4-
PHLASH; mid Sep–mid May
1000–1800, mid-May–mid
Sep 1000–2400.

SEPTA Tel: (215) 580-
7800.

Philadelphia is laid out on a strict grid formation and most attractions are found in clusters. As a result, walking is often the best way to get around. The **Phlash** minibuses also circle among most hotels and attractions. For non-attraction destinations, use the buses and streetcars operated by Southeastern Pennsylvania Transit Authority (**SEPTA**). Exact change is required. Discounted day passes can be purchased at the Visitors Center.

The **City Pass ($$$)** offers reduced-price admission to six museums, including the Philadelphia Museum of Art, the Franklin Institute Science Museum and Philadelphia Zoo. It is available at the Visitors Center and participating attractions.

Philadelphia Trolley Works $$–$$$ *Tel: (215) 925-TOUR; www.phillytour.com.*

Philadelphia Trolley Works offers a 90-minute city tour with a 40-minute excursion to Fairmount Park. The Fairmount Park tour, available separately, is a good way to get to Philadelphia Zoo and some of the park mansions.

Communications

Philadelphia uses 10-digit dialling, which means that local calls are dialled *with* the area code.

Below
Carriages at the Independence National Historical Park

Right
Love, the motto of Philadelphia

Sights

African-American Museum[*]

African-American Museum $$ *701 Arch St; tel: (215) 574-0380; open Tue–Sat 1000–1700, Sun 1200–1700.*

Artefacts, artwork and multimedia presentations document the history and culture of African-Americans, with an emphasis on the 20th century. The museum shop has a small selection of original contemporary art.

Arch St Friends Meetinghouse[*]

Arch St Friends Meetinghouse *320 Arch St; tel: (215) 627-2667; open Mon–Sat 1000–1600. Admission free.*

Although Pennsylvania was open to all faiths, the Quakers were the most numerous and prominent in the early years of its settlement. The Friends have used this property since 1693 and the current annual meetinghouse dates from the early 1800s, when Quaker women demanded equal facilities. The resulting structure, with separate men's and women's halls, is the world's largest Quaker meetinghouse.

Atwater Kent Philadelphia History Museum[*]

Atwater Kent Philadelphia History Museum $$ *15 S 7th St; tel: (215) 922-3031; open Wed–Mon 1000–1700.*

This small museum in the original Franklin Institute building owns 80,000 artefacts of city history, displaying a few hundred at a time in its limited gallery space. Larger galleries are devoted to temporary exhibitions on local history and popular culture.

Christ Church and burial ground[*]

Christ Church and burial ground *20 N American St; tel: (215) 922-1695; open Mon–Sat 0900–1700, Sun 1300–1700. Admission free.*

Completed in 1754, Christ Church was attended by Benjamin Franklin, George Washington and other prominent early Americans. It remains an active Episcopal parish. A Palladian window covering most of the altar wall highlights the graceful, voluminous interior. Two blocks west, the burial ground contains the graves of Benjamin Franklin and four other signers of the Declaration of Independence.

City Hall $ *Penn Sq. (Broad and Market Sts); tel: (215) 686-2840.* A 90-min tour of public rooms (*Mon–Fri 1230*) departs from Rm 121. The tour of the tower (*Mon–Fri 0930–1615*) is sometimes reserved for school groups (*Sept–June 1000–1200*).

Franklin Institute Science Museum $$$ *Benjamin Franklin Pkwy at 20th St; tel: (215) 448-1200; open daily 0930–1700.* Omniverse Theater tickets (*$$$*) are additional; advance reservation is recommended (*tel: (215) 448-1254*).

City Hall✦

Begun in 1871 and completed in 1901, City Hall occupies William Penn's Central Square and is the US's largest municipal building. Constructed in the effusive French Empire style widely used for grandiose American public statements in the late 19th century, the building is an undeniable engineering feat, although architects and art historians are divided about its aesthetic merits. The 538ft tower is the world's tallest masonry structure without steel reinforcement. Many visitors assume the 37ft, 27-ton bronze statue on top is Benjamin Franklin, but it is Philadelphia's founder William Penn. A gentlemen's agreement capped all other buildings at the brim of Penn's hat until a few towers from the 1980s reached a trifle higher. The City Hall tower observation deck, located just below Penn's feet, provides a spectacular 360-degree view of the central city. Timed tickets are given for the limited elevator space.

Franklin Institute Science Museum✦✦✦

Founded in 1824 to promote invention and mechanical arts, the Franklin Institute established a museum in 1934 to augment its activities. The current complex rates as one of the US's finest general science museums, living up to polymath Benjamin Franklin's own observation, 'watching, playing, asking questions – that's where all my inventions began'. Electricity exhibits and the walk-through heart are especially popular with children. The massive marble rotunda includes an oversized marble statue of Franklin and many of his effects. Franklin inventions on display include the glass armonica, bifocal glasses, cast-iron fireplace and swim fins. The Mandell Center relates sciences to contemporary technology (especially high-speed computers) with an accent on social implications. The Institute also has a major planetarium and a four-storey dome-screen Omniverse Theater.

Benjamin Franklin

Born in Boston in 1706, Benjamin Franklin spent his adult life in Philadelphia, where he became the American embodiment of the Enlightenment. A prodigious inventor and thinker, he was known by his contemporaries as a leading researcher on the properties of electricity. Nominally a printer by trade, Franklin advocated the establishment of the city's first library in 1731, the American Philosophical Society in 1743 and the Academy of Pennsylvania (now the University of Pennsylvania) in 1751. In 1753, Franklin became deputy postmaster general for the British colonies in charge of the mail for the northern colonies, expanding his political thinking beyond the merely parochial. A key figure in deciding on revolution against the English king and in drafting the Constitution, Franklin served the USA as postmaster general and as ambassador to France. French economist Anne-Robert-Jacques Turgot wrote of Franklin that 'he snatched the lightning from the skies and the sceptre from tyrants'.

Independence National Historical Park $ *Visitors Center on 3rd St between Chestnut and Walnut Sts; tel: (215) 597-8974 or TTY: (215) 597-1785; www.nps.gov/inde; most park buildings open daily 0900–1700. Admission free. Small fee charged at Second Bank building to support painting conservation. Frequent free ranger-led walking tours depart from Visitors Center (June–mid-Sept daily).*

Independence National Historical Park✦✦✦

Philadelphia sites associated with the American Revolution and the formation of the country lie within a few blocks of each other in 'America's Most Historic Square Mile'. Within these modest brick structures surrounded by green lawns in the heart of a busy city, the USA took shape. More than a dozen sites come under the park's purview, including some surviving colonial residences, but most visitors concentrate on a handful of buildings. The modernistic Visitors Center shows an overview film and guided tours depart from the lobby. The Second Bank of the United States, in the Greek Revival style chosen to associate the young country with classical democracy, houses a portrait gallery of early patriots, many painted by Philadelphia portraitist Charles Willson Peale. Carpenters Hall, still owned and operated by the Carpenters Company, was the meeting hall for the First Continental Congress, the colonial assembly which met in 1774 to address grievances against the king.

The cluster of buildings on Independence Square, however, were the crucible of the USA. Graceful Independence Hall was built between 1732 and 1756 as the Pennsylvania State House. The Second Continental Congress began meeting here in 1775 to authorise and approve the Declaration of Independence, first read to the public in Independence Square on 4 July 1776. The business of American government, including the drafting of the Articles of Confederation and the US Constitution, continued here (with brief hiatuses) until 1790. In that year, Congress moved next door to Congress Hall, where it remained until the US Capitol in Washington was ready in 1800. Timed tour tickets are issued for Independence Hall during peak visitation periods.

Over the generations, the Liberty Bell has become a patriotic icon. Cast in London in 1752 for the Pennsylvania State House, it cracked on arrival and was recast twice by a Philadelphia foundry. Rung for major national events – the surrender of Cornwallis at Yorktown, the

Opposite
City Hall

signing of the Treaty of Paris that ended the Revolution and the deaths of George Washington and Lafayette – the bell cracked again in 1835. It has not been rung since Washington's birthday (22 February) in 1846. The Liberty Bell used to tour the nation by train as a unifying symbol, a practice halted early in the 20th century to preserve it. Moved to a glass pavilion on Independence Mall in 1976, the bell receives more than 2 million visitors each year, many from nations who do not assume freedom as a birthright. Visitors may brush their fingers lightly on the 2 080lb bell.

Masonic Temple
1 N Broad St; tel: (215) 988-1916; guided tours Mon–Fri 1000, 1100, 1300, 1400, 1500; Sat 1000 and 1100. Admission free.

Museum of the Pennsylvania Academy of Fine Arts *$$ Broad and Cherry Sts; tel: (215) 972-7600; open Mon–Sat 1000–1700, Sun 1100–1700.*

Masonic Temple*

Philadelphia is the mother city of American Free Masonry, and its brethren thought big when constructing this architectural landmark just north of City Hall. Bristling with turrets and spires, the Temple claims to exemplify seven architectural styles, yet retains a resolutely Victorian sensibility. Stunningly excessive interior decoration, using Masonic mystic symbols as recurrent motifs, represents exemplary craftsmanship. All visits are guided, and include viewing of such artefacts as George Washington's Masonic Apron, embroidered by Madame Lafayette.

Museum of the Pennsylvania Academy of Fine Arts**

The museum's opulent Victorian Gothic building is a high-water mark in Philadelphia decorative arts. Opened in 1876 as a showpiece for the Centennial International Exposition, the first World Fair, the museum features voluminous, light-filled exhibition spaces, a grand marble stair and many sensuous marble statues, including a signature angel on the main staircase. The Academy was founded in 1805 as a teaching and collecting institution on the model of Britain's Royal Academy and its collections document three centuries of American art, beginning with portraiture and landscape of the Colonial and early Federal periods and progressing through the late 20th century. Paintings and sculpture in the 'Grand Manner' – ie, heroic narrative with classical models – claim much of the exhibition space in the entry hall and balcony galleries as permanent installations. Interior galleries are devoted to changing exhibitions. Although the Academy briefly embraced Modernism in the early 20th century, it became a stalwart defender of realism against the abstract tide. Outstanding works include paintings by Benjamin West, Mary Cassatt, Thomas Eakins and Robert Henri, all at one time associated with Philadelphia. Eakins and Henri also taught at the Academy.

Above
The Liberty Bell

Opposite
Philadelphia skyscape

National Museum of American Jewish History $$ 55 N 5th St; tel: (215) 923-3811; open Mon–Thur 1000–1700, Fri 1000–1500, Sun 1200–1700.

Independence Seaport Museum $$ Penn's Landing at Walnut St; tel: (215) 925-5439; open daily 1000–1700.

National Museum of American Jewish History✴

The only museum devoted to three centuries of Jewish experience in the USA, the small collection consists of display stations illustrating the Jewish contribution to the evolution of the country. Each exhibit includes personal artefacts, interpretative text, documents and photographs of individuals and families, creating an unusually intimate experience. Oral history videos probe American Jewish identity.

Penn's Landing✴

Like many American cities, Philadelphia was cut off from its waterfront by an Interstate highway. Penn's Landing redresses that mistake with a waterfront walkway (popular with joggers and rollerbladers), an amphitheatre and the **Independence Seaport Museum✴✴**. The museum relates the history of Philadelphia's seaport, 90 miles up the Delaware River from the Atlantic Ocean. The port was a major immigration site throughout the 18th and 19th centuries and became an important industrial and oil port with the discovery of petroleum in Pennsylvania in the 1850s. The walk-through exhibits are rich with artefacts that evoke seafaring days and the museum includes a workshop where small wooden boats are under construction. For an additional fee, visitors can tour the USS *Becuna*, a World War II submarine, and the USS *Olympia*, one of America's first steel ships and Admiral George Dewey's flagship during the Spanish-American War (1898).

Below
Independence Seaport Museum

Philadelphia Museum of Art $$

Benjamin Franklin Pkwy at 26th St; tel: (215) 684-7500; open Tue, Thur–Sun 1000–1700, Wed 1000–2045.

US Mint 5th and Arch Sts; tel: (215) 408-0114; open Mon–Fri 0900–1630. Admission free.

Philadelphia Museum of Art◆◆◆

Ranked among the US's leading art museums, the Philadelphia Museum might be best known for the cameo role played by the long steps of its eastern façade in the melodramatic boxing movie *Rocky*. The great strength of the collections lies in late 19th-century European painting, including extensive holdings of Cézanne and other Impressionists. Not least among them are the largely sweet canvases of Philadelphia-born Mary Cassatt, who worked primarily in France. The American holdings are likewise strong in local artists, notably the late 19th-century realist Thomas Eakins. Select exhibits of colonial silver and furniture hint at Philadelphia's erstwhile position as the largest and richest city of young America. The museum's holdings of medieval European art and Asian art are shown to particularly good effect surrounded by period architectural details. The 4-acre Azalea Garden on the west side of the museum bursts into spectacular bloom in late spring and early summer.

US Mint◆

The fourth US Mint in Philadelphia is the largest mint in the world. It stamps out more than $2 million in coins daily, and the self-guided tour proceeds along a walkway high above the operations. The mint also produces large numbers of commemorative medals. A round display on the ground level has examples of every US commemorative coin minted since 1892. The gift shop has some proof sets on offer, including the series of state-themed Washington quarters being issued at a rate of five per year until 2008.

Above
Philadelphia Museum of Art

Entertainment

Performing arts activities cluster on Broad St, also known as the 'Avenue of the Arts', where more than 20 facilities line a 3-mile stretch.

Academy of Music (*Broad and Locust Sts; tel: (215) 893-1999*) serves as home for the Philadelphia Orchestra, Pennsylvania Ballet, Opera Company of Philadelphia and the Philly Pops. The orchestra will move into the **Regional Performing Arts Center** at Broad and Spruce Sts when it is completed in 2001.

Merriam Theater (*250 S Broad St; tel: (215) 875-4800*) serves as a performance hall for touring Broadway shows and student productions of the University of the Arts.

Philadelphia Clef Club (*736–38 S Broad St; tel: (215) 893-9912*) is devoted to the preservation and promotion of jazz through performances, workshops, concerts and instrumental training.

Wilma Theater (*Broad and Spruce Sts; tel: (215) 546-7824*) produces innovative drama and performance art in a 300-seat hall.

Shopping

⊙ **Mummers Parade**
Tel: (215) 636-1666.
The New Year's Day folk parade of costumed participants and minstrel string bands on floats is a colourful century-old tradition. Final judging ($$) takes place at Pennsylvania Convention Center (*12th and Arch Sts*).

Principal downtown shops line **Walnut, Chestnut and Market Sts**, with upmarket boutiques located near Rittenhouse Sq. **Jeweller's Row** (bounded by Chestnut, Walnut, 7th and 9th Sts) is the US's oldest diamond district, established in 1851. More than 300 jewellery establishments are located here, most selling to the public at 30–50 per cent off retail prices. Pine St, between 9th and 13th Sts, is **Antiques Row**. Youth-oriented shops, tattoo parlours and counter-culture goods flourish on **South Street** from Front to 10th Sts.

Accommodation and food

Philadelphia is a major convention city and business centre with a strong complement of chain hotels. Business centre hotels often offer good weekend packages. Chains include Best Western, Clarion Suites, Comfort Inn, Doubletree, Four Seasons, Holiday Inn, Hyatt, Marriott, Omni, Ritz-Carlton, Rodeway, Sheraton and Wyndham.

Penn's View Hotel $$ (*Front and Market Sts; tel: (215) 922-7600*) fronts on the highway at the Market St entrance to **Penn's Landing**. This 38-room hotel offers good value and convenient location. Rates include continental breakfast.

Rittenhouse Bed and Breakfast $$$ (*1715 Rittenhouse Sq.; tel: (877) 545-1755 or (215) 545-1755*), in Philadelphia's most desirable central city area, has ten stylish rooms (and one suite), concierge service and luxury amenities.

Thomas Bond House $–$$ (*129 S 2nd St; tel: (800) 845-BOND*), an exquisitely restored 1769 Georgian town house owned by the National Park Service and furnished in late 18th-century style with modern comforts, has 12 rooms adjacent to **Independence National Historic Park**.

Philadelphia Flower Show *Tel: (215) 988-8776.* The early Mar displays at Pennsylvania Convention Center (*12th and Arch Sts*) are the oldest and largest in the USA.

Freedom Festival *Tel: (215) 636-1666.* A week of events around Independence Day (4 Jul) includes parades, fireworks and sporting events in locations throughout city.

Philadelphia's traditional markets are attractions as well as ideal places to purchase produce, meats and prepared foods. **Reading Terminal Market** (*Filbert St between 11th and 12th Sts*) closes by late afternoon, but includes many casual eateries, including **Rick's Steaks $**. **Italian Market** (*9th St between Catherine and Washington Sts*) is a district full of grocers, butchers and greengrocers and is most lively on Sat morning. **Butcher's Café $–$$** (*901 Christian St; tel: (215) 925-6200; no credit cards*) specialises in home-style regional Italian cooking. At 9th St and Passyhunk Ave. is 'Cheesesteak Junction', with **Pat's King of Steaks $** and **Geno's Steaks $** on opposite corners. Both specialise in Italian rolls filled with shaved beef, processed orange cheese and fried onions: the quintessential Philadelphia cheesesteak.

Northeast of Reading Market, **Chinatown** has a restaurant almost every two steps. An outstanding value is **Nice Chinese Noodle House $** (*1038 Race St; tel: (215) 625-8393; no credit cards*).

More elegant dining is concentrated on Walnut St between Broad St and Rittenhouse Sq. One less expensive option is the *prix fixe* at **Brasserie Perrier $$$** (*1619 Walnut St; tel: (215) 568-3000*), the casual restaurant owned by the city's best chef.

Above
Italian Market

Opposite
Antiques Row

Suggested walk

Betsy Ross House $
239 Arch St; tel: (215)
627-5343; open Tue–Sun
1000–1700.

Length: about 4 miles.

Duration: 2 full days.

Route: Begin at **INDEPENDENCE NATIONAL HISTORICAL PARK ❶** Visitors Center, proceeding west on Chestnut St to the **Second Bank of the United States**, on to **Carpenters Hall**, ending with a tour of **Independence Hall ❷**. Head north to the **Liberty Bell Pavilion**. Turn north up 5th St to Arch St to the **US MINT ❸**. Walk east, pausing at 4th St for the **ARCH ST FRIENDS MEETINGHOUSE ❹** and at 3rd St for the **Betsy Ross House ❺**, where widow seamstress Elizabeth Ross produced the first official flag of the USA. Go one half-block north on 2nd St to pass through **Elfreth's Alley ❻**, a narrow cobbled street of brick town houses continuously occupied from the early 1700s. At Front St walk south to Market St and turn left to cross over to **PENN'S LANDING ❼**. Walk south along the waterfront to Spruce St, using the walkway to resume going south on Front St for two blocks to **South St**, 'the hippest street in town' according to the 1960s pop tune. Stroll west on South St to 9th St.

Detour: Turn left and walk south for three blocks to reach **Italian Market ❽**.

Walk north from South St two blocks to Pine St and turn left. Walk through **Antiques Row ❾**, continuing to Broad St. Turn right and see the theatres and art centres of the **Avenue of the Arts**, ending at **CITY HALL ❿**. Turn right on Market St, then left on 12th St to reach **Reading Terminal Market**.

Right
South St

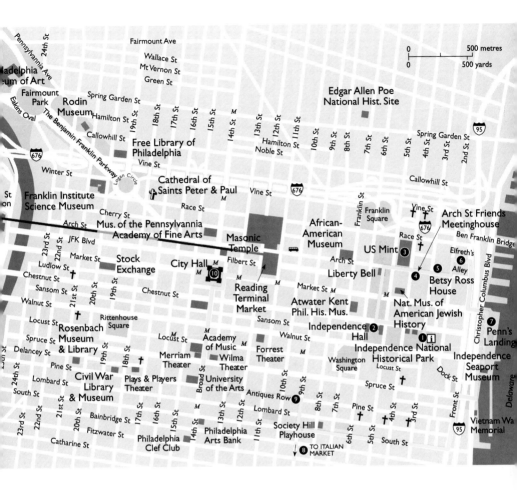

Also worth exploring

Fairmount Park, the largest landscaped urban park in the USA, covers more than 8 000 acres along the Schuylkill River northwest of the city centre. The park is criss-crossed with bicycle, walking and bridle trails. The site of the 1876 Centennial Exposition, the park contains extensive botanical gardens, a 10,000-seat amphitheatre, and several colonial mansions open to visitors. Also on the grounds is the **Philadelphia Zoo**, the oldest in the USA. The **Rodin Museum** on the Benjamin Franklin Pkwy at the entrance to the park holds 124 original sculptures and casts by Rodin, the largest collection outside Paris.

Valley Forge to Gettysburg

Ratings

Historical sights	●●●●●
Shopping	●●●●
Gastronomy	●●●
Art and museums	●●
Children	●●
Nature	●●
Beaches	●
Entertainment	●

This countryside tour begins at the edge of the Philadelphia megalopolis at Valley Forge, the crucible of American military might during the Revolution. It concludes at one of America's most solemn locales, the fields of Gettysburg, where brother met brother during the Civil War in the largest battle ever fought in North America. Between these venerated sites associated with America's two most traumatic wars lie the peaceful farmlands of Pennsylvania Dutch Country, where the pacifist Old Order Amish adhere to their traditional ways, seemingly oblivious to the high-tech, high-pressure rush of the modern world. The drive commences in urban traffic but gives way to uncrowded country roads where drivers might find themselves sharing the right of way with the old-fashioned horse-drawn buggies of the Amish and Old Order Mennonites. The unusual productivity of Amish farmers supports the hearty country cooking featured at almost every restaurant.

GETTYSBURG✦✦

ℹ Gettysburg Convention and Visitors Bureau 35 Carlisle St; tel: (717) 334-6274; www.gettysburg.com.

Ⓟ Gettysburg Town Trolley $$ Tel: (717) 334-6296; operates Apr–Oct.

Historic Walking Tour of Gettysburg $$ Greystone's American History Store, cnr Steinwehr and Baltimore Sts; tel: (800) 891-6541.

During 1–3 July 1863, Gettysburg witnessed the largest conflict ever fought on North American soil when massive Union and Confederate armies inadvertently collided. Even today, the Battle of Gettysburg defines the town, and it is hard to scratch the surface of Civil War commercialism to get at the honest community beneath. Start with the free downtown self-guided walking tour, reading the plaques to grasp what the battle meant to the 2 400 horrified residents.

Numerous commercial operations attempt to recreate some aspect of the battle, but few observe the scene on a human scale. At the **Schriver House**✦, built in the early 1860s and operated as a saloon during the Civil War, costumed guides interpret the life of the family while Confederate sharpshooters occupied the building and during the battle aftermath, when it served as a field hospital.

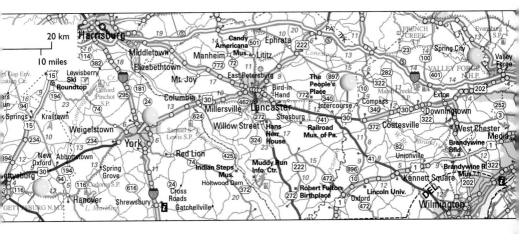

Accommodation and food in Gettysburg

Schriver House $$
309 Baltimore St; tel:
(717) 337-2800; open
Apr–Nov Mon–Sat
1000–1700, by appt in Dec
and Feb–Mar.

Gibson's Photographic Gallery 65 Steinwehr Ave.;
tel: (717) 337-9393. The
gallery continues the wet-
plate photographic
tradition of Civil War
portrait photographers.

The Horse Soldier Old
Gettysburg Village, 777
Baltimore St; tel: (717) 334-
0347; closed Wed. A shop
that specialises in high-end
Civil War military
antiques.

Memorial Day Parade Tel: (717)
334-6274. In a tradition
dating from 1867, the
parade concludes at
Gettysburg National
Cemetery where children
place flowers on graves.

Artillery Ridge Camping Resort $ 610 Taneytown Rd; tel: (717) 334-1288. The closest site to the attractions.

The Doubleday Inn B&B $–$$ 104 Doubleday Ave.; tel: (717) 334-9119. This is an upmarket country inn at Oak Ridge battlefield.

Abraham Lincoln's Gettysburg address

'Four score and seven years ago our fathers brought forth on this continent a new nation, conceived in liberty and dedicated to the proposition that all men are created equal. Now we are engaged in a great civil war, testing whether that nation or any nation so conceived and so dedicated can long endure. We are met on a great battlefield of that war. We have come to dedicate a portion of that field as a final resting-place for those who here gave their lives that that nation might live. It is altogether fitting and proper that we should do this. But in a larger sense, we cannot dedicate, we cannot consecrate, we cannot hallow this ground. The brave men, living and dead who struggled here have consecrated it far above our poor power to add or detract. The world will little note nor long remember what we say here, but it can never forget what they did here. It is for us the living rather to be dedicated here to the unfinished work which they who fought here have thus far so nobly advanced. It is rather for us to be here dedicated to the great task remaining before us – that from these honored dead we take increased devotion to that cause for which they gave the last full measure of devotion – that we here highly resolve that these dead shall not have died in vain, that this nation under God shall have a new birth of freedom, and that government of the people, by the people, for the people, shall not perish from the earth.'

Civil War Heritage Days *Tel: (717) 334-6274.* Battle re-enactments and encampment take place in late June and early July.

Anniversary of Lincoln's Gettysburg Address *Tel: (717) 334-6274.* On 19 Nov services commemorate Lincoln's speech at a cemetery dedication.

Below
Gettysburg battlefield

The Gettysburg Hotel $–$$ *One Lincoln Sq.; tel: (717) 337-2000.* A superb historic hotel, built in 1797, offering self-catering units in summer.

The Three Crowns Motor Lodge $–$$ *205 Steinwehr Ave.; tel: (800) 729-6564 or (717) 334-3168.* A budget 1940s motel, renovated in 2000, convenient for the National Military Park.

Dobbin House Tavern $–$$ *89 Steinwehr Ave.; tel: (717) 334-2100.* This historic property features continental fine dining and casual tavern fare.

Gettysbrew Pub and Brewery $–$$ *248 Hunterstown Rd; tel: (717) 337-1001.* Located at Montfort Farm, the building served as a Confederate field hospital in the Civil War. The pub brews its own ales, root beer and orange cream.

GETTYSBURG NATIONAL MILITARY PARK✦✦✦

Gettysburg Battlefield Tape Tour $$$ Sold at the Park Service Visitors Center.

Licensed Tour Guides $$$ *Park Service Visitors Center; tel: (717) 334-4474. Guides will drive your vehicle on a tour of Gettysburg battlefield.*

National Riding Stable $$$ *610 Taneytown Rd (Rte 134); tel: (717) 334-1288. Horseback tours through the battlefield.*

Visitors Center and Gettysburg Museum of the Civil War $ *Rte 134; tel: (717) 334-4474. Visitors Center open daily 0800–1700, battlefield 0600–2200 and cemetery dawn–dusk.*

Cyclorama Center $$ *Rte 134; tel: (717) 334-4474; open daily 0900–1700, shows hourly on the half hour, final show at 1630.*

General Lee's Headquarters Museum $$ *401 Buford Ave.; tel: (717) 334-3141; open mid-Mar–Nov 0900–1700.*

Eisenhower National Historic Site $$ *Shuttle from Visitors Center; tel: (717) 334-4474; open Apr–Oct daily 0900–1600, reduced hours remainder of the year.*

The Battle of Gettysburg ravaged 25 square miles of farmland and woods, now preserved by the National Park Service. The **Gettysburg Museum of the Civil War**✦✦ in the Visitors Center has one of the largest collections of Civil War artefacts, and its cool-headed interpretation outshines the histrionics of commercial sensationalisers.

Also in the Visitors Center, coloured lights on the Electric Map spell out troop movements over 1–3 July 1863. A more impressionistic overview of the battle is displayed next door at the **Cyclorama Center**✦. An 1884 painting in the round by Paul Philippoteaux depicts 'Pickett's Charge', the climactic action of the third day. The painting stands 26ft tall and stretches 350ft in circumference.

No amount of interpretation can compare with driving or cycling the battlefield. A free map covers the well-marked 18-mile tour, a trip that can be augmented with an audio cassette or a professional guide. More than 1300 monuments and markers spell out the action and pay tribute to both armies. The landscape has changed little in 140 years: stone walls and split-log fences mark the farm borders, cannons stand poised along ridges, and massive boulders, chipped by bullets, show where soldiers took refuge. Hiking trails include a 1-mile route from the Cyclorama through the area depicted in Philippoteaux's painting. On the property of a motel near Seminary Ridge, the stone house that served as the **Headquarters of General Robert E Lee**✦ contains a small museum of Civil War artefacts.

The most solemn stop is Gettysburg National Cemetery, where Abraham Lincoln gave his famous speech at the dedication on 19 November 1863. More than 3000 graves (of 51,000 casualties) fan out in a semicircle from Soldiers National Monument, a plan devised so that all are equal in death.

The Park Service also oversees the **Eisenhower National Historic Site**✦, the retirement home of the former World War II commander and American president.

PENNSYLVANIA DUTCH COUNTRY****

ℹ Pennsylvania Dutch Convention and Visitors Bureau *501 Greenfield Rd, Lancaster; tel: (800) PA-DUTCH or (717) 299-8901; www.padutch.com.*

Ⓠ Old Order Amish Tours $$$ *Tel: (717) 299-6535.* A guide joins you in your car to provide insight on the culture and to visit sites not otherwise open to outsiders.

Ed's Buggy Rides $$$ *Rte 896, 1.5 miles south of Rte 30, Strasburg; tel: (717) 687-0360.* A 3-mile tour on scenic back roads in an Old Order-style Amish horsedrawn buggy.

Strasburg Railroad $$$ *Rte 741, 1 mile east of Strasburg; tel: (717) 687-7522; operates July–Aug 1000–1900, Apr–June and Sept 1100–1500, Oct–Mar Sat 1100–1500, Sun 1200–1500.* A 9-mile, 45-min scenic trip.

🏛 Lancaster Museum of Art $ *135 N Lime St, Lancaster; tel: (717) 394-3497; open Mon–Sat 1000–1600, Sun 1200–1600.*

Demuth Foundation $ *120 E King St, Lancaster; tel: (717) 299-9940; open Feb–Dec Tue–Fri 1000–1600, Sun 1300–1600.*

The second-largest concentration of Mennonite and Amish 'plain folk' in the USA live in the rich farmland of Lancaster County. Descended from German religious refugees, many of these Pennsylvania Dutch belong to Old Order Amish and Old Order Mennonite sects that keep their distance from modern culture, eschewing electricity and internal combustion engines and dressing in a distinctive 'plain' style little altered from the 18th century. Black-frocked farmers on horse-drawn buggies share the roads with tourists drawn to the area by Amish and Mennonite crafts and foods.

With its central market dating from the 1730s, Lancaster is the market town for the area. The 19th-century city centre features three free museums. Housed in an 1840 Greek Revival mansion, the **Lancaster Museum of Art⁺** exhibits contemporary art. The **Demuth Foundation⁺** fills the home of American modernist artist Charles Demuth with his work. The **Heritage Center Museum⁺⁺** relates the history and complex culture of Lancaster County through furnishings and folk art. East of the centre, the **Amish Farm and Museum⁺⁺** occupies vestigial open farmland amid a forest of shopping malls. On the road to Bird-in-Hand, the factory tour at **Anderson Pretzels⁺** hits one of the region's chief culinary highlights.

Further east, the countryside opens into broad farmland, and most attractions are found along Rte 340 (Old Philadelphia Pike) in tiny Bird-in-Hand with its farm-products market and larger Intercourse, where **The People's Place⁺⁺** and its associated quilt museum provide clear and unsentimental information about Old Order Amish ways. Many Amish farms and Pennsylvania Dutch crafts shops line the highway to Paradise from Lancaster (Rte 30). More bucolic Rte 896 heads south into the spruced-up village centre of Strasburg. North of

Right
Amish farmer

Opposite
Bird-in-Hand craft shop

STURGIS
PRETZEL BAKERY

GIFTS · ANTIQUES · TOURS

the centre is **Amish Village**, a contrived complex depicting Amish life. East of the centre, the **Railroad Museum of Pennsylvania** displays locomotives and speciality train carriages.

Accommodation and food in Pennsylvania Dutch Country

Amish Country Motel $ *(3013 Old Philadelphia Pike (Rte 340), Bird-in-Hand; tel: (800) 538-2535 or (717) 768-8396)* is a modest motor inn between Intercourse and Bird-in-Hand, whose rates include a 2-hour tour of Dutch country.

Lancaster County Bed and Breakfast Inns Association *(tel: (800) 848-2994 or (717) 464-5588)* co-ordinates reservations for 16 properties.

ⓘ **Heritage Center Museum $** *13 W King St, Lancaster; tel: (717) 299-6440; open Apr–Dec Tue–Sat 1000–1700.*

Limestone Inn Bed and Breakfast $–$$ *(33 E Main St, Strasburg; tel: (800) 278-8392 or (717) 687-8392)* has six guest rooms (five with private bath) in a late 18th-century house in a historic district. With advance reservation, it will arrange an evening meal with an Amish family. No children under 12, no credit cards.

Amish Farm and Museum $$ *2395 Rte 30 E, Lancaster; tel: (717) 394-6185; open June–Aug 0830–1800, Apr–May and Sept–Oct 0830–1700, Nov–Mar 0830–1600.*

Quiet Haven Motel $ *(2556 Siegrist Rd, Ronks; tel: (717) 397-6231)* is an older motor hotel surrounded by farmland near Strasburg, Bird-in-Hand and Intercourse. No credit cards.

Anderson Pretzels $ *2060 Old Philadelphia Pike, Lancaster; tel: (717) 299-2321; factory tours Mon–Fri 0830–1600.*

White Oak Campgrounds $ *(White Oak Rd, off May Post Office Rd, Strasburg; tel: (717) 687-6207)* offers a choice of woodland or meadow camp for tents or RVs.

The People's Place $$ *Rte 340, Intercourse; tel: (717) 768-7171; open June–Aug Mon–Sat 0930–2000, Sept–May Mon–Sat 0930–1700.*

Your Place Country Inn $–$$ *(2133 Lincoln Hwy E (Rte 30), Lancaster; tel: (717) 393-3413)* is a modern motor inn with country décor on the busy section of Rte 30 but minutes from rural attractions.

Amish Village $$ *Rte 896, Strasburg; tel: (717) 687-8511; open summer daily 0900–1800, spring and fall daily 0900–1700, Nov daily 0900–1600.*

Large breakfasts and large midday meals are the rule in Pennsylvania Dutch Country; many restaurants stop serving 1800–2000.

Above
Sturgis Pretzel Bakery

Right
Bird-in-Hand

Railroad Museum of Pennsylvania $$
Rte 741, Strasburg; tel: (717) 687-8628; open Mon–Sat 0900–1700, Sun 1200–1700, closed Nov–Apr Mon.

Eldreth Pottery
246 N Decatur St (Rte 896), Strasburg; tel: (717) 687-8445. The pottery features salt-glazed stoneware and Pennsylvania redware.

Old Country Store Rte 340, Intercourse; tel: (717) 768-7101; closed Sun. Excellent selection of quilting books, fabrics and quilts.

Outlet centers Rte 30E, near Rte 896, Lancaster. More than 200 shops are housed here.

Zook's Quilts, Crafts and Furniture Rte 741E, Strasburg; tel: (717) 687-0689; closed Sun. An Amish-operated shop with superb quilts.

Above
Amish quilts

Two outstanding markets display local produce, meats, flowers and baked goods – **Bird-in-Hand Farmers' Market** (*Rte 340, Bird-in-Hand; no tel; open July–Oct Wed–Sat 0830–1730, Apr–June and Nov Wed and Fri–Sat 0830–1730, Dec–March Fri–Sat 0830–1730*) and **Central Market** (*120 N Duke St, Lancaster; tel: (717) 291-4723; open Tue and Fri 0600–1600, Sat 0600–1400*).

Dienner's $ (*2855 Lincoln Hwy E, Ronks; tel: (717) 687-9571; closes daily at 1800*) is an Amish-run restaurant featuring buffets at all three meals and generous portions of à la carte Dutch country food. A local favourite.

Good 'N' Plenty Restaurant $$ (*Rte 896, Smoketown (between Bird-in-Hand and Strasburg); tel: (717) 394-7111; closed Sun and Jan*) offers family-style seatings for traditional fare.

Jennie's Diner $ (*Lincoln Hwy E, Ronks; tel: (717) 397-2507*) is open 24 hours with low-cost large portions of classic diner food.

Market Fare Restaurant $$ (*cnr Grant and Market Sts, Lancaster; tel: (717) 299-7090*) has a casual take-away café upstairs (which closes at 1700), and traditional American fare in the downstairs dining room.

VALLEY FORGE**

① Valley Forge Convention and Visitors Bureau 600 W Germantown Pike, Plymouth Meeting; tel: (610) 834-7969.

ⓘ Valley Forge National Historical Park Rte 23 and N Gulph Rd, Valley Forge; tel: (610) 783-1077. Park $, Washington Headquarters $$. Visitors center open daily 0900–1700, park daily dawn–dusk; enquire for Washington Headquarters hours. Bus tour with taped narration, May–Sept, $$.

Valley Forge Historical Society $$ Rte 23 in National Historical Park; tel: (610) 783-0535; open Jan–Mar Wed–Sat 1000–1600, Sun 1300–1600, Apr–Dec Mon–Sat 1000–1700, Sun 1300–1700.

Washington Memorial Chapel $$ Rte 23 in National Historical Park; tel: (610) 783-0120; open Mon–Sat 0930–1700, Sun 1230–1700. Carillon recitals mid-Sept–mid-June after Sun 1115 service, July–Aug Wed 2000.

Mill Grove $ Audubon and Pawlings Rds, Audubon, Pennsylvania (adjacent to National Historical Park); tel: (610) 666-5593. Museum open Tue–Sat 1000–1600, Sun 1300–1600; grounds Tue–Sun 0700–dusk.

George Washington's 12,000-man Continental Army marched into camp at Valley Forge on 19 December 1777 after failing to save Philadelphia from British occupation. Undernourished and poorly clothed, 2000 soldiers died that winter and thousands more became unfit for duty. But thanks to the discipline of Prussian drillmaster Baron Friedrich Wilhelm von Steuben, they marched out on 19 June 1778 as a highly trained force that saved New York City by defeating the British at the Battle of Monmouth. The rolling landscape is now **Valley Forge National Historical Park**, a symbol of patriotic triumph over hardship. The Visitors Center shows a moving 18-minute orientation film and displays period military gear. A driving tour passes forts and earthworks, the artillery park, the parade ground where von Steuben rebuilt the army, and Washington's headquarters. The local community takes full advantage of the park's recreational amenities, including three picnic areas, 10 miles of bridle paths and a 6-mile bicycle/foot path. The Schuylkill River Trail begins in the park and connects to an 18-mile bikeway that follows an abandoned railroad bed to Philadelphia.

Privately owned attractions include the **Valley Forge Historical Society***, notable for its patriotic mementoes, and adjacent **Washington Memorial Chapel***, famous for carillon concerts.

The 175-acre **Mill Grove*** was John James Audubon's first home in America and his introduction to American birds and wildlife. The mansion displays Audubon paintings and illustrations and the artist's studio and taxidermy room are recreated in the attic. Miles of trails wind through the sanctuary, where more than 175 species of birds and 400 species of flowering plants have been identified.

Accommodation and food in Valley Forge

Most lodging lies 10 miles east near King of Prussia Mall on Rte 202, where major chains are represented.

King of Prussia Mall (Rte 202, King of Prussia) has two food courts with 20-plus vendors and 15-plus full restaurants. The mall bills itself as the largest shopping centre on the US east coast, with 365 speciality shops and eight major department stores, including Lord & Taylor, Bloomingdale's, Macy's, Strawbridge's, Nieman-Marcus and Nordstrom.

Lodge Restaurant $ (1371 Valley Forge Rd – 2 miles west of park on Rte 23; tel: (610) 933-1646; open Mon–Fri 0600–1430, Sat–Sun 0700–1400) does good homemade soups, and daily specials for breakfast and lunch.

Opposite
Valley Forge

HEADQUARTERS COMPLEX

THE HEADQUARTERS HOUSE, OVERLOOKING THE CONFLUENCE OF VALLEY CREEK AND THE SCHUYLKILL RIVER, WAS THE HUB OF MILITARY ACTIVITY. IT WAS FROM HERE THAT GENERAL WASHINGTON, WITH THE ASSISTANCE OF HIS STAFF, CONDUCTED THE DAILY ROUTINE OF THE ARMY. OFTEN THERE WERE MORE THAN TWENTY OFFICERS AND AIDES PRESENT TO ASSIST THE COMMANDER-IN-CHIEF IN HIS DUTIES.

YORK❖❖

ⓘ York County Convention and Visitors Bureau / Market Way E; tel: (800) 673-2429 or (717) 848-4000; www.yorkonline.org.

York County Colonial Courthouse $$ 205 W Market St; tel: (717) 845-2951; open Mar–Dec, Tue–Sat tours at 1000, 1200, 1400, Sun tours at 1300 and 1430.

Historical Society of York County Museum and Library $$$ 250 E Market St; tel: (717) 848-1587; open Tue–Sat 0900–1700. Entrance fee includes any two Historical Society properties.

Harley-Davidson Motorcycle Company $ Rte 30 east of exit 9E from I-83; tel: (877) 746-7937. Plant tours Mon–Fri 0930, 1030, 1230, 1330; Museum Sat 1000, 1100, 1300, 1400. Close-toed shoes required for plant tour.

⚫ York Fair Tel: (717) 848-2596. This September fair dates from 1765.

Located midway between Gettysburg and Lancaster in the Susquehanna River valley, York was settled in 1749. More than half the stone and brick buildings of the downtown are enrolled on the National Register of Historic Places, with the 1888 Central Market House the principal attraction. York was the American capital from 30 Sept 1777 until 27 June 1778, while Philadelphia was under British occupation. The Continental Congress met in the **York County Colonial Courthouse**❖ (now reconstructed) to adopt the Articles of Confederation and issue the first National Thanksgiving Proclamation. The 20-mile York County Heritage Rail Trail, a railroad bed converted to a foot and bicycle path, begins behind the courthouse.

Buildings owned by the Historical Society trace the development of the area. The Golden Plough Tavern, *circa* 1741, is York's oldest surviving structure. The General Horatio Gates House, *circa* 1751, is an English-style stone house. American Revolutionary War hero Gates lived here while attending the Continental Congress. The Bobb Log House, *circa* 1812, represents a sturdy country home of the early 19th century. The **Historical Society of York County Museum and Library**❖ includes exhibits on York's role as a centre for early automotive manufacturing.

Transportation history continues with the **Harley-Davidson Motorcycle Company**❖, which has built two-wheelers here since 1903. The plant tour shows the assembly of this American icon and the museum displays every model produced since 1906.

Accommodation and food in York

The Yorktowne Hotel $–$$ (*48 E Market St; tel: (800) 233-9324 or (717) 848-1111*) is a classic business hotel, built in 1925 and recently renovated.

White Rose Bar and Grill $ (*48 N Beaver St; tel: (717) 848-5369*) has a sandwich shop and tavern specialising in open-pit barbecued meats.

Central Market House (*cnr W Philadelphia and N Beaver Sts; tel: (717) 848-2243; open Tue, Thur, Sat 0600–1500*) is a good place to stock up on produce and baked goods as well as meats, cheeses and sausages. Local specialities include hotdog cooked in pretzel dough and 'wet-bottom' shoo-fly pie.

Above
Harley-Davidson assembly plant

Opposite
Harley-Davidson museum

Suggested tour

March-in Program
Tel: (610) 783-0535.
Activities on 19 Dec
commemorate
Washington's troops
entering Valley Forge.

Length: 108 miles, 138 miles with detour.

Time: 6 driving hours, 3 days with stops; add 1 hour driving time for detour.

Links: Area connects to Philadelphia (*see pages 254–67*) on the east, to Frederick, Maryland (*see page 195*), on the south.

Route: From **VALLEY FORGE** ❶, follow Rte 202 west for 17 miles to Rte 30, continuing 20 miles through several small towns to Rte 10. Turn right to go north 3 miles to Compass. Turn left on Rte 340 through **PENNSYLVANIA DUTCH COUNTRY** ❷, going 4 miles to Intercourse and another 10 miles to Bird-in-Hand.

Detour: Before entering Bird-in-Hand, turn left on Rte 896 through Amish farmland 3.5 miles to Strasburg. Turn left on Rte 741 to drive 10 miles east, then 0.5 miles north to Rte 30. Turn left on Rte 30 to enter Lancaster 16 miles west via shopping malls. To resume the route, continue west on Rte 340 for 3 miles into Lancaster.

Continue west on Rte 30 for 21 miles to pick up Rte 462 for 6 miles through the centre of **YORK** ❸. Resume westward travel on Rte 30 for 14 miles to **New Oxford**, self-proclaimed 'Antiques Capital of South-Central Pennsylvania' with 40 shops, some representing the wares of as many as 60 dealers. Rte 30 continues west another 10 miles to **GETTYSBURG** ❹. Rte 15 south connects to Frederick, Maryland, in 34 miles.

Also worth exploring

Opposite
Hershey's Chocolate World

Redolent with the smell of chocolate, **Hershey, Pennsylvania**, can be reached from Lancaster by driving 16 miles west on Rte 283, then 10 miles north on Rte 743. Top attraction is a tour of Hershey's Chocolate World to see how chocolate is made.

Photography in Amish country

Visitors often find the Amish lifestyle irresistibly picturesque, but the Amish themselves believe that photographs in which they can be recognised violate the Biblical injunction against making graven images. Moreover, they consider that agreeing to pose for a photograph constitutes the sin of pride. Officially, visitors are discouraged from making photographs or video images of the Amish. Unofficially, casual photography is tolerated if the image does not show a person's face and if the photographer shows discretion and respect.

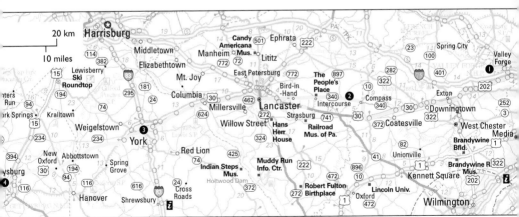

Capital speak

While the official language is English, Capital Region residents speak a peculiar blend of American, Southern and Political English, sometimes bearing only a confusing resemblance to the Queen's English.

DC-specific

Beltway insider (or *Inside the Beltway*) Someone inside Washington political circles.

-gate Washington reporters and politicians routinely add '-gate' to the name of a principal feature in the scandal of the moment. It comes from the Watergate Hotel, where Richard Nixon's operatives bungled a burglary and brought down his presidency.

Governmentality This approach to business emphasises paperwork over progress.

Spin doctor A political operative who informs others how to interpret the news in the best possible light for the politician who employs the spin doctor.

The Spur The northeast corner of the Beltway, also known as *The Spur Parking Lot* during commuting hours (0800–1000 and 1600–1900).

Wore-shing-tun Local pronunciation of the capital city of the USA.

General

Alternate is an Americanism indicating not 'every other' but an 'alternative' – as in 'alternate route' or 'alternate service' (as on an American timetable). *Alternative* is usually associated with *lifestyle*, connoting a sexual preference of which the speaker disapproves.

Bed and Breakfast (or *B&B*) Overnight accommodation in a private home or small inn, with or without rooms *en suite*.

Holiday Not a private holiday (which is called a vacation) but a public holiday such as Independence Day (4 July) or Labor Day (first Mon in Sept).

Lodging Generic term for all variety of accommodation.

Outlet shopping Shopping at large stores specialising in factory over-runs, returned goods and imperfect goods at reduced prices. 'Factory stores' are often cut-rate retail shops selling a special line of goods direct from the factory.

Food

Barbecue (variously spelled BBQ, barbeque or *bar-b-que*) Sliced, chopped or shredded beef or pork served with a tangy tomato-based sauce. Also beef or pork ribs basted with a similar sauce and cooked over charcoal or wood fire. *Pulled pork* is shredded roasted pork, often doused with a sweetened vinegar sauce.

Brewpub A tavern that brews its own beer. Contrast with *microbrewery*, which is a small brewery that produces high-quality beer or ale for local consumption.

Chips Crisps, usually made from potatoes, sometimes from corn (maize).

Crab The region's favourite crustacean can be served boiled or breaded and fried, but is often presented whole and steamed, leaving the diner to crack and dismantle it at the table. *Crabcakes* are usually a breaded blend of crab meat, onions, breadcrumbs and a binder, fried and served with a mayonnaise-based sauce. *Soft shell crabs* are those that have recently shed their shells. The new shell is tender and edible and considered a delicacy. The whole soft shell crab is usually battered and fried and often served in a sandwich.

Raw bar A section of some restaurants filled with uncooked seafood, especially raw oysters on the half shell. Many raw bars also have other seafood 'cooked' by being marinated in vinegar or citrus juices.

Rockfish A striped bass harvested wild from the Chesapeake Bay and its tributaries.

Index

Acknowledgements

Project Management: Dial House Publishing Services
Series design: Fox Design
Front cover design: Pumpkin House
Layout: PDQ Digital Media Solutions Limited
Map work: Polly Senior Cartography
Repro and image setting: PDQ Digital Media Solutions Limited
Printed and bound in Italy by: Rotolito Lombarda Spa

We would like to thank Ethel Davies for the photographs used in this book, to whom the copyright belongs, with the exception of the following:

Tom Bross (pages 13, 102B, 104, 111, 114, 116, 122, 123, 124, 125, 138, 148 and 152)

Delaware Art Museum (pages 20 and 241)

Pat Harris (page 268)

David Lyon (pages 238, 244, 252, 260 and 277)

Rogers Associates (pages 25, 32, 176, 178, 192, 194, 196, 197, 200, 201, 202, 203, 204, 206, 207, 208, 213, 214, 215, 217, 224 and 225)

Feedback form

If you enjoyed using this book, or even if you didn't, please help us improve future editions by taking part in our reader survey. Every returned form will be acknowledged, and to show our appreciation we will give you £1 off your next purchase of a Thomas Cook guidebook. Just take a few minutes to complete and return this form to us.

When did you buy this book? ....
....

Where did you buy it? (Please give town/city and, if possible, name of retailer)
....
....

When did you/do you intend to travel in Washington, DC, Virginia, Maryland and Delaware?..

For how long (approx)? ....

How many people in your party? ....

Which cities, national parks and other locations did you/do you intend mainly to visit?
....
....
....
....

Did you/will you:
❏ Make all your travel arrangements independently?
❏ Travel on a fly-drive package?
Please give brief details: ....
....

Did you/do you intend to use this book:
❏ For planning your trip?   ❏ Both?
❏ During the trip itself?

Did you/do you intend also to purchase any of the following travel publications for your trip?
Thomas Cook Travellers guides: ....
A road map/atlas (please specify) ....
Other guidebooks (please specify) ....

Have you used any other Thomas Cook guidebooks in the past? If so, which?
....
....

Please rate the following features of Signpost *Washington DC, Virginia, Maryland and Delaware* for their value to you (Circle VU for 'very useful', U for 'useful', NU for 'little or no use'):

The *Travel Facts* section on pages 14–23	VU	U	NU
The *Driver's Guide* section on pages 24–9	VU	U	NU
The *Highlights* section on pages 40–1	VU	U	NU
The recommended driving routes throughout the book	VU	U	NU
Information on towns and cities, National Parks, etc	VU	U	NU
The maps of towns and cities, parks, etc	VU	U	NU
The colour planning map	VU	U	NU

Please use this space to tell us about any features that in your opinion could be changed, improved, or added in future editions of the book, or any other comments you would like to make concerning the book:

....

....

....

....

....

....

....

....

....

....

Your age category: ❑ 21-30   ❑ 31-40   ❑ 41-50   ❑ over 50

Your name: Mr/Mrs/Miss/Ms ....

(First name or initials) ....

(Last name) ....

Your full address: (Please include postal or zip code)

....

....

....

....

....

Your daytime telephone number: ....

Please detach this page and send it to: The Project Editor, Signpost Guides, Washington DC, Virginia, Maryland and Delaware, Thomas Cook Publishing, PO Box 227, Peterborough PE3 6PU, United Kingdom.

We will be pleased to send you details of how to claim your discount upon receipt of this questionnaire.